Academic Quality Work

Academic Quality Work
A Handbook for Improvement

William F. Massy
Jackson Hole Higher Education Group

Steven W. Graham
University of Missouri System

Paula Myrick Short
Tennessee Board of Regents

ANKER PUBLISHING COMPANY, INC.
Bolton, Massachusetts

Academic Quality Work
A Handbook for Improvement

ISBN 978-1-933371-23-8

Composition by Julie Phinney
Cover design by Dutton & Sherman Design

Anker Publishing Company, Inc.
563 Main Street
P.O. Box 249
Bolton, MA 01740-0249 USA

Library of Congress Cataloging-in-Publication Data

Massy, William F.
   Academic quality work : a handbook for improvement / William F. Massy, Steven W. Graham, and Paula Myrick Short
      p. cm.
Includes bibliographical references and index.
ISBN 978-1-933371-23-8
1. Education, Higher—Aims and objectives. 2. Education, Higher—Evaluation. I. Graham, Steven W. II. Short, Paula Myrick. III. Title

LB2322.2.M37 2007
378.1—dc22   2006102154

To David Dill

Pioneer in the application of quality
principles to higher education

Table of Contents

About the Authors

William F. Massy is president of the Jackson Hole Higher Education Group, Inc., and a professor emeritus at Stanford University. He earned tenure as professor of business administration and then moved to Stanford's central administration as vice provost for research and later vice president for business and finance. In 1987 he became a professor of higher education and founded the Stanford Institute for Higher Education Research, where he worked on education quality, resource allocation, finance, and mathematical modeling of universities. He served as a trustee of EDUCOM (predecessor to EDUCAUSE, 1973–1976), and on the Yale University Council (1979–1992), the Hong Kong University Grants Committee (1991–2003), and the board of directors of Diebold, Inc. (1984–2007). Since 1997 he has served on the board of the Forum for the Future of Higher Education. His book with David Hopkins, *Planning Models for Colleges and Universities* (Stanford University Press, 1981), received the Operations Research Society of America's Frederick W. Lanchester Prize for 1981, and in 1995 he received the Society for College and University Planning's annual career award for outstanding contributions to college and university planning. His more recent books are *Resource Allocation in Higher Education* (with collaborators, University of Michigan Press, 1996), *Honoring the Trust: Quality and Cost Containment in Higher Education* (Anker, 2003), and *Remaking the American University: Market-Smart and Mission-Centered* (with R. Zemsky and G. Wegner, Rutgers University Press, 2005). Dr. Massy holds a PhD in economics and an MS in management from the Massachusetts Institute of Technology, and a BS from Yale University.

Steven W. Graham serves as associate vice president for academic affairs and director of the President's Academic Leadership Institute in the University of Missouri System. In that role he is responsible for leadership development, academic program review, new degree program approvals, and a variety of other university-wide academic affairs issues. He holds the rank of professor in educational leadership and policy analysis at the University of Missouri–Columbia. He has more than 25 years of experience in higher education as an administrator, professor, and consultant. He has written approximately 70 articles and papers on leadership development, manager coaching, college outcomes research, adult learning, adult development, professional education, and business training effectiveness; he has conducted numerous research projects evaluating the effects of training in the industry. For the past 20 years he has consulted with a variety of clients in banking, telecommunications, and computing, as well as various colleges and universities. He has received several awards, including the 2002 UCEA National Research and Scholarship Award for significant contributions to the literature and professional practice, several UCEA National Outstanding Research Awards, a $10,000 University of Missouri Special Research Award, and the University of Missouri–Columbia Provost's Award for Excellence. Dr. Graham earned a bachelor's degree in psychology from Coe College, a master's degree in college personnel, and a doctoral degree in higher education administration with an emphasis in organizational behavior from the University of Iowa.

Paula Myrick Short is vice chancellor for academic affairs for the Tennessee Board of Regents, the sixth-largest higher education system in the United States, with 182,000 students and 45 institutions. She previously served as associate vice president for academic affairs for the University of Missouri System. Dr. Short was a tenured professor and former department chair in educational leadership and policy analysis at the University of Missouri–Columbia, where she brought the department to a national ranking of 15th in the *U.S. News & World Report Graduate Rankings*. She also has held tenured faculty positions at Auburn University and the Pennsylvania State University. A nationally recognized scholar and researcher in the field of educational administration, Dr. Short was chosen as the recipient of the 1993 Jack A. Culbertson Award, given nationally by the University Council for Educational Administration to the outstanding professor of educational administration who, within the first 10 years in the professorship, made distinguished contributions in research. She has published more than 75 scholarly articles and 7 books, and made more than 110 national and international presentations. Her leadership with academic audit has also been recognized by the Australian Universities Quality Agency through her selection as an auditor. In 2006 she was honored internationally by the Chair Academy as an exemplary leader. Her current research focuses on leadership and organizational development, and change in higher education and higher education policy. Dr. Short received her PhD in administration in the Department of Organizational Development and Institutional Studies at the University of North Carolina at Chapel Hill.

Foreword

Although a willing member of the Spellings Commission on the Future of Higher Education, I became a somewhat disappointed signer of its 2006 final report, *A Test of Leadership: Charting the Future of U.S. Higher Education.* In crafting a call for fundamental change, the commission's chairman, Charles Miller, and his staff faced the same two challenges every effort to reform or recast American higher education confronts: the need to state clearly and concisely the problems to be fixed, and the need to specify, again clearly and concisely, the mechanisms or processes by which the necessary change is to be accomplished. On both counts, *A Test of Leadership* comes up short.

Historically, those who would reform our colleges and universities have been either exhorters or lamenters—the former focusing largely on the challenges that lie ahead, the latter on the failures of the past. The Spellings Commission report more often than not settled for mild lamentation, arguing that despite their notable successes American colleges and universities were in need of "urgent reform." The system's failings were forthrightly catalogued:

- Too many secondary students were not prepared to succeed in college. Too many students were shopping blind, having been denied adequate information. At the same time they faced costs they could not afford, while confronting a federal system of financial aid that was both "confusing" and "spends too little on those who need help the most" (p. vii).
- Once in college, too many students wasted time—"and taxpayer dollars" (p. vii)—engaged in remedial education. Too many students who started failed to finish a degree—or took too long mustering sufficient credits to graduate.
- Particularly disadvantaged were those students from low-income families and from racial and ethnic minorities.
- There was a fundamental absence of transparency and hence a scarcity of "reliable information about the cost and quality of postsecondary institutions, along with a remarkable absence of accountability mechanisms to ensure that colleges succeed in educating students" (p. vii).

A Test of Leadership continued:

> As if this weren't bad enough, there are also disturbing signs
> that many students who do earn degrees have not actually
> mastered the reading, writing, and thinking skills we expect
> of college graduates. Over the past decade, literacy among
> college graduates has actually declined. Unacceptable numbers
> of college graduates enter the workforce without the skills
> employers say they need in an economy where, as the truism
> holds correctly, knowledge matters more than ever. (p. vii)

In leveling this charge, the report of the Spellings Commission
faced a curious conundrum. Having declared that neither the American public writ large nor those responsible for the management of the
nation's colleges and universities had sufficient information to judge
the quality of the product, *A Test of Leadership* nonetheless came down
four square on the side of "not good enough and getting worse." No
doubt understanding that to lament the declining quality of American
higher education without confirming evidence would, at best, appear
quixotic, the commission's chairman had talked eagerly and willingly
about the need for better tests of educational outcomes, provoking
across higher education a renewed interest in standardized testing.
There were even bad jokes about the chairman's penchant for testing.
At The University of Pennsylvania one wag suggested the commission
had as its mandate "No College Left Behind."

But there was real give and take as well. Midway through the commission's deliberations Derek Bok added his voice to the debate that
Chairman Miller had provoked. Writing in *The Washington Post* Bok
began by noting that greater accountability on the part of higher education was long overdue, partly at least because of a growing body of
research that indicated American college students weren't really learning what they needed to learn. Spending four years in college resulted in
only a marginal improvement in one's critical thinking. "Tests of writing and of literacy in mathematics, statistics and computer technology
suggest that many undergraduates improve these skills only slightly,
while some actually regress" (Bok, 2006b, p. B07). Bok and others were
taking Miller and his commission seriously. They were joining Miller in

proclaiming that business as usual was no longer acceptable. They were lending their prestige to the search for a better understanding of learning outcomes, and, in the process, were bestowing on Miller's quest a legitimacy it could not have otherwise claimed.

Ironically, this linkage with Bok only highlighted the other problem Miller faced in crafting *A Test of Leadership*: the need to specify a real strategy for getting large numbers of higher education institutions to do things differently. In his op-ed in the *Post* as in his book *Our Underachieving Colleges* (2006a), Bok had warned:

> Useful reforms can come only from within the universities. Academic leaders will have to work with their faculties to develop methods of assessing student learning that are appropriate to their institutions. They will need to provide funds to experiment and evaluate new teaching methods. They can offer more extensive training of graduate teaching assistants and young faculty members. Above all, they should try to emulate other well-run organizations by initiating a sustained process of improvement in which they continuously evaluate their educational programs, identify weaknesses and experiment with new ways to remedy their deficiencies. (p. B07)

Miller disagreed. In an email to members of the commission that called attention to Bok's op-ed in the *Post,* the commission's chairman noted:

> While much of what is needed to improve student learning and improve assessment will have to be accepted at the academy, it is not likely that this will happen only if and when and how it is decided in the academy. Dr. Bok has made a great contribution to this issue overall, however most of the "pressure" for change has come from outside sources. (Email communication from Cheryl Oldham on behalf of Charles Miller, March 5, 2006)

Indeed, throughout the life of the commission, Miller would argue that no reform strategy would prove successful unless the proponents of change began by getting higher education's attention. The way to do that was to use what Miller called "strong language," forcefully identifying the enterprise's many flaws and broken parts—in short, a strategy of jolt and shame, roughly the educational equivalent of shock and awe.

Which brings me at last to the volume you have before you. Academic *Quality Work: A Handbook for Improvement* shares with the report of the Spellings Commission a belief that now is the time to sound the alarm: "American universities may be the envy of the world, but the world is passing us by in the areas of academic quality assurance and improvement." But unlike the drafters of *A Test of Leadership*, the authors of *Academic Quality Work* know how to foster the kind of changes the Spellings Commission believed important. They have the same advantage over Derek Bok who, though he argues eloquently that meaningful change must begin and end with the faculty, has yet to foment the transformation he has called for. Professors Massy, Graham, and Short, on the other hand, know of where they speak. They have been there and done that, working with two diverse, often underfunded systems of public higher education. More importantly, they have taken seriously Bok's dictum that it is the faculty who are the key to meaningful reform. Only by making the conversation about quality a faculty conversation that focuses first on principles and educational purposes will change occur. Only by making quality faculty work will there be a systematic and documented improvement in the quality of educational processes and outcomes. What you have before you is in fact A Handbook for Improvement—a step-by-step process for getting and keeping faculty involved. The fundamental difference between this volume and the report of the Spellings Commission—and it is a difference with a vengeance—is that Academic Quality Work presents a fully tested mechanism for change.

Robert Zemsky
Professor and Chair
The Learning Alliance for Higher Education
The University of Pennsylvania

References

Bok, D. (2006a). *Our underachieving colleges: A candid look at how much students learn and why they should be learning more.* Princeton, NJ: Princeton University Press.

Bok, D. (2006b, March 5). A test colleges don't need. *The Washington Post,* p. B07.

U.S. Department of Education. (2006). *A test of leadership: Charting the future of U.S. higher education.* Washington, DC: Author.

Preface

The genesis for this book occurred in Missouri in February 2000 when Paula Short produced a report on academic program review. Paula at that time was associate vice president for academic affairs at the University of Missouri System, reporting to Vice President Steve Lehmkuhle. She had searched the literature, reviewed practices in different states, and interviewed chief academic officers, deans, and department chairs from the university's four campuses. The main themes in her report were that the reviews tended to be retrospective and not focused on future planning, not participatory (the department chair often prepared them), done for someone else (hence with little ownership by faculty), and protective of the department rather than giving it direction and purpose for the future; and these reviews had little if any value added for the dean, the chief academic officer, the university system, or the state's Coordinating Board for Higher Education.

Paula then invited David Dill to Columbia, Missouri, to give a talk on education quality. A professor of public policy at the University of North Carolina (UNC) at Chapel Hill, David is a world-renowned expert in the field. His talk described the alternative approaches to quality assurance and improvement being practiced around the world. It included Hong Kong's Teaching and Learning Quality Process Review (TLQPR), a variant of academic audit developed by Bill Massy and his colleagues on the region's University Grants Committee (UGC). David was familiar with the TLQPR from having served on an external panel appointed by UGC to review the process's first round.

Paula and Steve Lehmkuhle became excited about the prospect of piloting academic audit at the University of Missouri. They asked David whether he would consult on such a project, but his responsibilities at UNC precluded his accepting the assignment. He recommended Bill, who had taken early retirement from Stanford University a few years earlier to found the Jackson Hole Higher Education Group (JHHEG, online at www.jhheg.com). Bill accepted, and the project began during the summer of 2001.

By this time, however, Paula had left Missouri to become vice chancellor for academic affairs at the Tennessee Board of Regents (TBR). Enter Steve Graham, who had been running the university's leadership development program for Steve Lehmkuhle and now received the assignment to manage the academic audit pilot project. Bill and Steve Graham approached each other with some apprehension—Bill worried about the switch from Paula and Steve, wondering, "Who is this dude, and will I be able to work with him?" All turned out well, however. Steve and Bill bonded during a road show across Missouri, during the early fall of 2001, to introduce the audit idea to the departments on each of the university's four campuses. As in so many good collaborations, they found themselves reacting the same way to questions and even finishing each other's sentences. Steve became the university's champion of academic quality work and audit, and in a couple of years his expertise reached the point where he could operate independently.

The first round of the Missouri audit project took place during 2001 and 2002. The initial task was to adapt Hong Kong's institution-level TLQPR to the department level. Once this was accomplished, the next tasks were to bring the four pilot departments along on their self-studies and then to select, train, and deploy the auditors. Interestingly, Missouri proceeded somewhat gingerly with respect to use of the word *audit*. The memo introducing the project used the word in the subject line but called it "a pilot review program referred to as academic audit." Discussions with departments and the materials developed that fall generally did not refer to "audit."

The first-round project was judged to be successful, due in no small way to the dedication and energy of participating faculty. A second round was soon launched. That, too, was successful, but there was a groundswell of concern about excluding research and scholarship from the audit. Bill had resisted this idea because of his concern that research would overshadow teaching in the self-studies and site visit conversations. Chapter 7 describes how we overcame this difficulty. The third round of audit at Missouri included research and scholarship and subsequent rounds also will do so. The word *audit* has moved back into the university's vernacular as well.

Meanwhile, Paula was stirring the pot in Tennessee. She invited Bill to speak on education quality to the TBR during the fall of that year and then continued the conversation with the chancellor, her colleagues in the systems office, and academic officers on the campuses. Another talk by Bill, this time to the campus academic officers during the fall of 2003, marked the beginning of the TBR Academic Audit Pilot Project. The program, which Paula had decided to call "audit" unequivocally, involved volunteer departments and programs from 11 of the system's 19 campuses. Paula decided to handle the hands-on work herself, and she soon became not only the champion but also the resident expert on quality work and audit.

The TBR project presented two entirely new challenges. First, the program spanned the institutional range from a research university, to a variety of four-year colleges, to community colleges. (The programs in Missouri and Hong Kong had been limited to research universities and liberal arts colleges.) Sally Vaughn of JHHEG, one of Bill's colleagues, helped us surmount this difficulty by conducting interviews on a representative sample of campuses. She brought back many good examples of education quality work and concluded that the audit approach could be applied across the spectrum of campuses without significant modifications. Second, the sheer number of programs to be included raised the matter of logistics to a whole new level. TBR is the nation's sixth-largest higher education system, and the pilot involved some 36 units spread across a very long state. We surmounted this difficulty by running our road shows in three locations (Memphis, Nashville, and Knoxville), to which all participating campuses sent representatives, through a liberal use of conference calls, and by creating a team of Super Dudes (described in Chapter 5) to serve as local resources in the regions. Steve Graham came from Missouri to assist with the road shows.

The first-round program in Tennessee proved to be successful beyond expectations. The concepts of education quality work were embraced by all the participating units, and the audit methodology worked well in both large and small units on all types of campuses. Much of the credit for this goes to the many TBR faculty members and administrators, including but not limited to the Super Dudes, who devoted so much time and energy to mastering the ideas and making those ideas work in their units. Space doesn't permit us to cite each name individually. We do, however, want to acknowledge Harriette Bias-Insignares, Maxine Smith Fellow at the TBR central office, who compiled and edited *Reflections on the TBR Academic Audit Pilot Project* (2005). The book contains many useful insights about quality work and audit that have proved invaluable as the program proceeded. At this writing the program has completed its second round and is going into its third, for which Steve is assisting Paula on the addition of research and scholarship to the agenda. This latest round involves all the system's campuses and has been incorporated in the state's performance funding program.

Chapters 1, 2, and 3 present the motivation and conceptual basis for education quality work and academic audit. Chapter 4 describes how faculty members become engaged in the process. The examples come mainly from Missouri, but many similar ones exist in Tennessee. Chapters 5 and 6 present the nuts and bolts of an audit: how to prepare the self-study and how to handle the audit visit and report. Here most of the examples are from Tennessee. Chapter 7 describes how Missouri extended quality work and audit to include research. Chapter 8 further extends the ideas to include institution- or campus-level audits—reviews that incorporate department-level audits on a sampling basis. Chapter 9 distills our experience into a set of policy recommendations that we believe are relevant for colleges and universities everywhere.

The successful applications of audit in Missouri and Tennessee are what, literally, made this book possible. They drove the refinement of concepts and methods of application far beyond what Bill had described in *Honoring the Trust* (Massy, 2003c). Most important, though, they provided proof for the approach's practicality and usefulness in the United States and at the department level. The three of us came together on this conclusion at the Association for the Study of Higher Education conference in November 2005, where we gave a presentation. Out of that came this book.

William F. Massy
Jackson, WY

Steven W. Graham
Columbia, MO

Paula Myrick Short
Nashville, TN

September 2006

1

Quality Matters

The finger food had been consumed, and the deans and others attending the earlier session had returned to their offices. Now it was the advisory panel, the president, and the provost. The view from the window was of a vibrant and boundlessly optimistic Asian city, but it could have been America, Europe, Australia—any part of the world that takes its universities seriously. The panel's job was to advise on strategic issues, and this year the most strategic of all issues was the quality of undergraduate education.

The recently retired vice chancellor of one of England's oldest and most famous universities spoke first. "They just don't get it," he said of the professors he had interviewed earlier in the day. "There's no consideration of what undergraduate education is *for*. They think only of the academic discipline, not what the students need to take away from their studies—or, at least, the 99% who won't go on to get a PhD." "I found the same thing," said the president of a major American university known for its scholarly orientation. "Faculty have no view about the outcomes of an undergraduate education. They never reflect on them—don't seem to care." "Everyone's caught up in research," added the Australian vice chancellor emeritus. "They think their teaching is fine as long as no one complains." "And the research," chimed in the president of an upstart eastern European university, "is too often divorced from context. Faculty talk about what will most easily qualify for an alpha journal, not what could be important for solving the world's problems."

That such a conversation actually took place in 2006 is important for several reasons. For the university in question, it led to some quick remedial action. This relatively new institution is well on its way to

1

becoming world-class in research, but it recognizes that undergraduate education is a central part of its mission—and that its future depends on doing, and being seen to do, an outstanding job with its undergraduates. The president welcomed the feedback, not because it was something he wanted to hear, but because it confirmed his fears that the school the panel had visited was lagging behind the rest of the university in teaching. Stronger leadership was needed from the dean and the university's senior academic officers—leadership that he assured the panel would be forthcoming, starting with himself.

But the conversation is noteworthy for a broader set of reasons. It reflects a growing worldwide impatience with the quality of education and, indeed, with university outcomes generally. And as the story reveals, the impatience comes from within the academy as well as from outside. It can no longer be dismissed as ranting from the uncaring or uninformed. It is not anti-intellectual, anti-research, or anti-academic in any way. What it does represent is a genuine and well-meaning effort, increasingly by insiders, to improve the university's contributions to society.

This book is about how to bring such ideas to fruition—to reduce the theories to practice. It is about how the academy can reform itself from within while at the same time preserving its cherished and important freedoms. It describes lessons learned by the three of us while actually doing the job. We believe these lessons will be valuable in a number of ways: by demonstrating that change is possible, by providing a road map for how to organize the effort, by offering materials and templates that can be adapted to local circumstances, and by alerting change agents about the pitfalls and how to avoid or overcome them. This is a how-to book; it's literally a handbook for change agents. But we believe it is more, that it breaks new ground on what it means to be an academic in the 21st century. We invite the reader to share what has been an exciting journey for each of us.

Could Quality Be Better?

Faculty can be forgiven for asking the critics to justify their claims about shortfalls in teaching quality, let alone in academic quality in general. After all, higher education enjoys strong and growing demand.

People want a college education, and most families are willing to pay for it. Students are not in revolt, and indeed course evaluations tend to be fairly good for most faculty most of the time. On the research side of the enterprise, many professors do get published, do go to conferences, and do achieve a certain amount of recognition. There is no crisis, no loud noises or smoking guns—just a slow drip, drip, drip of criticism that will not go away no matter how hard the academy tries to "educate" the nonbelievers.

Critical Voices

Three books describe higher education's current quality problems. Derek Bok's *Our Underachieving Colleges* (2006) takes "a candid look at how much students learn and why they should be learning more." We'll describe how his work relates to ours in this chapter and the next. *Declining by Degrees* (Hersh & Merrow, 2005; also a PBS documentary) cites a range of ills, including weaknesses in curricula and student engagement—"Caveat Lector: Unexamined Assumptions About Quality," the title of one of the essays in that book, could well have been a subtitle to our book. Brent Ruben's *Pursuing Excellence in Higher Education: Eight Fundamental Challenges* (2004) also resonates with our message. One of his challenges is that universities should become more effective learning organizations, particularly in regard to the development of environments that value and support student learning. Another concerns the integration of assessment, planning, and improvement. Our proposals speak directly to both challenges.

The latest expression of concern comes from the U.S. Secretary of Education's Commission on the Future of Higher Education (or Spellings Commission), which reported in September 2006. After an opening paragraph that lauds the past accomplishments of America's colleges and universities, the commission sounds an alarm:

> Despite these achievements, however, this Commission believes U.S. higher education needs to improve in dramatic ways. As we enter the 21st Century, it is no slight to the successes of America's colleges and universities thus far in our history to note the unfilled promise that remains. Our year-long examination

of the challenges facing higher education has brought us to the uneasy conclusion that the sector's past attainments have led our nation to unwarranted complacency about its future. (U.S. Department of Education, 2006, p. vi)

Elaborating on this theme a few paragraphs later, the commission asserts that there are

> disturbing signs that many students who do earn degrees have not actually mastered the reading, writing, and thinking skills we expect of college graduates. Over the past decade, literacy among college graduates has actually declined. Unacceptable numbers of college graduates enter the workforce without the skills employers say they need in an economy where, as the truism holds correctly, knowledge matters more than ever. . . .
>
> Compounding all of these difficulties is a lack of clear, reliable information about the cost and quality of postsecondary institutions, along with a remarkable absence of accountability mechanisms to ensure that colleges succeed in educating students. (U.S. Department of Education, 2006, p. vii)

While disagreeing with the commission's core recommendation about quality, we believe it was right to sound the alarm. American universities may be the envy of the world, but the world is passing us by in the areas of academic quality assurance and improvement. This book describes our proposals for remedying the situation—proposals that we believe will be much more effective than the ones put forward by the commission.

Reports such as the commission's have the greatest impact among those who already believe there is a problem. Professors on the firing line don't see a problem, let alone perceive themselves as part of it. Many departments appear healthy; any malaise can easily be attributed to a lack of resources, poorly performing students, or some other external cause. The reaction to outside criticism, like that from the Spellings Commission, is most often to circle the wagons and search ever more urgently for ways to justify the academy's special circumstances and privileges. There is also a growing lament that, like the late comedian Rodney Dangerfield, we get no respect.

Which brings us to the matter of evidence. Much of the critics' evidence tends to be fragmented and anecdotal: "Students don't work hard enough"; "graduates don't know this or that." Such evidence isn't convincing, and efforts to get hard benchmarks like national tests have failed for practical and political reasons. So the skirmishes continue (and occasionally erupt into outright warfare), with neither side being able to mount a convincing argument for the merit of its position.

The Way Forward

We come from a different place, one that is rooted in hands-on experience buttressed by a deep study of quality and what's required to produce it. Our experience is that, when departments address academic quality in a systematic way, they *conclude for themselves* that improvement is possible. They develop their own evidence about what needs to be improved, evidence they simply cannot ignore. They experiment with change, study the results, and then use the new evidence to inform additional experiments. And with such evidence they can convince others that quality is in fact improving. These "others" join with the department in celebrating the improvements, and a virtuous circle is established. We've seen this begin to happen—and indeed have been part of the process. Both the journey and the results are satisfying for everyone involved.

Our Underachieving Colleges (Bok, 2006) calls for just such changes. It describes the purposes of undergraduate education, how schools fall short on achieving those purposes, and what should be done by way of improvement. As a former law professor and Harvard president, Bok cares deeply about the academy. But he also cares about evidence and logic, and the evidence and logic he presents are compelling. We recommend that everyone who cares about academic quality read his book from cover to cover. Our book is a handbook for raising the priority of academic quality improvement within departments and institutions—that is, for accomplishing the goals Bok sets out.

We have yet to find a department where systematic quality improvement efforts don't pay off. Often the improvements are substantial and come with expending few if any additional resources. This results in a win for all concerned—for students, for faculty, for the institution, and even for the critics. Why the critics? Because by showing that improvement is possible without spending more, such outcomes demonstrate that the critics' concerns were in fact well founded. But before "we told you so" rings through the academy, let's all remind ourselves that although the concerns were right, the proposed interventions were wrong. To pursue its mission effectively the academy must reform itself from the inside, not have change imposed crudely from the outside.

Smart academics can punch holes in any assertion by outsiders that teaching or research should be reformed in a particular way. What we can't do, at least if we're honest with ourselves, is to claim it's impossible to do better without having seriously tried to do so. It's honest to assert, as the three of us have heard often enough, that improving quality is too difficult or that it will take time away from other activities. But this speaks to trade-offs rather than facts. When one finishes haggling about priorities, the case for spending at least a little time on systematic quality improvement is very strong.

We don't wish to suggest that universities are uniformly indifferent to quality improvement. There is progress in curricula, for example—witness the renewed attention to general education and greater emphasis on science and mathematics at many schools. And of course research quality improves steadily as evidenced by advances in the sciences. Our point is that quality could be materially better if universities and departments gave it more systematic attention. This is especially true for undergraduate education, where attention to purposes, teaching methods, assessment, and quality assurance often leaves much to be desired. It also applies to how research is approached in many departments.

Bok (2006) puts it this way:

> Although the attacks on college professors seem clearly overblown, there is a subtler problem with faculty behavior. . . . However much professors care about their teaching, nothing forces them or their academic leaders to go beyond normal conscientiousness in fulfilling their classroom duties. There is no compelling necessity to reexamine familiar forms of instruction and experiment with new pedagogic methods in an effort to help students accomplish more. (p. 22)

"Good enough isn't" has become an axiom of the quality movement. Yet Bok's characterization, which we agree is accurate, amounts to "good enough is." Once stated, such an attitude about education becomes indefensible. As the recipients of large societal investments and as objects of hope for so many people, universities have an obligation to be the best they can be. Doing so requires more than lofty rhetoric about quality. What is needed is for faculty to become more self-conscious about quality and more continuously involved in its improvement.

The Importance of Mental Models

The first step is to examine one's mental models of quality. Conventional wisdom holds that quality is a black box—opaque except for the "obvious" truth that spending more (e.g., raising faculty-student ratios) improves quality. Although more money certainly confers additional degrees of freedom, what's done with the money also is important. Other bits of conventional wisdom that don't stand scrutiny are that "good teachers are born, not made," and that "good researchers aren't or need not be good teachers." On the research side, it's a mistake to believe that the best research is that which is most divorced from societal problems. Worthy problems addressed with the most advanced theories and tools can produce results that are just as exciting as "pure" research—results that include extensions to theory and methodology. The point is not that academics shouldn't be free to choose the problems on which they'll work, but that they should cast their net as widely as possible.

What these problems have in common is the academy's tendency to narrow both the issues it believes can fruitfully be addressed and the range of stimuli that can be admitted into consideration. That such narrowing may have in the past served a purpose is beside the point. No one doubts that more faculty lines can help a department improve education quality, but the quest for more money should not crowd out efforts to use what one has as effectively as possible. Focusing on immediate worldly problems can blind one to broader scientific and social issues, but that doesn't mean such problems shouldn't be a source of ideas or that the academy doesn't have a comparative advantage in solving them. We celebrate and protect basic research in the sciences, for example, but important breakthroughs also come when scientists address problems, like AIDS and global warming, from outside their discipline.

Another bad mental model is to assume one already knows everything that's important about an issue. The purpose of an undergraduate education is a case in point. Many professors, recalling their own undergraduate experiences and steeped in the values of their disciplines, assume that undergraduates should learn from the perspective of a budding professional in the field—thinking of science as scientists do, economics as economists do, and so forth. The Holy Grail of teaching is to interest and prepare a student to do graduate work in the discipline. Unfortunately, this "mini-me" approach ignores the vast majority of undergraduates who never will go on to study science or economics, but who want or need to understand the subject for other reasons. A moment's reflection would reveal this fact, and a few moments more would begin to generate solutions. However, the moments never come because the answer is (uncritically) assumed to be known.

Some would say the academy's quality problems lie in its culture and that convenient whipping boy, tenure. We don't see it that way. Most faculty want to do a good job with their teaching and, of course, with their research. Most are able and willing, indeed eager, to collaborate on finding solutions to difficult problems—witness the degree of collaboration on research projects. The academic culture supports these values, and tenure does not inhibit acting them out except in the case of a few people whom everyone recognizes as deadwood. Business firms and government agencies strive mightily to build workforces that have the self-starting capacity, not to mention the intellectual horsepower, of university faculty. The problem is not deadwood faculty, tenure, or an uncaring culture—as the most strident of the academy's critics would have it—but inappropriate mental models.

This book presents mental models that, if internalized and acted on, will materially improve a department's teaching and research quality. The models are informed by the so-called quality movement in business, government, health care, and the like, but their focus is on colleges and universities. They are rooted in the experience of real academics, not just ourselves, but the growing cadre of colleagues who "get it" when it comes to quality.

Our observations about mental models apply as much to academic leaders as to rank-and-file faculty. Because leaders in colleges and universities almost always come from the faculty, they share the faculty's mental models. Indeed, many department chairs, program directors, and deans see articulating, enforcing, and defending the standard mental models as an important part of their job descriptions. It should come as no surprise, therefore, that the standard mental models are built into the academic incentive and reward system. This makes it harder to change the models, but once changed, the incentive and reward system will follow. It may also be possible for enterprising leaders to change incentives and rewards up front, as part of a broader system of quality reform. We strongly advocate such changes but do not believe they're a sine qua non. We have seen departments recast their mental models and effect significant quality improvement under the radar of a conventional incentive and reward system.

One final word about academic culture: While agreeing that an organization's culture is the sum of its beliefs and values, we don't accept the idea that culture is exogenous or immutable. Too many researchers in higher education consider culture the end of the line—that one or another behavior results from culture and nothing can be done about it. But history shows that the most successful leaders are those who not only diagnose their organization's culture correctly but also figure out how to change it. For us those aspects of the academic culture that inhibit quality improvement stem from defective mental models. We have enough faith in our colleagues to believe that the defects can be identified and corrected, and that changing the models will change the culture.

Economic Considerations

Although our primary concern is with improving departments' mental models of quality and helping them apply the models effectively, we cannot ignore economic factors. It is widely believed, for example, that the only way to improve quality is through additional spending. But this mental model is not only wrong, it is self-defeating. To think only about getting more is to ignore possibilities for using the current resource base more effectively. Another model, widely held in political circles, is that universities spend too much and that quality attained per dollar of tuition and state appropriation can be improved by putting universities on a strict, even draconian, revenue diet. This view is dangerous because quality improvement becomes vastly more difficult when an institution is starving. We'll discuss the proper role of funding-based sticks and carrots in later chapters.

The real problem lies in the markets' failure to reward academic quality, especially education quality, sufficiently enough to counter the proclivity of academics to pursue their own interests. These market failures, coupled with the university's nonprofit governance structure, inhibit (but do not prevent) the application of quality principles. Institutions that take quality seriously will find ways to mitigate these difficulties. They will restructure their internal economies and cultures to reinforce quality improvement even when such actions aren't immediately rewarded in the marketplace. And over the long run, one may hope that markets will become better informed so they can reward quality more effectively.

Cost and Quality

The idea that spending more will improve quality is deeply rooted in academe. The logic is straightforward. More money permits a department to hire more professors. More professors will cover the subject matter of the discipline more completely. (The growing importance of specialization in most disciplines and the desires of professors to teach their specialties means that more teachers will be required, over time, to achieve the same degree of coverage.) Having more professors also allows the department to offer more sections and thus cut average class size or, perhaps more likely, reduce teaching loads—two more actions that are believed to enhance education quality.

The logic is correct as far as it goes, but it obscures two very important truths. First is the idea of cost-effectiveness. Take undergraduate education, for example. To what extent will the capacity created by new faculty hires be used to improve teaching as opposed to research? One shouldn't be optimistic on this score. Research on the "academic ratchet" (Massy & Zemsky, 1994) suggests that added capacity is used to reduce teaching loads across the department and that the time freed up goes more to research than to education quality improvement. And does the time that does go to education result in quality improvement that's commensurate with the extra cost? Unfortunately, departments rarely consider these issues: They just want the extra faculty lines.

The second truth is one we referred to earlier: that thinking first and foremost about resources—faculty lines in this example—blinds departments to how they use the resources they have. A member of the advisory panel whose story we recounted at the beginning of this chapter observed that faculty in the department he visited were amazed that his mission was not to find out what additional resources they needed, but rather to ask about their mental models. The obsession with resources has another, even more perverse, consequence. It makes quality improvement the responsibility of "someone else"—the keeper of the purse. If there's no new money, there's no quality improvement. The department is absolved of all responsibility except to make the case—some would say beg—for "more."

Richard Vedder, in *Going Broke by Degree* (2004), juxtaposes higher education's unbounded appetite for spending with lagging education quality. In other words, students are paying more and getting less. No one should be surprised by the appetite for spending. Not only is this appetite apparent from observation, it derives ineluctably from the intrinsic character of universities. Those who seek to blunt the appetite have it wrong. To succeed would be to kill the very essence of the academic enterprise. The challenge is to channel spending into uses that are most productive for society—and specifically into the kinds of quality improvement that matter for those who pay the bills.

Nonprofit Enterprise Theory

Understanding the university's appetite for spending requires its own mental model—the theory of nonprofit enterprises (Hopkins & Massy, 1981; Massy, 1996, 2003a; Zemsky, Wegner, & Massy, 2005). The theory holds that universities maximize what economists call a "utility function"—that is, the value created by the enterprises' activities. Utility functions are abstractions, but useful ones. The inputs are lists of possible activities, each with an associated set of consequences. The outputs rank-order the consequences, from best to worst, according to the institution's values. Value determination depends on governance processes—which are subjective, messy, and often controversial. For now it's enough to say the university does have values and that (one would hope) they reflect its mission and nonprofit status.

Maximizing utility involves more than simply picking the alternative that has the highest-ranked consequence. Cost is also a factor because each alternative specifies a set of activities, and each activity incurs costs. The cost of the chosen activities can't exceed the funds available, on average over time, or the university will bankrupt itself. And with cost comes the question of productivity. Why? Because it's the consequences produced by the activities that are important, and *productivity* is shorthand for the connections between inputs, activities, and consequences. A productive department will produce more and better consequences than one that is less productive. Many academics mistrust the idea of productivity. They associate it with profit-making and thus violations of the university's value system. The fact is, however, that productivity looms just as important for nonprofit as for-profit enterprises. Lower productivity means the best affordable alternative produces fewer good consequences and thus lower utility.

University behavior also depends on markets. Again the reason is simple and inexorable: People pay universities for services like teaching and sponsored research. Universities sell their services in the market-place and always have. Sales produce revenue, which helps defray the cost of activities. That universities are so heavily involved with markets threatens some academics, but it's clear that market success produces revenue that can be recycled into producing value. The challenge is not to constrict the institution's capacity to raise revenue, but to ensure that market success doesn't become an end in itself. Economist and former Williams College provost Gordon Winston describes this tension as between "university as church" and "university as car dealer." It's a tension that will have to be managed indefinitely since the prospect that the modern university, with its manifold range of activities, will be funded entirely by generous benefactors and governments is nil.

Nonprofit enterprise theory applied to universities proves what has become known as Bowen's Law: Universities will raise all the money they can and spend all the money they raise. Rooted in experience as well as theory, the law holds even for the most productive of institutions and those that are most successful in the marketplace. A productive institution always can put extra money to good use, and money saved by increasing productivity further will produce even more good consequences. Value generation is limited only by the ability of an institution's faculty to create exciting new alternatives, which in a good school is essentially unbounded. To ask a university to deny such aspirations as a matter of principle is to ask it to abandon its birthright. Universities will limit tuition increases as a result of market forces, and they will invest in need-based financial aid because access for low-income students is part of their value system, but they will never take a self-denying ordinance on spending.

Market Failure

So what do universities spend money on? Vedder and others have complained that too much goes to things that don't contribute directly to quality—for example, administrative overhead and lavish amenities for students and faculty. Critics also complain that too much goes to faculty research and scholarship, which may boost research quality but not the quality of undergraduate education. Space does not permit an examination of these concerns, but we believe there's more than a grain of truth in them. The references in this book's bibliography provide a good overview.

Why do universities spend money as they do? The short answer is, "Because they want to." In terms of nonprofit theory, they're spending on things that weigh heavily in their utility functions. Although research and scholarship fall under that rubric, amenities like climbing walls surely do not. In fact, most faculty and many others involved in university governance rail against such expenditures. Hence one must add another line to the short answer: ". . . or the market makes them do it."

The academic marketplace is unusual to say the least. First, it suffers from a dearth of relevant information about quality. Take prospective freshmen, for example. For them, the most relevant information would be how their investment of time and money will pay off in future income and quality of life. Such information is readily available for the so-called medallion schools. Going to such a school increases expected future income (often through access to an elite graduate or professional school) and opens doors to certain kinds of personal and cultural associations. Indeed, the ability to confer these benefits is the defining feature of a medallion school—the quintessential element of prestige.

But beyond the medallion schools the key question is, how much value added is provided by one's college experience? What has been learned, inside and outside the classroom, that will boost one's chances in later life? Value added doesn't matter so much for the medallions because prestige creates its own rewards. (Cynics sometimes characterize the medallions as observing the Hippocratic oath: "They get top-notch students and do them no harm.") But for students who don't go to a medallion school, value added is all-important—not just in general terms, but in the degree to which the school caters to the student's particular objectives and capacities. That there are big differences from institution to institution seems intuitively obvious. So what kinds of information are available?

Unfortunately, the huge industry that supplies information to prospective freshmen addresses value added indirectly or not at all. Data about inputs (faculty-student ratios, library holdings, endowment, and the like) exist in abundance, as do data on admissions selectivity, faculty research reputation, and athletic performance. One can even learn about an institution's ranking on the "party scale." But aside from lists of majors offered, which helps match the school to broadly defined student interests, information about the value added through teaching is hard to obtain.

It's no wonder that people choose schools on the basis of prestige and quality of student life rather than educational performance. What else can they do given the dataset? The students aren't at fault—neither are the suppliers of information. The problem is that data about value added don't exist. Even in fields with built-in performance metrics (like pass rates on licensure exams), one can't control for incoming student quality—which makes the assessment of value added impossible. So where might data on value added be found? In the universities, of course—or more precisely, in their departments and faculties. But here one runs into a brick wall. Colleges and universities don't have the data either. Worse, the mental models about quality that inform today's academics provide no impetus for collecting such information.

But we have yet to plumb the depths of market failure. Markets that depend heavily on prestige tend to be what's called "winner-take-all." Such markets array competitors on a single dimension, where to be second is to miss out on the best students and the ability to charge a premium price. Instead of differentiating themselves across the many dimensions of education quality, institutions concentrate on doing well in the prestige sweepstakes. And because prestige correlates with spending, institutions are motivated to spend more…and more…and more. The biggest spending payoffs in terms of prestige lie in the areas of faculty research prowess, visible student amenities, and merit-based financial aid that can be used to "buy" good students. The result is a classic arms race where each gain is soon canceled by the gains of others.

Little of the extra spending targets education quality. Better faculty-student ratios produce positive effects, but much of the benefit is realized in research and scholarship. Although better research also tends to improve education, it doesn't improve things as much as a more direct focus on academic quality would. Finally, the extra spending does nothing to improve market information. R&D investment on measuring value added remains minuscule. Indeed, the institutions that could most afford such investments have no incentive to make them—such institutions have nowhere to go but down if prestige is supplanted by evidence about value added.

These are strong assertions, and we have presented little evidence to support them. Our purpose is to *improve* academic quality, not document the current shortfalls. Readers who don't believe current practice needs improvement should consult Bok (2006), Massy (2003a), and Zemsky et al. (2005). Better, they should read on and then ask themselves why improvement would not be worthwhile even if current quality levels aren't as bad as the preceding discussion suggests. The same logic extends to schools on the upper end of the current quality distribution. We suggest they ask themselves why they shouldn't try to do even better.

A Program for Academic Quality Improvement

Our program for academic quality improvement is at root straight-forward. Faculty reflect on how they can work collegially within their departmental or program units to improve teaching and research quality. Then they put their ideas into practice and track results. The combination of reflection, experimentation, and results-tracking is powerful, especially when practiced in a collegial way. It is even more powerful when repeated regularly. Reflection and the ability to act collegially improve with practice, and each round of experimentation and performance data produces new insights. Finally, reflection, collegiality, experimentation, and the collection of evidence are quintessential academic values. There is nothing in the process that poses the slightest threat to academic freedom.

Of course, the devil is in the details. How does one get the process started? What conceptual structure can best aid reflection? How can potentially attractive initiatives be identified and impediments to their implementation overcome? What measures can be used to track results? How can the departmental efforts be brought to the attention of deans and higher-level administrators, and how can administrators be induced to reward exemplary performance? Perhaps most important, how can the improvement effort be sustained and build momentum in the face of competing demands on faculty time—including professors' inexorable requirement to perform well on their own research?

We offer answers to these questions and others that will arise as the program is put into practice. All answers are found in academic quality work, academic audit, and the quality improvement cycle.

Academic Quality Work

Quality doesn't just happen. The fundamental message of Deming and other quality pioneers is that sustaining, assuring, and improving quality requires systematic effort—effort we will call "quality work." Quality work is distinguishable from the tasks required to produce the good or service whose quality is being addressed. In many consulting firms, for example, one group is responsible for doing an assignment while a separate group is charged with reviewing it. The first group performs a primary task (doing the project), and the second does quality work (in this case providing a check on the methodology and results). This example illustrates what's called "quality assurance"—an after-the-fact checking of performance. However, there are many other kinds of quality work. Mentoring young consultants is a type of quality work, as is reflecting on the team's experience with a project in an effort to make improvements with the next one. The quality assurance function itself also can be viewed as improvement oriented, since the reviewer is performing a teaching as well as checking role.

The essential idea is that "doing the work" and "assuring and improving its quality" are distinguishable tasks—that is, academic quality work is not the same as teaching and research. Both are essential. The first great lesson from the now-famous quality movement was that being more conscientious on the doing side of an activity is no substitute for systematic quality work. Being conscientious will propel quality to a certain point, but getting past that point requires organized effort and specialized skills. The other great lesson is that "good enough isn't"—which means no organization should be satisfied with the quality levels achievable simply by trying harder.

Academic quality work (AQW) is our term for the systematic effort required if departments, programs, campuses, and institutions are to maximize teaching and research quality. We have noted that AQW is different from teaching and research. Faculty must be the prime movers of AQW at the department level, but it's crucial that they think about the two roles separately. Failure to do so almost surely means that AQW will atrophy.

Developing a conceptual structure and practical tools for AQW has loomed large in our work. We shall report these results in subsequent chapters. For now it is enough to say that AQW involves *subject matter* ("focal areas of activity"), *normative principles* for working with the subject matter ("quality principles"), and *criteria* for evaluating performance ("AQW maturity levels"). We have developed variants on the AQW tools to apply specifically to teaching and to research—hence the inclusive name "academic quality work." Finally, and in contrast to some quality programs elsewhere, our program is oriented toward quality improvement rather than quality assurance. Nevertheless, energetic

AQW at multiple levels in a higher education system will satisfy most quality assurance goals.

Academic Audit

The question is, how do we get started? Faculty tend to like AQW once they get into it. They find the questions stimulating and the results satisfying. Because most of them care deeply about their students and their field, they can embrace the idea of working systematically to improve the delivered quality of their department's education and research. But these feelings lie fallow until a critical mass of people in a department actually begin working together on AQW tasks.

AQW can be likened to a great wheel. The wheel is attached to an axle, which can be thought of as the administration. But most of the mass is near the circumference—that is, with the faculty. When the wheel is at rest (no AQW), a great deal of energy will be required to overcome inertia and get it moving. Transmitting this energy through the axle will be difficult, and trying to do so quickly may exceed the axle's capacity to handle stress, but applying the energy nearer the circumference generates greater leverage. And once the wheel is moving, its inertia (now thought of as momentum) tends to keep it spinning.

The challenge, then, is to apply energy near a department's "circumference"—which means faculty member to faculty member rather than from administration to faculty. Academic audit provides a way to generate this kind of energy.

To illustrate the chronology let's assume the university (or a campus, a school, or even a department chair) has decided to mount a campaign to improve AQW. The first step is to explain AQW to the campus community and ask for volunteer departments or programs to participate in a trial run. Faculty in the volunteer units are briefed on AQW concepts and discuss the ideas in a half- or full-day workshop. Then they're asked to do three things:

- Reflect on their current AQW activities (such as they are), identify opportunities for improvement, and agree among themselves on which opportunities should be tackled first.
- Write up their conclusions in a short self-study report.

- Discuss the report with an audit team, mostly made up of faculty from other departments, who will visit for a day in six to nine months.

The audit team's job is to ask probing questions about AQW and act as a sounding board for the department, in much the same way as research seminars provide feedback for principal investigators and their teams. The auditors sum up their conclusions and recommendations in a report to the department. Sometimes the department invites team members to return in a year or two to discuss its progress in implementing the agreed changes.

Because the auditors don't assess a department's teaching or research, they don't have to come from the same discipline as the faculty members being visited. Indeed, it's helpful if most of them aren't steeped in the discipline because they're more likely to ask out-of-the box questions. The auditors receive a thorough briefing on AQW concepts and what to look for in an audit visit. The workshops usually include a role-playing exercise on how to engage department faculty in meaningful conversation about AQW as opposed to the primary tasks of teaching and research. Experience shows that it's not hard to fill a day with meaningful conversation, and that a single day is enough to make a difference.

To go back to our metaphor, the prospect of a visit from faculty peers provides the impetus needed to start the AQW wheel spinning. No professor wants to come across as foolish or unprepared in conversations with peers. The timeframe for the audit visit is set at the time of the initial workshop, which introduces a deadline effect.

Creation of audit teams greatly expands the number of people who become versed in AQW. It's not uncommon for auditors to introduce AQW concepts into their own departments and perhaps volunteer to be audited in subsequent rounds. Likewise, faculty in departments being audited frequently serve as auditors.

Academic audit elicits structured conversations about how well the AQW concepts are understood and applied. Conversations are important because the complex issues of teaching and research quality are best addressed through dialogue. Structure is important because the conversations must cover all the relevant topics and allow the audit team to produce a coherent report. Above all, the conversations must not be allowed to degenerate into bull sessions that reinforce prejudices instead of stretching minds.

Academic audit bears a superficial resemblance to the program reviews that have become familiar features of the academic landscape. The department prepares a self-study, the report is discussed during a visit by the review team, and the team submits a report. But there the resemblance stops. Program reviews assess the department's primary activities—teaching and research—whereas an audit looks at its AQW. Program review teams are mostly populated by disciplinary experts from outside the university, whereas audit teams of the kind discussed here mostly are university insiders from other disciplines. Program review reports are addressed to deans, provosts, and presidents, whereas audit reports are addressed to the department. In short, program reviews are designed to help the administration evaluate the quality of a department's teaching and research; academic audits are designed to help departments improve their quality work.

Audits do not eliminate the need for program reviews. However, a robust program of academic audit and quality work may allow institutions to reduce the frequency of program reviews. Later chapters will show how departments with good AQW are able to produce better evidence about quality than those with poor AQW. The availability of such evidence reduces the need for external review. Audits also have the advantage of focusing on what can be done with existing resources, whereas program reviews often focus on the perceived need for new resources. Finally, audits are much less expensive than program reviews because they rely on insiders and last only a single day. These considerations suggest that all departments should be audited regularly with program reviews being conducted less frequently or, perhaps, when there is reason to believe a problem exists.

The Quality Improvement Cycle

AQW needs to be part of an ongoing cycle of departmental activity. One-off efforts may produce flurries of improvement, but quality breakthroughs require sustained effort. This is more than a matter of time on task. We have referred often to "systematic quality work," where *system* implies a set of interconnected parts. Many forces work against quality. To counter them requires organized effort, a system in which the whole is greater than the sum of its parts.

The quality improvement cycle depicted in Figure 1.1 is just such a system. As in our earlier metaphor, the cycle is represented by a wheel. AQW's objective is to keep the wheel spinning. The department moves from event to event (which are represented by type blocks on the wheel), with each event building on the ones before it. Completing the transit embeds a new increment of delivered quality, after which the cycle begins again. Another metaphor is that of an orbit. Not only does forward movement need to be maintained, there must be enough centripetal energy to counter inertial tendencies that, unchecked, would cause faculty to abandon the program. These inertial tendencies are shown as italicized blocks at the ends of arrows, which depict centrifugal forces. The events are designed to mitigate the inertial tendencies. Failure to do so risks breaching the quality cycle—which would cause AQW to founder and quality improvement to stagnate.

Figure 1.1 The Quality Improvement Cycle

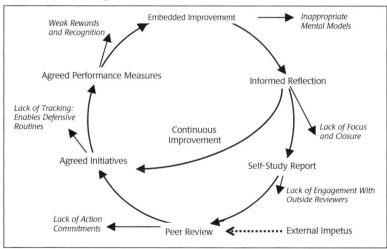

Starting at the top of the figure, we find inappropriate mental models to be the first problem. Faculty who believe that spending more is the only way to improve quality will be disinclined to engage in quality work, for example. Another killer belief is that failure to learn is the student's fault, that there is little a faculty member can or should do to solve the problem. Although it's true that some students are badly motivated or find learning difficult, professors should see this as a challenge rather than a reason to give up. Blaming the student should be a last resort, exercised only when all else has failed.

Informed reflection, the first event in the quality cycle, provides the mitigation for inappropriate mental models. Faculty become informed about quality and quality work and use this information when reflecting on their department's behavior. But reflection without focus and closure is less than fully effective. Therefore, the second event is to produce a written report on the subject. As in all scholarly activities, the act of writing focuses one's own mind as well as facilitates communication with others. Clear communication within the department is essential for a collegial activity like AQW, and of course it is required for the audit team as well.

The next event, denoted by "Peer Review" at the bottom of the figure, is the academic audit visit. The visit tests the department's thinking through structured conversation. It also provides a deadline for completing the report. But even the most serious engagement will fail to produce improvement unless it leads to a commitment for action. Therefore, the next event is to agree on specific initiatives—actions the department will undertake to improve quality during the next year. And because initiatives that can't be tracked invite claims that success has been achieved when it hasn't and enable other defensive routines, it's essential to agree in advance about how the department will gauge success. Normally the initiatives and tracking measures will be identified in the self-study report and discussed with the audit team, but they're set out as separate events in the figure because of their importance.

Now the dean comes into the picture. He or she should take a keen interest in the department's AQW, particularly in its initiatives and tracking measures. (Sharing the audit report with the dean will stimulate interest and provide context for the initiatives and measures.) Although the faculty's intrinsic motivation can do much to drive quality improvement, weak rewards and recognition can undermine the process. The dean is a pivotal figure in providing rewards and recognition, so he or she plays a key role in getting closure on the quality cycle. Deans—or provosts or presidents, for that matter—who don't care about AQW are telling the faculty they shouldn't care either, which dooms the process to failure.

We spoke earlier about the need to inject energy near the circumference of the quality improvement wheel and academic audit's role in so doing. That accounts for the dotted arrow leading into the "Peer Review" event—that arrow represents the impetus needed to get AQW embedded in departmental routines.

External impetus becomes less important once the quality wheel is spinning—once the department has developed a "culture of quality." Such a culture spawns reflection spontaneously, and the reflection leads directly to initiatives and tracking measures. This is what's meant by "continuous improvement," the mantra of the quality movement. Continuous improvement is depicted by the interior arc that cuts across the figure. Rewards and recognition still are necessary, but quality improvement tends to proceed by itself without the formalities of written reports and audit visits. Unfortunately, the friction of day-to-day events will cause even a mature AQW system to run down over time unless fresh injections of energy are forthcoming, so it is necessary to revisit the outer circle from time to time. We believe that written self-studies followed by academic audits should be repeated on approximately a five-year cycle, with decanal reinforcement of continuous improvement in the intervening years.

Plan for the Book

As indicated earlier, our purpose is to provide a how-to guide for those who wish to introduce AQW at their institutions. Our main focus is on AQW at the department level. Beginning there has several advantages. First-line quality work must take place at the grassroots, since faculty are the ones ultimately responsible for quality. (We speak of departmental AQW because that's where most faculty have their appointments. However, the techniques work just as well for interdepartmental programs.) Chapters 2–7 address department-level work. Work at higher organizational levels is covered in Chapter 8.

Chapters 2 and 3 describe AQW as applied to education. The former elaborates on the purposes of quality work and its five focal areas, all of which need to be addressed if quality work is to be successful. Chapter 3 introduces a set of normative principles, such as the use of evidence, which should govern education quality work. Next we present a maturity scale for AQW, which can be used by department members and others to gauge progress toward an embedded culture of quality. The chapter concludes by considering quality work above the department level—that is, how deans, provosts, and others can spur improvement throughout the institution.

The next three chapters address the practicalities of AQW for education. They elaborate on the principles discussed earlier with examples from the University of Missouri System and the Tennessee Board of Regents—entities with which we have hands-on experience. Chapter 4 describes the briefings and workshops used to introduce AQW and academic audit in these venues and the kinds of questions raised by faculty in the sessions. It presents sample questions that can be used to jump-start conversations about quality work and our ideas about rewarding faculty engagement in the process. Chapter 5 describes the development of self-studies: how to organize for the self-study and guidelines to facilitate the process. Chapter 6 addresses the audit and audit report. Topics include the selection and training of auditors, planning the audit day, and guidelines for report-writing. Examples of self-studies and audit reports are provided in their respective chapters.

Chapter 7 extends AQW to include research and scholarship— that is, moving from *education* quality work to *academic* quality work. We begin with the University of Missouri's decision to make the change and the reasons for doing so. Revision of the quality principles and sample questions so they apply to research comes next. This is followed by the changes needed to audit research as well as education in a single day.

Chapter 8 describes how departmental audits can be extended to the campus level and how this is being done in overseas venues. The chapter ends with a discussion of the National Consortium for Continuous Improvement's program for advancing academic and administrative excellence—a program that we believe offers opportunities to carry forward the ideas contained in this book.

Chapter 9 provides a summary of the book, a discussion of return on investment in higher education, and the findings of the Spelling Commission. We conclude with a set of policy recommendations—practical actions that can be taken to enhance quality in higher education.

2

Academic Quality Work

Derek Bok, the long-time president of Harvard whose book we cited in Chapter 1, asks why faculty should not regularly engage in cycles of education quality improvement: "Is something wrong with continuous evaluation and experimentation?" (Bok, 2006, p. 310). The answer, of course, is that there's nothing wrong with continuous improvement. The reasons it doesn't happen on most campuses stem from errors of omission rather than conscious decisions. It is one of those "good works" that just falls through the cracks.

AQW provides the antidote for such errors of omission. Distinguishing quality work from the "doing" of teaching and research gives it a separate focus and invites targeted time investments. Such focus and investment significantly increase the time spent on quality improvement tasks. But while time on task is important, the biggest benefits come from organizational learning, when faculty *learn how to improve education quality*—a subject that is notoriously lacking in programs that train PhDs.

A department's AQW is easier to observe than teaching and learning. It may sound strange to "assess the quality of quality work," but that's a perfectly sensible concept. Assessments of departmental AQW maturity can provide the impetus needed to sustain focus and spur organizational learning.

AQW Defined

AQW extends the idea of *education quality work* (Massy, 2003c, Chapters 6 & 7) to include research and scholarship. This term was coined by the Swedish Academic Quality Agency in the early 1990s to describe the subject matter of its academic audits. Because the translation from Swedish to *education quality work* appeared awkward to some, there was considerable experimentation with alternatives—for example, *teaching and learning quality processes* and *education quality processes.* In the end, however, the original term seemed to sum up the idea best.

Academic quality processes can be defined as follows (adapted from Massy, 2003c, p. 159):

> Academic quality processes are *organized activities dedicated to improving and assuring education and research quality.* They systematize a university's approach to quality instead of leaving it mainly to unmonitored individual initiative. They provide what higher education quality pioneers David Dill (1992) and Frans van Vught (1995, p. 13) call "a framework for quality management in higher education . . . drawn from insights in Deming's approach, but grounded in the context of academic operations."

We have already noted that academic quality processes should not be confused with the acts of teaching and research. Course development is not the same as teaching, for example, nor is improving the department's research environment identical to doing one's own research. One might say that quality processes plan and govern the improvement and monitoring of teaching and research.

This chapter describes the educational side of AQW—that is, education quality work. The amount of application experience is greatest in this area, and one can argue that the problems are the hardest. To avoid the awkwardness of terms like *educational AQW,* we'll simply use *EQW.* The ideas presented here will be extended to research and scholarship in Chapter 7. This chapter concludes with a discussion of how departments can apply the same kind of collegial thinking to cost issues as they do to AQW.

Myths About Education Quality

A less formal description of quality work, applicable especially in its early stages, is that of myth-busting. The myths at issue are unexamined but widely held mental models about teaching and research. Such myths can kill a department's ability to improve quality.

Quality work subjects the myths to scrutiny. The grains of truth can be retained, and the erroneous or misleading parts can be discarded. And because quality work is a collegial activity, its myth-busting benefits can touch a critical mass of department members. We will describe the teaching-related myths briefly to provide motivation for what comes later.

> *Myth 1: Quality depends mainly on spending.* "Reducing class size and/or teaching loads is the best if not the only ways to improve quality. Doing so requires more faculty lines or smaller enrollments. More lines also will enable us to cover the discipline better and concentrate on teaching our specialties."

We introduced the quality-spending myth in Chapter 1. It belies the whole idea of EQW by saying that what one *does* with the money (other than adding faculty) doesn't matter. It says, "Purposes and curricula don't matter. Teaching and assessment methods don't matter. Quality assurance doesn't matter. Just get the faculty, and quality will follow." The truth is that what professors do *does* matter. "If you build it, they will come" worked in *Field of Dreams,* but it can't be counted on in the real world of education quality. Getting additional resources can be a worthy goal, especially if a department is understaffed, but getting the best from what one has also is important.

> *Myth 2: Research automatically improves teaching.* "Next to adding faculty, the best way to improve quality is to boost faculty research. As researchers we bring up-to-date facts and concepts to our teaching and involve undergraduates in the research itself. The vibrancy associated with a research-active faculty enriches the undergraduate curriculum and energizes the students. These benefits more than make up for the time we spend on research—which in any case is offset by the lower teaching loads afforded by a larger faculty."

The research myth has more than a grain of truth, but its uncritical acceptance obscures some very real issues (Massy, 2003c, Chapter 5). Professors don't need to publish at the cutting edge of their specialty to keep up with the field. Indeed, high degrees of specialization may make it harder to give undergraduates what they really need. Only small numbers of undergraduates ever participate seriously in faculty research projects—for them the experience can be life-changing, but what of the vast majority of students? How does the vibrancy of a research faculty trade off against the fact that research-active professors often are inaccessible to undergraduates? Quality work addresses such issues. It seeks to maximize the synergies between teaching and research instead of leaving them to the vagaries of chance.

> *Myth 3: Good teachers are born, not made.* "Some professors are inherently good teachers, and others are not. The ability to teach well is more of a trait than a learned behavior—it's nice to have but not something to train for. And because being a master of subject matter is what counts in a professor, we don't hire or promote on the basis of teaching ability, especially the ability to teach students who lack preparation and/or motivation."

The born-not-made myth absolves professors from trying to improve their teaching skills and departments from pressing them to do so. But it has two big holes. First, teaching involves consideration of educational purpose, the design of curricula and pedagogies, and the assessment of student performance—none of which depend on stand-up personality characteristics. Second, the ability to empathize and communicate can be learned, at least to a point. The fact that graduate programs ignore such learning does not make it irrelevant to the faculty member's job. Once again, quality work can address these issues in a straightforward and compelling way.

> *Myth 4: It's the best and most motivated students that matter.* "Teaching is the professor's job; learning is the student's. It's not my fault if students lack preparation or don't study hard enough. My goal is to draw out the best students, uphold

standards for the rest, and not waste my time with the laggards. What's important is the degree of attainment at the top of the class, not what happens at the bottom."

The issue here is, where do you draw the line? There's no doubt that some students are unwilling or unable to perform adequately in a university setting, and that after a certain point they're not the professor's problem. But it's easy to overextend the argument—to blame the students for what in fact is the teacher's failure to impart motivation or present content in meaningful ways. We spoke of professors' desires to replicate themselves (the "mini-me" objective) in Chapter 1; this is another manifestation of the it's-the-best-students myth. Quality work focuses on the value added by education for all students, not just the attainment of those in the top percentiles.

> *Myth 5: Teaching is a lone-wolf activity.* "What goes on
> behind the classroom door is a private matter between me
> and my students. I usually prepare alone and teach without
> peer presence. I may know or suspect that a certain colleague
> isn't teaching well, but it isn't my job to do anything about
> that. Academic freedom goes beyond the question of
> teaching controversial material. It includes my choice of
> teaching and assessment methods and rules out most forms
> of quality assurance." (And in extreme interpretations,
> "Academic freedom includes the freedom to teach badly.")

Asserting that teaching is a private matter between teacher and students is like saying medical care is a private matter between doctor and patient. That may have been true at one time, but modern medicine asserts an overarching professional responsibility to enhance and safeguard the patient's interests. It is presumptuous to say that individual doctors can do their jobs effectively without input from colleagues. The doctor-patient consultation may remain one on one, but good doctors are quick to consult with one another about diagnoses, treatments, and outcomes. The same is true in virtually all professions—except higher education. Quality work aims to correct that shortfall by making education quality a departmental responsibility.

Myth 6: Quality is good absent evidence to the contrary. "The students aren't complaining, and the dean hasn't taken me to task about my course evaluations. Therefore, my teaching must be all right."

Such attitudes reflect a passive approach to quality and one that focuses on achieving minimum standards instead of doing a truly good job. A proactive approach would be to seek out new evidence and then act on it energetically. The absence of complaints would be seen as the threshold for minimum acceptable performance, not an indicator of good performance. A shortage of evidence would be seen as a danger sign rather than one that all is well—rather like driving at night with a poor set of headlights.

Myth 7: Education quality can't be measured. "Teaching is too complicated for the results to be measured effectively. Besides, the outcomes won't be known until much later in the students' lives—many years from now. People who try to assess learning often come up with confusing or contradictory results. Measurement invites 'teaching to the test,' which everyone knows is bad. I know quality when I see it, so why bother with less-than-perfect measurements?"

Many externally mandated learning assessment programs have foundered on just such objections. Quality work approaches measurement from the opposite perspective: "How do we, as faculty members, know whether we're achieving our goals?" The assertion "I know quality when I see it" is shown to be inadequate through probing conversations with colleagues. Academic ingenuity can find ways to make sense of the evidence and uncover new evidence, if the process proceeds collegially and the purposes of the educational task are clear.

Design and Implementation Quality

People who study quality have learned to distinguish between *design quality* and *implementation quality* (D. H. Maister, personal communication, February 1985). *Design quality* refers to the specifications for the product or service: the way things are *intended* to work. *Implementation quality,* on the other hand, refers to how well a product or service *actually* works as compared to the intent. Sustaining and improving quality requires that both design and implementation be considered explicitly. It does little good to improve course design if teaching is lackluster. Likewise, the best teaching in the world may not be able to overcome a flawed design—for example, one that misses the purpose of the educational program.

Outcomes may differ from intentions for two reasons. First, the design may simply be impractical to implement given the time and resources available. Cramming too much content into a course design, for example, is a common problem. The material may be in the syllabus and even "taught" after a fashion, but it is not learned. The second reason is the quality of the implementation itself. The teacher may be unprepared, or the classroom may be crowded and uncomfortable. The two reasons interact. A content-crammed syllabus may be teachable by the best instructors, for example, but not by those with lesser skills. It's obvious that solving such problems depends critically on finding the correct diagnosis. Confusing design and implementation quality leads one to look in the wrong place for solutions.

High-quality designs are what experts call "fit for purpose." One starts with the functions the product or service is supposed to perform and the context or conditions in which the performance will take place. Doing so implies that beyond a certain minimum there is no absolute standard of what counts as design quality. Take cars, for example. All cars need to meet minimum standards of performance, safety, and durability. Beyond that, however, design quality should be gauged relative to the car's target functionality and price. Although the design of a luxury sedan can be viewed as embodying more absolute quality (e.g., power and handling) than a subcompact, the latter's design quality may be just as high given its purpose (basic transportation) and target price (low). One lesson for universities is that building up the faculty's research prowess does not necessarily improve the design quality of its education. One must go further and ask whether the extra research would add value to the institution's particular student body. Universities that can afford only low levels of expenditure per student can have high design quality if their offerings are truly fit for purpose.

Design quality also speaks to the difficulty of producing the product or service. A device whose features cannot be manufactured reliably is not said to have good design quality. In higher education the University of Phoenix prides itself on designing courses that can be taught effectively by adjunct faculty. (Phoenix also carefully matches its courses with the needs of its particular students.) How many traditional universities can say the same? How many courses that would work well if taught by professors end up being taught by adjuncts or graduate students?

Mature EQW might well identify such disconnects through a systematic analysis of design and implementation quality. It may also identify cases where implementation simply isn't up to reasonable standards. Anyone who has purchased a "lemon" knows that even a well-designed car can be produced poorly. High implementation quality requires that all cars be produced to specification, even when the workforce may lack focus (e.g., on Monday morning) or when production levels strain capacity. In higher education the best course designs will produce poor outcomes if facilities and teaching standards aren't maintained. Well-designed curricula taught by poorly trained and poorly motivated adjuncts or graduate students will not produce the desired learning outcomes.

AQW Focal Areas for Education

The definition of *academic quality work* speaks to systematizing a university's approach to quality. *Systematizing* implies a body of content that must be considered before an analysis can be accepted as complete. We call that body of content the "focal areas" of quality work.

EQW covers five focal areas: 1) learning objectives; 2) curriculum; 3) teaching and learning methods; 4) student learning assessment; and 5) quality assurance. (The focal areas for research and scholarship will be discussed in Chapter 7.) Failure to address all five means the work is incomplete and therefore flawed. For example, curricular design can't be done effectively without explicit consideration of, and agreement on, the objectives of the learning experience. Teaching and student assessment methods should depend on learning objectives as well as curricular content. And by omitting quality assurance a department ignores the question of whether its intentions are being carried out as planned.

We introduce each focal area with a short list of questions that faculty might ask themselves as they address EQW for the first time. These questions were used in Missouri and Tennessee to good effect. Subsequent commentary provides a framework for thinking about the focal area and some examples of how such thinking can improve teaching and learning. The discussion only scratches the surface, however. We cite additional examples in later chapters, and Bok (2006) provides many more.

Learning Objectives

What knowledge, skills, and values should students acquire from their educational experience? How will this experience pay off in employment, societal contributions, and quality of life? Are the objectives based on the needs of actual or potential students rather than some ideal student?

This first area speaks to the purpose part of fitness for purpose. It's the question from which all else follows, yet too few departments consider it systematically. Too often, learning objectives are assumed to be mastering the discipline's core facts and concepts. The all-important "why" question is never asked, so the facts and concepts are presented as self-evidently important. Worse, perhaps, which facts and concepts to present is dictated by the disciplinary professional rather than the needs of students—most of whom will never become professionals in the field.

Derek Bok (2006) describes what he considers to be the eight core purposes of undergraduate education writ large. These purposes are relevant to every major, as well as to general education, in every undergraduate institution. In addition to their intrinsic importance, considering them will stretch one's mind beyond normal disciplinary boundaries. The question should be, how can the facts and concepts of our discipline contribute to learning with respect to these purposes? The eight purposes, together with brief expository phrases adapted from Bok, follow, although we encourage readers to consult the original:

- *Learning to communicate:* learning to write and speak. "Expressing oneself with clarity, precision, and, if possible, style and grace."
- *Learning to think:* critical thinking, quantitative reasoning. "Asking pertinent questions, recognizing and defining problems, identifying the arguments on all sides of an issue, searching for and using relevant data, and arriving in the end at carefully reasoned judgments."
- *Building character:* teaching moral reasoning, strengthening the will to act morally. "Teaching students to think more carefully about ethical problems by having them discuss dilemmas that arise frequently in personal and professional life."
- *Preparation for citizenship:* countering apathy, developing informed choices. "The distinctive role of civic education is to give students enough knowledge to make the thoughtful, informed choices that enlightened citizenship requires."
- *Living with diversity:* race, ethnicity, and gender. "Broadening experience and improving critical thinking through response to different values and perspectives. A successful democracy demands tolerance and mutual respect."
- *Preparing for a global society:* international subjects, foreign languages, international students, education abroad. "Building the groundwork for international expertise, responsible citizenship, travel abroad, and understanding one's own country."
- *Acquiring broader interests:* general education, extracurricular activities. "Awakening intellectual interests and helping students understand the world and their place in it with greater understanding than achievable through study in a single area."
- *Preparing for a career:* choosing a career, acquiring work-related knowledge and skills. "Reconciling study in liberal arts subjects with the need to prepare for life-shaping work."

So many colleges and universities cite career preparation as an important goal, and so many professors lament this fact, that it is worthwhile to consider the subject in slightly greater depth. John Seely Brown, former chief scientist of Xerox and director of the Xerox Palo Alto Research Center, and his colleague Paul Duguid put the matter of career preparation into perspective by citing two critical distinctions:

between "learning to be" and "learning about" and between "know how" and "know that" (Brown & Duguid, 2000, p. 128). The best career preparation is to learn to be successful in the relevant areas. This is much broader than learning about career-oriented subject matter. Indeed, for most careers it's no stretch to incorporate many of the liberal arts values into learning to be. Brown and Duguid also point to the need for learning through practice, that know-how does not come simply through accumulating information. "And, similarly," they say, "through practice, we learn to be" (p. 128). We take these arguments as supporting not only the need for carefully thought-out purposes in higher education but also the need for active learning, as will be discussed later.

Higher education's repertory of purposes applies differentially across majors and, of course, to general education. But while not every department will subscribe to all of these purposes or find ways to further each in its discipline, every one should consider them when setting the learning objectives for its major. It's one thing to consider and decide that certain objectives are more important. It's another to assume that without any analysis.

One can imagine going even further—that a school or campus will work proactively to ensure that each purpose is achieved in the aggregate for students in every major. Such consideration would emphasize that all faculty bear a degree of responsibility for all the purposes, not just the faculty teaching general education courses. Bok (2006, Chapter 12) makes a point of recommending this. We'll recommend a way of accomplishing it in Chapter 8.

Curriculum

How does the curriculum relate to the program's learning objectives? What is being taught, in what order, and from what perspective? Does the curriculum build cumulatively on students' prior knowledge and capacity? To what extent does the cocurriculum support the curriculum and the program's learning objectives generally?

No department is without experience in curricular design, and few professors have never put together a course syllabus. (We include course development under the rubric of curriculum.) Unfortunately, however, curricula that are informed by detailed learning objectives are more the exception than the rule. Deeper reflection on the mapping of objectives to curriculum is needed.

The purpose of a curriculum is to convert learning objectives, which by nature are fairly abstract, to specific and tangible content. For example, the develop-critical-thinking objective could be mapped into lists of required courses or, at the course level, sets of problems and the facts and concepts needed to solve them. The communication objective might be implemented through a writing-across-the-curriculum program. The character-building objective might lead course designers to identify sets of ethical dilemmas and collections of readings that illuminate those dilemmas from various perspectives. Learning objectives and subject matter knowledge provide the input to curricular design. Specification of the content to be taught and the materials to be assigned to students provide the output.

Curriculum designers always suffer from an embarrassment of riches. There's never enough space in the course or program to include everything with a reasonable claim to importance. Designers must select from the range of alternatives. But how? One way is to use the established canon of the discipline. Obviously the level must be appropriate to the student's preparation, but the criteria for importance come from the discipline itself. We, however, advocate a different approach. Start with the learning objectives—student needs—and see how the discipline's armamentarium can help. Maybe the results turn out to follow the canon, but maybe not.

Cramming the available space with content while ignoring skill development is a common problem. Maybe this occurs because so many designers start with lists of content items rather than clear-cut skill development goals:

> Although almost all faculty members claim to give highest priority to helping students learn to think critically, they spend most of the time in their curricular reviews arguing over which courses to offer and which to require. [Educational] researchers, on the other hand, find that the arrangement of

courses, per se, has little effect on the development of critical thinking. What matters more is the way in which courses are taught and the effort the students and faculty devote to the educational process. (Bok, 2006, p. 144)

The same point applies to the design of individual courses.

The best designers carry the mapping of objectives one step further. Every item of learning content should serve not one but a number of objectives. Operations researchers call this a "knapsack problem." Suppose you'll be in the wilderness for a long time with nothing more than what you can carry on your back. The things you might take vary in size and value, and an item's value increases if it can serve multiple purposes. Finding the collection that maximizes value while fitting into the available space isn't easy, but it pays dividends when camping. Thinking about how a given curricular element can serve multiple purposes also can pay dividends for one's students.

Teaching and Learning Methods

What teaching methods are used—for example, for first exposure to materials, for interpreting materials and answering questions, for stimulating student involvement, and for providing feedback on student work? Is learning active? Is it collaborative? Is technology being used, and if so, is it exploited effectively?

It's surprising that so many courses are taught by the lecture method— some 80% by some estimates. Lectures do little to stimulate critical thinking, and research has shown them to be ineffective even for imparting content. For example, one study reports that "students retain only 42 percent of the information when [a lecture] ends and only 20 percent one week later" (Bok, 2006, p. 123). So much for the idea, widely held in academe, that "once I, as the lecturer, state the material clearly, my job is done." This is an example of poor design quality. It's fine to say that learning is up to the students, but it's the professor's job to create situations where learning can be effective. Study after study shows that sitting passively is a poor way to learn content and no way at all to learn critical thinking skills.

So what works better? The short answer is "active learning," but that requires elaboration. Active learning requires students to think about the material from a variety of perspectives and to apply it in a variety of contexts. Students need stimulation and reinforcement. They need substantive feedback while the material, and what they did with it, is fresh in their minds. These things can be accomplished through class discussion, collaborative work on assignments, and provision of timely comments on student work—anything but passive lectures followed by memory tests at midterm and end of term.

Barbara Walvoord, professor of English at Notre Dame and a nationally recognized expert on teaching and assessment, offers a good example of how professors can improve their course designs. (Bok, 2006, Chapter 5, provides additional examples.) She organizes educational tasks according to phase of learning and type of "faculty-student space" involved, not just by units of content (Walvoord & Pool, 1998, p. 38):

Phase of learning:
- *First exposure:* when students first encounter new information, concepts, or procedures
- *Process:* when students analyze the material, synthesize it, use it to solve problems, apply it to actual situations, and so on
- *Response:* when the teacher or peers respond to a student's attempts at synthesis, analysis, problem solving, or application

Faculty-student space:
- *Synchronous space:* simultaneous effort by students and teachers, either face-to-face as in a conventional class or through telecommunications
- *Student space:* activities like studying and paper-writing, done alone or in groups but without real-time input from the teacher
- *Teacher space:* preparation, grading, and other activities performed by professors and course assistants while not in direct contact with students

Walvoord advises professors to organize their courses so each assignment can be handled in its own uniquely effective way. Some assignments would cover first exposure, others would stimulate and facilitate process-related activities, and still others would provide the responses students need to solidify their learning. Each assignment should use the space that is most cost effective for that phase of learning.

Because most students either don't read the textbook before class or don't get what they need from it, traditional lectures rely on professors to handle first exposure in synchronous space. Then students are sent home to perform the all-important process activities in student space—that is, to synthesize their notes, write papers, solve homework problems, and read or reread the course materials. (Discussion sections may facilitate these activities, but such sections often are delegated to teaching assistants.) Responses in the form of grades and comments on papers are prepared in teacher space, one student at a time, and often returned to students only after considerable delay.

Although outstanding lecturers can inspire and motivate students, thus creating active learning in what otherwise would be a passive setting, most lecturing is more mundane. Such lecturing puts the cart before the horse:

> It uses the time of the most highly paid and experienced person—the faculty member—for *first-exposure* lecture and leaves the more difficult *process* part of learning to students alone or to students in recitation sections with less experienced teaching assistants.... It requires the faculty member or teaching assistant to mark and comment on one paper at a time to one student alone, in an exchange that takes place without the benefit of face-to-face contact....
>
> Because teachers and teaching assistants are so pressed by sheer numbers of student papers, responses may be "hasty, unreadable, truncated, or hostile." Because response must be made one on one on the teacher's own time, any increase in class size or number of assignments exerts a heavy price in teacher or teaching assistant time. (Walvoord & Pool, 1998, p. 39)

Student time commitments to first exposure and processing often are skimpy—less than six hours of preparation a week for all classes, according to one study (Warren, 1997). Class time often can't be used for interactive processing or responding to student work because students are poorly prepared or teachers feel they must lecture on new material.

Walvoord's work illustrates the results of thinking seriously about teaching and learning methods. That most departments don't engage in such thinking evidences the immaturity of their quality work. It's easier to continue along the familiar path, but that path is becoming less defensible as research on learning effectiveness accumulates. One objective of EQW is to bring the same standards of scholarship to teaching and learning that are insisted on for disciplinary content.

Student Learning Assessment

What measures are used to assess student learning? Are they constructively aligned with your learning objectives? Do they compare beginning and ending performance to ascertain value added? Who is responsible for student learning assessment? Are the assessment results trending upward or downward? Do they inform quality improvement efforts, and if so, how?

Assessment serves three purposes. The first is formative: providing feedback to students—the "response" function in Walvoord's scheme. The second is summative: grading students' performance. The third is diagnostic: providing teachers with feedback about the learning process. The first and second functions fall under the rubric of teaching itself, not EQW. The third is a key element, some might say *the* key element, of quality work. Unfortunately, few departments or faculty think about it that way.

That faculty should experiment with new teaching and learning methods, *and evaluate those methods' results,* is one of Bok's main points. The idea of evaluation taps one of the quality movement's central themes: "If you can't measure it, you can't improve it." In other words, the feedback provided by diagnostic assessment is essential. Although value-added assessment is controversial, the idea is beginning to take root. For example, the National Association of State Universities and Land-Grant Colleges and the American Association of

State Colleges and Universities have called for the use of value-added assessment measures (McPherson, 2006). They also note that although externally normed tests have many advantages, being able to observe trends within one's own unit may be just as important as comparisons with external benchmarks.

Why is such assessment the exception rather than the rule? It's partly a matter of time on task. Faculty are busy with other things and aren't thinking about diagnostic assessment. But it's more than that. As Bok points out (2006), too often "the best . . . is the enemy of the good" (p. 310). Applying rigorous experimental procedures like matched control groups and randomized selection is difficult or impossible in the educational setting. It's similarly hard to get agreement on ways to measure, say, improvements in writing and critical thinking. Seeing how hard it is to achieve standards like those they apply in research, most faculty abandon the effort to obtain systematic diagnostic assessments. But that throws the baby out with the bathwater. Our EQW experience fully supports Bok's characterization of the matter:

> The proper test for universities to apply is not whether their assessments meet the most rigorous scholarly standards but whether they can provide more reliable information than the hunches, random experiences, and personal opinions that currently guide most faculty decisions about educational issues. By this standard, there are surely many important forms of intellectual development that can be described and measured well enough to conduct useful studies to evaluate existing educational programs and assess new methods of instruction. If faculties are willing to examine their students and record the results on official transcripts, it is hard for them to argue that they are incapable of devising methods of assessment reliable enough to evaluate the effects of their teaching on student learning. (p. 310)

Many states and all six regional accreditation associations have instituted requirements for universities to assess student learning. However, the so-called assessment movement has produced only limited results. In 1999, for example, the National Center for Postsecondary Improvement queried 1,393 public-sector chief academic officers about how their institutions "support, promote, and use student-assessment data to improve student learning and institutional performance" ("Revolution or Evolution?," 1999, p. 53). The results were not encouraging. Many academics feel the development of such measures is too difficult and "resistance at the institutional and/or faculty levels hindered the effectiveness of states' assessment policies" (Nettles & Cole, 1999, p. 11). Things are no better in the private sector. Institutions have learned to meet accreditation requirements, but efforts to embed and use assessment have not been successful. Charles Cook, director of the New England Association of Schools and Colleges' Commission on Institutions of Higher Education (a regional accreditation association), summed things up this way: "Millions have been spent by thousands going to hundreds of assessment workshops, and you need a microscope to find the stuff" (qtd. in McMurtrie, 2000, p. A31).

The problem is that an external requirement for assessment puts institutions and faculty in a compliance mode. Assessment is viewed as something to "get out of the way" rather than to diagnose and meet the faculty's own objectives. Embedding assessment in a regimen of EQW makes all the difference. Faculty will find ways to get feedback on student learning once the need for doing so becomes internalized.

Quality Assurance

How do faculty and departments assure themselves and others that the designs for curricula, teaching and learning methods, and student assessments are being implemented as intended? How do they assure themselves that other priorities don't push the education quality to the sidelines?

Teaching matters, no matter how well designed a course or curriculum may be. Most faculty members want to do a good job of teaching, but good performance depends on more than good intentions. To hone and, where necessary, develop one's teaching skills requires systematic effort. So does resistance to the dulling effects of routine and competing demands on one's time. These efforts should be viewed as the shared responsibility of individual professors and the department as a whole. This is what we mean by *quality assurance.*

The term *quality assurance* (QA) evokes images of inspection or in higher education perhaps intrusive external evaluations or standardized tests. But this view is too narrow. One of the lessons from the quality movement is that you can't inspect quality in at the end of a process. QA should be viewed as an ongoing process of getting feedback to detect the problems that crop up during any complex activity. Such feedback is essential for making midcourse corrections; even when it's too late for midcourse corrections, one can avoid repeating the problems the next time around. Without systematic QA processes, faculty members are likely to repeat the same errors semester after semester. Indeed, without feedback the problems are likely to get worse over time.

Student course evaluations are the most prevalent form of QA, and most campuses and departments require some kind of end-of-term evaluation. This represents a good start, but it's not sufficient. Students can evaluate certain aspects of teaching—whether explanations seem clear to them, for example—but they lack the expertise to make deeper judgments. End-of-term evaluations are too late to allow for midcourse corrections. Students don't always take the evaluations seriously, and even when they do the inherent limitations of written evaluations constrain their ability to communicate.

Professors who take their QA responsibilities seriously have a variety of methods at their disposal. They may assign so-called minute quizzes, perhaps several times in a class session, to gain feedback about how particular concepts are being understood. Technology has extended this idea: students respond with handheld wireless devices, and results are displayed on the professor's console or a classroom video display. To get at broader or deeper issues, faculty can meet with small groups of students several times during the semester for a conversation about how things are going in the course. Such actions not only produce good feedback, they signal that the professor cares about students' learning. Professors responsible for large courses can insist that their teaching assistants (TAs) seek such feedback and meet with them weekly to process the results. (Such actions have the added advantage of passing the techniques to the next generation of teachers.) Perhaps more ambitiously, professors who teach multiple sections of a given course can agree to get feedback and then meet regularly to compare notes.

Departments that take their QA responsibilities seriously can encourage faculty members to take the actions just described and schedule time at department meetings to discuss lessons learned and to effect improvements. They can create formal faculty-student consultative committees for large introductory courses and for students in the major. They can encourage, or perhaps even require, the peer evaluation of teaching for junior and even for senior faculty. (Such evaluations should not be viewed as threatening when conducted collegially for formative purposes.) They can mentor junior faculty on teaching skills and encourage faculty at all ranks to seek help if the feedback being obtained indicates a recurrent problem.

QA is not a punitive proposition. When used in the context of EQW, it is inherently formative. However, there is no denying that data produced in the process of assuring and improving quality can be used for purposes beyond the department's purview. The most important use is to provide evidence to deans and provosts (and by extension, accreditors and oversight boards) that the department cares about implementation quality. The key questions pertaining to such evidence are 1) whether the department is collecting QA information, and 2) whether it is acting on the information. Negative feedback is no cause for alarm unless there is a failure to act. However, failing to generate the feedback to begin with does represent cause for alarm. The myth that no news is good news should not obscure the need for transparency with respect to departmental and faculty QA efforts.

Balancing Cost and Quality

The myth that education quality can be improved only by spending more isn't consistent with the facts of quality work. Quality can almost always be improved by making better uses of current resources. But what about the idea of spending less? Might a department economize in certain courses and still maintain their quality? Might quality actually be improved while spending less? The answer to both questions is yes. It's not unrealistic for departments to set savings goals sufficient to offset the cost of their quality work—or perhaps to go even further.

Activity-Based Costing at the Course Level

The approach is to extend EQW's teaching-methods focal areas to include a variant of activity-based costing (ABC). Businesses use ABC to model the cost of all kinds of processes. The idea of applying it to college courses seems to have originated in the early 1990s with Jack Wilson at Rensselaer Polytechnic Institute (Wilson, 1997). It was picked up by EDUCOM (a predecessor to EDUCAUSE) soon afterward (Massy & Zemsky, 1994) and since then has been adopted widely—for example, through the Pew-funded Program in Course Redesign; the Teaching, Learning, and Technology Group (Ehrmann & Milam, 1999; Milam, 2000); the National Center for Higher Education Management Systems (Jones, 2004); and the BRIDGE cost simulation model developed by Frank Jewett of the California State University System. In Britain, the methodology has been used as part of institutional costing programs by the higher education funding councils of England, Scotland, and Wales. Northwest Missouri State University has run a successful pilot program linking ABC directly to its quality work.

Course-level ABC involves four commonsense steps (Massy, 2003c, Chapter 9). The steps can be applied to one of the department's current teaching methods or to a method that has been proposed but not yet adopted:

1) Identify the activities needed to teach the course using the current or proposed method.
2) Describe the resources consumed by each activity.
3) Find out how much the resources cost.
4) Cost out the resources consumed by each activity, and add the results to get the total cost of the process.

Steps 1, 2, and 4 can easily be accomplished within departments as part of their EQW. Step 3 can be done by a staff group, and the results can be supplied to the department in the form of standardized unit cost data.

We'll illustrate the steps by applying them to a conventional lecture-discussion course of the kind used at many colleges and universities. Figure 2.1 identifies the activities required to teach the course (Step 1). The shaded boxes depict what happens during each of the semester's

Figure 2.1 **Activity Schedule for a Conventional Lecture-Discussion**

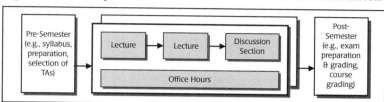

15 weeks: two lectures followed by a breakout discussion section, plus office hours. (Quizzes, papers, and midterm exams are ignored for the sake of simplicity, but they easily could be added.) Other activities, including syllabus preparation and the selection of TAs, take place before the start of the semester. Still others—including exam preparation, grading, and the finalization of course grades—occur after the semester is over. Taken together, the activities compose the course's activity schedule.

Figure 2.2 fulfills Step 2 by describing the resources needed for each activity. Let's assume that each class is one hour long, and that tenure-line professors teach the lectures and TAs teach the discussion sections. Professors estimate that on average they spend three hours of preparation for each lecture (six for the whole week) and that they provide two office hours a week for each section they teach. Economies in preparation accrue if a given professor teaches two sections. Similar

Figure 2.2 **Weekly Resource Requirements for a Conventional Lecture-Discussion Course**

A. *Assumptions*

Gross hours/section	Lecture	Discussion	Office hours	Preparation	Max. sections per teacher
Professor	2	0	2	6	2
Teaching assistant	0	1	4	2	3
Normal class size	110	20		Total enrollment	500

B. *Results*

	Lecture	Discussion		Professors	TAs
Number of sections	5	30	Max. hours	50	210
Facilities hours	10	10	Min. hours	38	170

assumptions apply to TAs and to pre- and post-semester activities, but the latter are not included in the table.

Next comes the question of how many professors and TAs will be required to teach the course. This depends on the number of students enrolled (the so-called driver variable), which we assume equals 500. Suppose the lecture room assigned to the course holds 110 students and that this number is judged by the faculty to be acceptable from a quality perspective. Suppose also that the faculty wants no more than 20 students per discussion group and that all the students in a given group must come from the same lecture section.

Doing the math shows that 5 lecture sections and 30 discussion sections will be required. This translates to 38 faculty hours and 170 TA hours a week if maximum preparation economies are achieved (if there are no such economies, the requirements would be 50 faculty hours and 210 TA hours). In addition the lecture room will be tied up for 10 hours a week, and breakout rooms will be occupied for 30 hours a week.

Step 3 requires cost accounting judgments that need not concern us here. The numbers can be supplied by university planners. These costs should reflect the department's particular circumstances, and they should be updated every year, but they need not be accurate to the penny.

Step 4 involves simple spreadsheet calculations. The result, given in Figure 2.3, shows total cost to be $144,507, or $289 per enrollment. (Pre- and post-semester costs aren't included, but they would be built up from their own activity analysis if this had been a real case.) Simple sensitivity analysis can provide additional insight. Interestingly, the largest element of cost in this case is not faculty, but rather TAs. Department members might wonder whether the financial aid component of such a cost is worth preserving, but they will have learned that TAs aren't exactly free goods.

Rensselaer pioneered the application of course-based ABC when considering whether to adopt its new Studio Physics course in place of the conventional lecture-discussion format (Wilson, 1997). Although the motivation behind Studio Physics was quality improvement, the change achieved a 33% reduction in the faculty's contact time with

Figure 2.3 **Total Cost and What-If Analysis for a Conventional Lecture-Discussion Course**

Base case (Based on maximum preparation hours)			Variations from the base case (Alternatives for reducing cost per enrollment)		
	Hours	Total		Total cost	Cost/enr.
Faculty cost	750	$ 50,000	Min. preparation hours	$118,093	$236
TA cost	3,150	$ 75,674			
Lecture hall cost	150	$ 5,521	Incr. lecture size by 25%	$128,137	$256
Breakout room cost	450	$ 3,313	Incr. breakout size by 25%	$131,343	$263
Pre and post cost		$ 10,000			
Total cost		$144,507	Cut office hours by 25%	$131,197	$262
Cost per enrollment		$ 289	Incr. enrollment by 25%	$171,409	$274

classes—which saved between $10,000 and $20,000 per semester. On the quality side, more topics were covered, and students performed as well as or better than students in the traditional courses. Student response was enthusiastic. Faculty evaluations in the studio format were far higher than in the traditional mode, and, when asked whether the course should be taught in the studio format versus some other way, 91% of students voted for the studio format. Class attendance increased from 50%–75% to 75%–80%, pre-semester test scores improved by 10%–13% compared to post-semester scores, and retention increased from 70% to 80%. Similar successes were achieved with other studio courses.

Faculty Time

Rensselaer's experience illustrates the importance of including faculty time when doing course-level ABC. But including faculty time raises two important questions. First, how should one estimate the time required for particular teaching and learning processes? Second, what happens to any time saved by adopting a more cost-effective approach?

Time estimation should be viewed as a judgmental exercise, not as something that requires detailed measurement. We're not talking about time logs, which are anathema to most professors. Rough averages usually suffice—for example, "How much time per session, on average, do I spend preparing for my Econ 101 lectures?" Indeed, when Zemsky et al. (1999) asked professors to provide time estimates at about mid-semester, those professors provided stable and consistent data and felt that the exercise was meaningful.

What to do with time saved presents a thornier set of issues. People often view faculty resources as fixed because tenure and other contractual commitments prevent time saved during a given semester from being turned into cash. However, it's the scarcity of faculty time rather than its financial fungibility that makes course-level costing work.

Most faculty members are, or at least feel, overworked. Faculty time is the university's scarcest resource, so it behooves departments to make the best possible use of it. Teaching processes that require less faculty time are better than those that require more, if other factors are equal. It doesn't matter that the savings can't be cashed out—most professors will redeploy their effort to worthwhile uses, including other education-related tasks, EQW, and research. To ignore the faculty time input to educational processes is to miss an important opportunity for disproving the quality-spending myth. It also ignores opportunities for mitigating the workload pressures associated with the improvement of EQW.

3

Quality Principles and Their Application

When the idea of EQW was first introduced in Hong Kong and Sweden in the early 1990s, decisions about what represented good performance were left to the universities and their departments. This stemmed more from practicality than conviction. The protagonists of quality work didn't really know what to look for, but they felt they would know good work when they saw it. It was enough to devote attention to the newly defined EQW focal areas. Reflecting on the department's work in each area would illuminate shortfalls and spawn ideas for improvement.

Nondirected reflection served well enough as a first step, but requests for guidance didn't take long to emerge. Now, more than a decade later, the guidance notes and discussion questions prepared to facilitate various academic audits have been reduced to a set of principles of good practice for quality work. The principles can guide a department in its reflection and improvement efforts; they also can guide auditors in evaluating a department's work. An analogy with financial auditing is apt: The people who manage a company's accounts and those who audit them operate from a single set of generally accepted accounting principles (GAAP). Although the principles that govern AQW are necessarily more subjective than GAAP, their role is the same. In time higher education may come to think of them as "generally accepted academic quality principles"—or the unpronounceable acronym GAAQP.

This chapter introduces principles of best practice for quality work, followed by a discussion of AQW maturity, the degree to which departments apply the principles daily. The chapter concludes by examining quality work above the department level—that is, by deans, provosts, system-wide administrators, trustees and regents, oversight boards, and accreditors.

Quality Principles

Research at Stanford University's National Center for Postsecondary Improvement identified seven principles of good practice for quality work. The principles have their roots in business, government, and health care, but they have been adapted to and tested in academe (Massy 2003a; Massy & French, 2001). They are consistent with the preponderance of ideas expressed in the literature on quality in higher education (cf. Ruben, 1995). We state each principle first and then discuss it using language adapted from the business literature. Applications to higher education will be elaborated in later chapters.

Define Quality in Terms of Outcomes

Learning outcomes should pertain to what is or will become important for the department's students. Exemplary departments carefully determine their students' needs and then work to meet those needs. They know that student learning, not teaching per se, is what ultimately matters.

Defining quality in terms of outcomes brings the fitness-for-purpose principle, from Chapter 2, to life in higher education. *Outcomes* means student learning and its consequences. Therefore, *education quality* means the extent of learning and its relevance to what is or will become important for the student. Put more provocatively, education quality should be defined as meeting "customer" needs and wants. Doing so provides purpose and direction for the organization, improves competitiveness and goodwill, and contributes to long-term institutional success.

In the business literature, a customer is anyone who receives the benefits of the output from another individual or organization. The definition includes both external and internal customers. Surely students qualify as customers by this definition:

> There can be little doubt that there are many "customers" of higher education.... At the origin of the views of quality there is ... a student: a researcher being prepared for science and industry, a new teacher being prepared for ... our schools, a city manager completing a master's program in public administration, an attorney returning to learn about computers, or a farmer or plant manager being served by an agricultural or manufacturing extension service. (Bogue & Saunders, 1992, p. 270)

Quality champions believe that making customer focus the defining aspect of all jobs can play an important role in shaping and changing organizational culture. Customer focus provides an external purpose for an activity. It encourages people to move from being inwardly directed to being externally directed. Customer focus also helps instill values of cooperation and service, both of which improve products and services and boost operational efficiency. The notion of customer focus has taken hold not only in business but also in government and other nonprofit organizations such as health care (Rosenbluth & Peters, 1992; Whiteley, 1991; Zeithaml, Parasuraman, & Berry, 1990; Zemke & Schaaf, 1989). Quality-disciplined enterprises satisfy customers by exceeding their needs and expectations, or even by providing products and services they did not know they needed but end up appreciating (Berry, 1991; Deming, 1986; Joiner, 1994; Juran, 1989; Senge, 1990; Whiteley, 1991). Such enterprises call this "customer delight."

In education customer focus doesn't imply that the customer is always right. Anyone who has graded an exam or paper knows that the student is not always right. Most academics resist using *customer* for exactly this reason. Yet the idea of being externally focused transcends this interpretation. It stands in sharp contrast to the more inward-focused definition of *quality* so often espoused by academics—that is, "mastering the academic discipline."

We prefer to describe students as "clients" rather than "customers." The clients of lawyers, accountants, and consultants are not always right. In fact, such clients usually know relatively little about the subject in question. It is the professional's job to study the client's problem and apply his or her knowledge and skills to provide the best possible solution. Is it any different with professors? The fitness-for-purpose principle holds that professors should ascertain the needs of their students and then apply their expertise to meet those needs.

Focus on How Things Get Done

> *Departments should carefully analyze how teachers teach, how students learn, and how they all approach learning assessment. Departments should consult their discipline's pedagogical literature and collect data on what works well and what doesn't. They should stress active learning, exploit information technology, and not hesitate to experiment with new teaching and learning methods. Faculty should be quick to adopt their colleagues' successful innovations, which should become part of the department's modus operandi and form the baseline for future experimentation and improvement.*

All activity is process, and teaching, learning, and assessment are activities. Yet professors view education quality mostly in terms of content, not activity (Stark & Lattuca, 1997). They take process more or less for granted—believing, for example, that content is the responsibility of professors and learning is the responsibility of students. But even if this view was valid when access to higher education was limited to a select few, increased participation has made it obsolete. Today's average undergraduate has neither the preparation nor the inclination to "sit at the feet of scholars," as academic tradition would have it. The second quality principle, then, is to stop taking process for granted and give it equal status with content.

In the business literature, a *process* is any activity or group of activities that takes inputs, transforms and adds value to them, and delivers an output to an internal or external customer (Davenport, 1993; Deming, 1986; Harrington, 1991; Joiner, 1994; Lareau, 1991; Melan, 1993; Scholtes, 1988). Processes have specific purposes that produce value for customers or stakeholders. Effective processes have distinct start and end points, and they consist of actions that are definable, repeatable, predictable, and measurable. One begins thinking about quality improvement by studying how processes work and how their elements interact. Then one identifies the causes of quality defects and figures out how to mitigate them. As Einstein said about physics, "God is in the details."

Process design refers to the specifics of determining how various resources—people, materials, and machines—can be brought together to produce the desired outcomes with minimal defects. *Process design* also refers to the redesign or reengineering of an existing set of activities.

Process design tends to involve certain identifiable steps (Davenport, 1993; Hammer & Champy, 1993; Juran & Gryna, 1993; Scholtes, 1988). First, one uses flowcharting and other analytical techniques to develop a clear understanding of the current process and what might be wrong with it. Second, one develops ideas for design or redesign in response to clearly defined requirements for the new process. Such requirements might include improved effectiveness or accuracy, reduced cycle time (the elapsed time between key process steps), fewer failures, or the use of technology to leverage people's time. Once a new process is up and running, someone can benchmark its performance against similar processes in other enterprises.

In the production of services, tight process design does not imply the loss of humanity or spontaneity. Key process elements are controlled, but people can act independently within these limits when such independence benefits the customer. For example, Nordstrom employees are encouraged to interact with customers in a spontaneous and friendly way even as they maintain the rigorous standards needed for process integrity, including provision of accurate information about products and enforcement of store policies. In education professors can interact spontaneously and proactively with students even as they maintain design standards for content coverage and timing, provision of skill development experiences, and assessment. Without process design standards, on the other hand, providers can do whatever they wish whenever they wish. This makes it hard to compare results with expectations, refine the process through systematic analysis, and build cumulatively on successful experience.

Work Collaboratively

Professors should demonstrate collegiality in education-related work, just as they do in research. For example, working in teams brings an array of talent to bear on difficult problems, disseminates insight, and allows members to hold each other accountable for team assignments. This makes the department a learning organization not only for disciplinary content but also for education quality processes.

Strange as it may seem in light of the academy's stated emphasis on collegiality, professors rarely work together on the design, implementation, and QA of teaching and learning. This is consistent with the so-called organized anarchy that many authors associate with academic processes (Cohen, March, & Olsen, 1972). One experienced commentator put it this way: "Academic specialists retreat into the forts of their specialized knowledge-fields and they are no longer concerned with the relationships of their work to that of colleagues" (van Vught, 1995, p. 10).

The resulting isolation and fragmentation has a chilling effect on education quality. Former Cornell president Frank Rhodes described the problem as follows:

Without community, knowledge becomes idiosyncratic: the lone learner, studying in isolation, is vulnerable to narrowness, dogmatism, and untested assumption, and learning misses out on being expansive and informed, contested by opposing interpretations, leavened by differing experience, and refined by alternative viewpoints. (qtd. in Vedder, 2004, p. 118)

Substitute *quality work* for *learning,* and one sees the overwhelming importance of collegiality in EQW.

Working collegially implies what's called "teamwork" in the literature on quality—that is, working together in groups to achieve a common objective. Teams provide mutual involvement and support, aid communication, and minimize duplication of effort. Teamwork helps eliminate destructive internal competition and contributes to a culture where everyone works together to benefit stakeholders. Effective teamwork requires training in a variety of skills—for example, interpersonal communication, organizing meetings, group decision-making, using improvement tools, and handling difficult people. Surprising progress can be achieved when people work in teams (Manz & Sims, 1993; Orsburn, Moran, Musselwhite, & Zenger, 1990; Scholtes, 1988). To quote Bill Creech in *The Five Pillars of TQM* (1994), "Organizational change is imperative, and the team approach is the most effective way to reorganize" (p. 12). It's ironic that although many faculty work together effectively in research, they rarely do so in education-related tasks.

Some may argue that universities already have too many teams—except that we call them "committees." Most schools do have too many committees, but there is a fundamental difference between a team and a committee. A committee usually is charged with policy-making or advice-giving—that is, directing others' activities. In a team, members already are committed to achieving some important outcome. The team's purpose is to help its members do a better job or do the job in less time. This changes the dynamics dramatically. It's hard to hold a committee accountable for results, but team members already have accepted responsibility.

Base Decisions on Evidence

Departments should monitor outcomes systematically—for example, by collecting data from students, graduates, and employers. Data on student preparation and learning styles can be helpful as well. The data should be analyzed carefully in light of disciplinary standards and the faculty's professional experience, and findings should be incorporated in the design of curricula, learning processes, and assessment methods.

People who study quality believe that information should drive decision-making. Information serves a number of important purposes. It provides knowledge about external circumstances that may affect performance. It provides feedback on the results of process changes, without which processes cannot be controlled or improved. Information also focuses discussion and helps team members develop a common view of reality. For example, it may call out discrepancies between the team's current view of reality and the external environment—discrepancies that invite constructive reinterpretation and problem solving. Finally, data in the form of trends can help a team assess progress toward goals, identify areas that need greater attention, confer a sense of challenge or closure, and provide a basis for extrinsic rewards.

Visit a quality-oriented manufacturing facility, and you will see evidence of "fact-based management." Production teams routinely track output levels, machine performance, defect rates, attendance, time lost due to accidents, and other measures they deem important in their circumstances. They may collect the data themselves or they may track data collected or processed by others, but in every case the team members "own" the data and believe that information is essential for day-to-day effectiveness. Team members continuously improve the data sources and displays as part of their overall responsibility for quality (Deming, 1986; Harrington, 1991; Joiner, 1994; Juran, 1989; Miller & Krumm, 1992; Pitt, 1994; Senge, 1990; Sonnenberg, 1994). If fact-based management can work on the shop floor—and it does— one can expect even greater success with highly trained professionals.

Making better use of evidence has become the most widely discussed idea for improving teaching and learning since the publication of *Scholarship Reconsidered* (Boyer, 1990). Applying the quality principles requires using evidence effectively. Indeed, evidence usage lies at the heart of process effectiveness. Simply put, evidence supports a belief that something is true. The *Evidence Guide* published in 2002 by the Western Association of Schools and Colleges, a regional accreditor, describes how people responsible for quality processes can improve their use of evidence. It starts by listing five characteristics of good evidence:

- *Evidence should be intentional and purposeful.* Evidence should be advanced to address deliberately posed questions that are important to the department. It should stimulate dialogue among decision makers, ideally in a way that helps them achieve consensus.
- *Evidence entails interpretation and reflection.* Because evidence does not speak for itself, presenters should do more than list the facts. They should reflect on the evidence's meaning and interpret it appropriately to support conclusions.

- *Good evidence is integrated and holistic.* The best evidence involves information drawn from disparate sources that reinforce one another. Hence judgments need to be made about a body of evidence as a whole—the "weight of the evidence," in common parlance.
- *Evidence can be both quantitative and qualitative.* What is considered as evidence need not be confined to numbers. Relevant quantitative data is powerful, but measurement is not the be all and end all. It is better for evidence to be meaningful than for it to be numeric.
- *Good evidence can be either direct or indirect.* Evidence does not necessarily depend on specially designed instruments and samples. Indirect evidence based on existing data—for example, from ongoing institutional processes—can be more powerful than direct evidence, and it usually is less expensive to obtain.

Figure 3.1 provides an example of how the evidentiary principles can be applied in quality work—in this case, to student assessment.

Although few faculty members would dream of violating the evidentiary guidelines when doing research, such violations occur all too often in education. Like other aspects of quality work, better use of evidence requires a degree of systematization that has yet to be embraced by most departments.

Strive for Coherence

> *Departments should view learning through the lens of the students' entire educational experience. Courses should build on one another to provide the desired depth and breadth. Students' portfolios of educational experiences also should reflect coherence. For example, a mix of large lectures and small seminars may produce better learning than a succession of medium-size classes that consume the same amount of faculty time.*

W. Edwards Deming's theory of profound knowledge underpinned his entire view of quality. The concept of coherence between activities was one of the cornerstones. Two of the requirements for coherence are that the activities must have an aim or purpose and that they must

Figure 3.1 **Applications of Evidentiary Principles to Student Assessment**

Cover knowledge and skills taught throughout the program's curriculum.
The unit of analysis should be the cumulative experience of the student at the time of graduation, not simply averages based on work done in individual courses.

Include multiple judgments of student performance.
Departmental assessments should represent the considered judgment of a faculty team, not a single individual. They should be discussed by the team members before finalization.

Provide information on multiple dimensions of student performance.
There should be more than a single summative performance measure. Information should instead be collected on a variety of performance dimensions. Reports should include profiles of the relevant student population, not simply averages or data for the top few percent of the class.

Include more than surveys or self-reports of competence or growth by students.
Surveys asking students to rate their satisfaction, strengths and weaknesses, and/or areas of perceived growth, though helpful, are not adequate as the primary metric for education quality.

Source: Western Association of Schools and Colleges, 2002

be managed. The secret to that management is "cooperation between components toward the aim of the organization" (Deming, 1986, p. 54). Coherence requires that processes be viewed as systems. Designers should concentrate less on what the separate parts are doing and more on how interactions between the parts affect overall performance. They should enhance synergies between elements, reduce redundancies and complexity, and mitigate negative interactions that impede performance.

Peter Senge, author of *The Fifth Discipline: The Art and Practice of the Learning Organization* (1990), also puts the systems view at the heart of his thinking. He developed a series of archetypes that characterize critical behavior patterns in organizations. For example, certain feedback loops and choice points can enhance or undermine efforts to produce quality. By focusing on these archetypes, one can more effectively diagnose organizational problems and discover what changes will have the greatest leverage for improvement.

Coherence has been a hot topic in academe since the curricular destructuring that took place in the 1960s (Zemsky, 1989; see also Bok, 2006, p. 41; Sykes, 1988, pp. 79–82). Although student demands for choice triggered the initial destructuring movement, they were not the only cause. In the 1980s, for example, the Association of American Colleges and Universities (1985) stated that lack of a clear sense of mission in many colleges and universities had led to a "marketplace philosophy . . . a supermarket where students are shoppers and professors are merchants of learning" (p. 2). The report placed much of the blame on faculty who had become "protectors and advocates" (p. 4) of their interests (including the desire to protect jobs and teach their specialties) at the expense of institutional responsibilities and curricular coherence. Although there has been some increase in coherence in recent years, many commentators believe that today's curricula are still unduly fragmented (cf. Bok, 2006).

Less discussed is what one might call "learning process coherence"—the juxtaposition of activities within a student's program. For example, having students learn a statistical tool in one course and then immediately apply it in another reduces cycle time and boosts learning. Situations like this one do occur, but high levels of student choice and the rigid structure of semester-long courses make it hard to coordinate assignments. The problem also stems, however, from faculty inattention to process-coherence issues.

The Quality Assurance Agency for Higher Education (2000), a UK organization, works with a code of practice that provides some good standards for coherence:

> [Faculty should consider] the overall coherence and intellectual integrity of the programme, . . . [which] should be designed in a way that will ensure the student's experience has

a logic and integrity that are clearly linked to the purpose of
the programme. (p. 14)

[The curriculum should promote] an organised progres-
sion so that the demands on the learner in intellectual challenge, skills, knowledge, conceptualization, and learning
autonomy increase. (p. 13)

Departments that adopt these standards would significantly improve
the quality of teaching and learning. The same is true for programs like
general education.

Learn From Best Practice

*Faculty should identify and analyze good practices in compa-
rable departments and institutions and then adapt the best to
their own circumstances. They should compare good versus average or poor practices within their own departments, assess the
causes of the differences, and seek ways to improve the subpar
performers.*

Searching out best practice and adapting its lessons to the local situation
is called "benchmarking." By identifying best practice one is, in effect,
setting up a goal. Studying how others achieve that goal provides insights
into how to achieve it oneself. The idea is not, as some skeptics put it, to
force-fit others' work to the local situation. It is to think outside the box,
to gain stimulus and insight. Such stimulus and insight need not come
from the same type of institution or even the same field. For example, the
learning of certain skills may have invariant elements across disciplines
and types of universities. One should consider the process itself, not necessarily the entity or context in which it is applied.

When properly done, benchmarking follows a structured set of
steps. These steps include 1) identifying precisely what the organization will benchmark; 2) creating a list of benchmarking candidates; 3)
comparing data that highlights differences between the organization's
activity and the benchmark; and 4) establishing goals and action plans
for improvement based on what the organization has learned from the
benchmarking project. Without such discipline, benchmarking can
degenerate into "industrial tourism."

Benchmarking dates from the dawn of the quality movement. Originally it was used in engineering, manufacturing, and scientific research, but it is being applied to service functions with similarly good results (Bogan & English, 1994; Boxwell, 1994; Camp, 1989; Spendolini, 1992; Watson, 1993). Entities like the American Productivity and Quality Center, which brings together groups of clients to achieve economies of scale in benchmarking, have honed the methodology to a fine art. Universities like Northwest Missouri State, a pioneer in applying quality concepts to higher education, will not launch a significant quality improvement initiative without systematic benchmarking.

Learning from best practice also involves the analysis of quality variations within one's own area of responsibility. The idea is simple: Find the best-performing entity and then work to bring others to the same standard. Reinforcing the causes of positive variation and mitigating the negative ones will allow average performance to move upward. This should be a central goal of quality work (Deming, 1994; Joiner, 1994; Miller & Krumm, 1992).

The idea that variations in learning performance present quality improvement opportunities seems foreign to academics who believe such variations stem from differences in students' ability or motivation. We have already seen, however, that many of these variations are in fact controllable by the teacher. This opens the possibility that faculty can learn from the variations in performance that are bound to occur among teachers as well as students.

Make Continuous Improvement a Priority

> *Departments should strive to improve teaching and learning regularly. Although many professors will continue to place strong emphasis on research, they should spend enough discretionary time on EQW to maintain an impetus for improvement. Personnel committees should consider the results of such work, along with research and teaching performance, as important evidence for promotion and tenure.*

Quality experts believe that all processes present opportunities for incremental improvement. Indeed, continuous quality improvement (CQI) has become a cornerstone of the business quality movement.

Known as *kaizen* in Japan, CQI holds that organizations can continuously improve all processes and activities through the application of systematic techniques. This requires a disciplined process that includes, first, a commitment to excellence and, second, ongoing efforts to identify and eliminate all defects, inefficiencies, and nonconformance to stakeholders' needs and legitimate expectations.

Continuous incremental improvement contrasts with episodic change, in which the current process is replaced with a new and improved design. (Such changes are sometimes called "process reengineering.") Although episodic change can pay dividends in some situations—as when curricula are being reformed or radically different technology options are being considered, for example—it's not the only option. Indeed, because reengineering rarely gets things right the first time, follow-on incremental improvement becomes essential. Sometimes the cumulative effect of CQI eliminates the need for disruptive episodic change. Organizations that allow the quality and utility of their offerings to become static will become targets for competing organizations. Competitors may add benefits or find new ways to deliver the benefits. Or they may reduce costs and lower prices, which boosts value for money.

Despite these obvious advantages, many in higher education regard *continuous quality improvement* as irrelevant or offensive jargon. They feel that education quality is fine as it is and resent assertions that it can and should be improved. The root problem, however, is that CQI takes time—time that many faculty, and their departments and institutions, would rather spend on research. CQI is threatening because it exposes a contradiction in the work lives of many professors.

Most professors care deeply about their teaching and their students. Even at institutions where teaching is less important than research, *teaching is not unimportant.* Many professors feel caught between wanting to do a better job teaching and mentoring students, and what it takes to further their own careers. They resolve this tension by 1) placing their first priority on teaching until they've achieved "good" or at least "acceptable" performance, and 2) then turning their attention to research (Massy & Wilger, 1995).

Richard Cyert and James March (1963) coined "satisficing" as the descriptor for this tension-reducing strategy. Rather than trying to do the best job possible (e.g., on teaching), a satisficer commits only enough effort to attain an acceptable threshold of performance. The threshold may be fairly high, but in effect it puts an upper limit on quality. Satisficing is a fancy way of saying, "Good enough is OK." This contradicts the CQI mantra, "Good enough isn't."

But that's not the worst of it. Unless one is careful or lucky, the press of other priorities may cause the quality threshold itself to erode over time. Such erosion is most likely when, as in teaching, the threshold is more a personal standard than an externally driven one. Even the strongest wills find it hard to resist the pressures for publication asserted by their universities, departments, and colleagues—not to mention their own intrinsic interests. A corner may be cut here and another there, and if no demonstrably negative consequences accrue, such behavior may become the new standard. Erosion of the satisficing threshold for teaching exemplifies what has come to be called the "academic ratchet": the steady irreversible shift of faculty allegiance away from broad institutional goals toward those of an academic specialty and from teaching toward research (Zemsky & Massy, 1990).

Calls for continuous improvement in education quality escalate the faculty's job stress because, instead of accepting the ratchet as an implicit fact of academic life, they drive *up* the definitions of "good" and "acceptable" teaching, usually without diminishing the expectations for research. But while CQI requires effort over and above what it takes to achieve acceptable quality, such efforts need not be overwhelming. Because it is collegial, quality work distributes the burden among department members. It also makes the job intellectually stimulating and satisfying so it becomes less of a burden. Universities should provide rewards for quality work and recognize that, for some faculty some of the time, it requires trade-offs against other activities. They should do this because it's hard to sustain CQI when most or all of the responsible people are satisficing on educational tasks.

Maturity of AQW

Although primarily intended to improve practice, the principles also can be used to mark progress toward quality process improvement. For example, one might note a lack of attention to outcomes, inadequate use of facts, lack of coherence, or indifference to best practice. Or one might see great collegiality, strong focus on teaching and learning, effective learning assessment, and commitment to continuous improvement. Few who reflect seriously about education quality have difficulty distinguishing between the good, the bad, and the ugly when it comes to the application of these principles. Likewise, it isn't difficult to discern whether the principles are being applied in all the focal areas of quality work.

The capability maturity model developed at Carnegie Mellon University provides a useful set of categories for gauging quality processes' maturity. Developed to track the prowess of advanced software development teams, the maturity idea applies equally well to education quality. High maturity implies strong understanding and commitment, and vice versa. Chairs and their executive committees can use the maturity categories as benchmarks for evaluating their progress. So can deans, presidents and provosts, boards, and oversight agencies.

Our model lays out five levels of quality process maturity at the department level (Massy, 2003c, p. 228). It was tested in Hong Kong during 2002 and 2003 (a similar model applies to decanal and institutional quality process maturity):

- *No effort.* The department asserts little responsibility for education quality and does not have systematic quality processes. Quality improvement and assurance are unmonitored and approached mostly in traditional ways.
- *Firefighting.* The department responds to problems, but mostly with ad hoc methods. The five focal areas are not covered systematically, and the quality and evidentiary principles receive little attention.
- *Informal effort.* Individual professors experiment with the principles, but few colleagues pay much attention. Coverage of the focal areas remains spotty, and the department has yet to become a learning organization with respect to the quality and evidentiary principles.
- *Organized effort.* Departments plan and track quality process initiatives in all five focal areas. Emergent norms encourage consideration of the quality and evidentiary principles, and methods for gauging performance are under development.

- *Mature effort.* The quality and evidentiary principles have become embedded in the department's culture and the idea of regular improvement in all five focal areas is a well-accepted way of life. The department has accepted planning, tracking, and performance evaluation of quality processes as important elements of peer accountability and has developed effective methods for doing so.

The categories can be assigned numerical scores, but quantification is not necessary for most purposes. Suppose a dean, president or provost, board, or oversight agency has made it clear that quality process improvement is a high priority. Now imagine the tough-minded discussions that could occur between department chairs and deans, or between chairs and professors, if performance has been evaluated as unsatisfactory. What chair would feel comfortable defending "no effort" or "firefighting" to the dean? What dean would like to defend poor maturity ratings to the provost? What institution would like to defend them to the coordinating board or accreditors, students, and the public?

We'll see in later chapters how mature EQW demonstrably changes how faculty approach teaching and learning. Indeed, the maturity of a department's EQW will be readily apparent to anyone who bothers to look. EQW cannot be faked. Engaged faculty will be able to describe their activities in detail and present evidence about outcomes, whereas those who are not engaged will soon sputter into silence or empty rhetoric. Deans, provosts, and auditors can learn to distinguish between the maturity levels, a fact that underpins quality work above the level of the department and the academic audit at all levels.

Quality Work Above the Department Level

Our descriptions of quality work to this point have focused on departments because they "work at the coal face" (as the British would say). But that's not where the idea originated. The first academic quality audits—in the United Kingdom, Hong Kong, Sweden, and New Zealand—covered whole campuses. Why? Auditors represented oversight bodies like Hong Kong's University Grants Committee. Such bodies focus on institutions first and departments second. (U.S. academic audit applications, in contrast, were initiated by individual institutions and thus focused on departments.) The fact that such audits have been successful at the higher level, however, implies that it's possible to define quality work above the department level.

A Tiered System of Quality Work

The basic idea is simple: Each tier seeks to spur improvement in quality work at the level directly beneath it. Deans spur the quality work of departments, provosts spur that of schools or faculties, and so on right up to the level of oversight boards. A well-functioning system will demonstrate good quality work at all levels. The efforts at each level will reinforce the level below and be reinforced by the one above. The whole will be greater than the sum of its parts.

In contrast to department-level quality work, which begins with reflection, work at higher levels begins with fact-finding. Deans need to learn the facts about quality work in their departments, for example. They need to know whether departments are addressing all five focal areas and whether the principles of good practice are being applied. If not, it is the deans' responsibility to get departments to improve their performance.

Provosts should learn whether the deans give quality work a high priority and what they're doing to assure and improve it. And because the role of the deans is pivotal, provosts should intervene where necessary to cure shortfalls in decanal performance. The same can be said for system-wide chief academic officers. They should stay informed about the provosts' quality work and intervene to improve it where necessary. The role of trustees and regents, and oversight boards, is similar—with one caveat. They need to insist that institutional heads and chief academic officers pay sufficient attention to quality work, but their interventions should be made at arm's length, befitting their oversight role. Indeed, efforts by external entities to micromanage academic quality almost always turn out badly (Massy, 2003c, Chapter 7).

Applying the Quality Principles

Deans, provosts, and others will find the seven quality principles to be useful touchstones for their work. For one thing, they can inquire about how the principles are being applied in the units for which they are responsible. A dean might ask departments to describe how their curricula are informed by learning objectives, for example, and what kinds of evidence they use to gauge success. They might ask about collegiality—who is involved in quality work and with what intensity? Coherence questions might focus on the linkages between assessment and learning objectives. Probing the faculty's knowledge of best practice and what's been done to expand it gets at the question of benchmarking.

All these are legitimate academic questions. Although resistance may be encountered, it can be overcome by approaching questions in a conversational rather than inquisitional way. Deans who take a real interest in such questions will encourage departments to do likewise. Unfortunately, the converse also is true. Topics that don't arise in conversations with the dean are less likely to be seen as important. In addition to their benefits for quality work, such conversations put the relationship between deans and departments on a stronger and more academic footing than the usual back-and-forth over administrative details and resources.

We have already noted that it's impossible to fake the answers to questions about quality work. A rich set of examples will come to mind if the principle is being applied seriously. Such examples simply cannot be made up, and if one attempts to do so, the lie will easily be exposed. Deans should insist on transparency in their conversations about quality work and take appropriate steps if that isn't forthcoming.

Provosts might ask how deans respond to interdepartmental variations in the effectiveness of quality work. Significant variation was observed when such questions were asked in Hong Kong's first round of academic audits, for example. Certain deans knew that some departments were better than others and were helping the laggards improve their performance. Other deans were blissfully ignorant of the variations but accepted responsibility when the differences were pointed out by the audit team. Still others were aware of the variations but were doing nothing to address them. This last group said yes when asked whether departments with effective quality work delivered better value to students but accepted no responsibility in the matter. The idea that performance variations within their schools represented a call for action hadn't sunk in. Such views illustrate a common though critical lapse in EQW above the department level.

The Quality Improvement Cycle Revisited

The quality improvement cycle presented in Figure 1.1 of Chapter 1 applies to deans, provosts, and so forth, with only minor variations. First substitute "Fact-Finding" for "Informed Reflection," "Consideration and Consultation" for "Self-Study Report," and "Intervention" for "Peer Review" in the figure's right-hand hemisphere. Fact-finding performs the dual role of informing the dean (or other officer) and sending signals down the line. Such signals may be sufficient to spur improvement once a culture of quality has become embedded, but the dean should not take that for granted. He or she also should consider the evidence and perhaps consult with faculty advisors or the provost about it. The result may be a decision to intervene—for example, by urging the chair and faculty to give higher priority to quality work or to correct a particular problem. This provides the external impetus for change shown at the bottom of the figure, one that may include the possibility of consequences. (We'll discuss these possibilities in Chapter 8.) The rest of the cycle works as before: from interventions to initiatives to performance measures to (one would hope) embedded improvement.

That cycle describes what might be called a "line-responsibility approach" to quality work. Because the dean bears ultimate responsibility for departmental performance, he or she needs to stay well informed and intervene directly and forcibly when shortfalls become apparent. Likewise, provosts should know about quality work at the decanal level and take steps to cure shortfalls where necessary. Although a dean or department may resist such interventions, to assert they have no place in university governance is an extreme view of academic autonomy.

Arm's-length relationships like those involving oversight boards, trustees and regents, and system-wide officers provide neither the information nor legitimacy required to intervene directly at the local level. (Provosts in large institutions may be reluctant to intervene at the department level for similar reasons.) Yet such officers need to assure themselves that the quality work at all levels below them is being performed satisfactorily. Academic audit at the level of the whole institution provides a way to accomplish this, a topic that will be taken up in Chapter 8.

Appendix: Context-Defining Questions for Teaching

Learning Objectives

What knowledge, skills, and values should students acquire from their educational experience? How will this experience pay off in employment, societal contributions, and quality of life? Are the objectives based on the needs of actual or potential students rather than some ideal student?

- *Define quality in terms of outcomes.* Have you systematically considered what students need to be successful in their chosen field and lead meaningful lives?
- *Focus on how things get done.* Are your learning objectives consistent with the processes you're actually using? If not, is it the objectives or the processes that need to be changed?
- *Work collaboratively.* To what extent do you collaborate effectively on the determination of learning objectives?
- *Base decisions on facts.* Do you look beyond the standards of your discipline to seek input on learning objectives? For example, do you use surveys or focus group interviews with employers or former students? Are the results documented so you can learn from the experience?
- *Strive for coherence.* Do your learning objectives reinforce one another? Do they appear coherent to colleagues, students, and employers, or do they appear discrete and disconnected?
- *Learn from best practice.* Do you identify and evaluate the learning objectives of comparable departments in other institutions?
- *Make continuous improvement a priority.* Do you reconsider your learning objectives regularly? Does anyone else in the university encourage you to do so?

Curriculum and Cocurriculum

How does the curriculum relate to the program's learning objectives? What is being taught, in what order, and from what perspective? Does the curriculum build cumulatively on students' prior knowledge and capacity? To what extent does the cocurriculum support the curriculum and the program's learning objectives in general?

- *Define quality in terms of outcomes.* How effectively does the curriculum reflect your learning objectives?
- *Focus on how things get done.* Is the curriculum well aligned with your chosen teaching and learning assessment methods? For example, do assigned materials facilitate active learning, or do they mainly involve conventional reading? Do they invite the behavior you seek to assess?
- *Work collaboratively.* Do colleagues collaborate effectively on curricular design? Are you able to reach agreement on the essential elements of design, or does the design represent a compromise of expediency?
- *Base decisions on facts.* Do you look beyond the content standards of your discipline to seek input on curriculum? For example, do you consult curricular experts to help align the curriculum with the needs of your students?
- *Strive for coherence.* Do the various parts of the curriculum reinforce each other? Does the curriculum appear coherent to students, or does it look like a smorgasbord?
- *Learn from best practice.* Do you seek out and evaluate the curricula of comparable departments in other institutions?
- *Make continuous improvement a priority.* Do you reconsider your curricular decisions regularly? Does anyone else in the university encourage you to do so?

Teaching and Learning Methods

What teaching methods are used—for example, for first exposure to materials, for interpreting materials and answering questions, for stimulating student involvement, and for providing feedback on student work? Is learning active? Is it collaborative? Is technology being used, and if so, is it exploited effectively?

- *Define quality in terms of outcomes.* Do you evaluate teaching methods in terms of their effects on student learning as well as on your own workload? Do you analyze learning outcomes and use the results to revise teaching and learning processes?

- *Focus on how things get done.* Do you try to understand how your students learn? Do you systematically examine your teaching and assessment methods—for example, by developing flowcharts and debating what-if options? Do you solicit ideas for change and act promptly on them?
- *Work collaboratively.* Do you work together on teaching method design? Do your designs represent consensus or expedient compromise? Do you achieve organizational learning, or is teaching method improvement a lone-wolf activity?
- *Base decisions on facts.* Do you research the teaching literature in your discipline and related areas? Do you actively solicit inputs from students about their experience with alternative teaching methods? Do you run tryouts or experiments to test alternatives and then document the results?
- *Strive for coherence.* Do teaching activities reinforce each other? Do teaching and learning processes appear coherent to students?
- *Learn from best practice.* Do you push beyond the familiar methods of your discipline to examine exemplary processes within and outside your institution?
- *Make continuous improvement a priority.* Do you reconsider teaching and learning processes systematically and regularly? Does anyone else in the university encourage you to do so?

Student Learning Assessment

What measures are used to assess student learning? Are they constructively aligned with your learning objectives? Do they compare beginning and ending performance to ascertain value added? Who is responsible for student learning assessment? Are the assessment results trending upward or downward? Do they inform quality improvement efforts, and if so, how?

- *Define quality in terms of outcomes.* Have you defined key quality indicators based on your educational objectives? Do your assessment measures provide the data needed to track these indicators?

Do they measure the value obtained from your course or program as opposed to the student's talent and preparation?

- *Focus on how things get done.* Do you focus on the way assessment is conducted? Do your methods avoid measurement noise and bias? Do they work smoothly and connect seamlessly with the processes of teaching and learning?
- *Work collaboratively.* Do you work together on the design of assessment methods? Is there collective action on program-wide assessment results?
- *Base decisions on facts.* Are your assessment processes grounded in the literature wherever possible? Can you defend your choice of assessment measures by some appropriate combination of theory, experience, and experimentation?
- *Strive for coherence.* Are your assessment measures aligned with your learning objectives? Are they consistent with each other? Do they reinforce teaching and learning? Does assessment appear coherent to students?
- *Learn from best practice.* Do you identify and evaluate the assessment practices of comparable departments at other institutions?
- *Make continuous improvement a priority.* Do you reconsider your learning assessment methods systematically and regularly? Does anyone else in the university encourage you to do so?

Quality Assurance

How do department and program leaders assure themselves and others that the designs for curricula, teaching and learning activities, and student assessments are being implemented as intended? How is teacher performance evaluated?

- *Define quality in terms of outcomes.* Does QA focus on student outcomes as well as curriculum and teaching methods—for example, by tracking student learning and the history of graduates?
- *Focus on how things get done.* Have QA methods been thought through with the same intensity as curriculum and teaching methods?

- *Work collaboratively.* Do you collaborate effectively on the design of QA methods? Do you work with colleagues to interpret the results and follow up on issues?
- *Base decisions on facts.* Do QA methods go beyond student course evaluations to include more intense and objective fact-finding— for example, peer evaluation of teaching and student-faculty consultative committees?
- *Strive for coherence.* Do the various QA methods reinforce each other? To what extent does implementation QA appear coherent to students and staff?
- *Learn from best practice.* Do you identify and evaluate the QA practices of comparable departments in other institutions?
- *Make continuous improvement a priority.* Do you reconsider your QA processes systematically and regularly? Does anyone else in the university encourage you to do so?

4

Engaging Faculty in Education Quality Work

Today's discussions about higher education often focus on the high costs of attending college and providing access to students, learning through distance education, and the competition between traditional institutions and the private for-profit institutions that are becoming important on the national and global scenes. Although such issues are important, addressing them will make little difference if America's traditional colleges and universities do not deliver high-quality education and scholarly performance. All the resources in the world will not promote better quality without purposeful and focused thinking on how we can do this better.

Colleges and universities employ many of the brightest and most talented people available in the workforce, but usually they're not trained to think about teaching as a professional activity. Most faculty want to do a good job on their teaching, but many feel frustrated by the issues they confront each year. Often they get little support from their institutions or even their departmental colleagues (Massy, 2003c). For college professors most teaching is a private activity that occurs behind closed doors. Faculty conversations about teaching often focus on the core curriculum rather than the purposes of education, how to improve the quality of what's taught, or ways to address the needs of different types of students. Faculty research activities may be more collaborative, although in many fields scholarship is still considered an independent accomplishment that can best be described as a lone-wolf activity. Faculty members may see themselves as independent entrepreneurs, and most do not focus on strategic campus goals—mind-sets that can distract from the ability to focus energy on the common campus purposes. This culture is becoming more problematic. Some even suggest that America's ability to maintain its world-class standing depends on raising the priority of quality improvement across a broad spectrum of teaching-related activities (Lovett, 2002).

When chairs, deans, and provosts discuss ways to improve the quality of teaching and learning, the typical response from faculty members is to argue for smaller class sizes, lower teaching loads, and fewer adjunct faculty. Most of these recommendations come without careful scrutiny and often require hiring more tenure-track faculty or additional operating funds. Such suggestions are likely to be disregarded because of limited resources, inflexible administrators, or even skepticism stemming from a lack of concrete evidence that such strategies have worked in the past to improve the quality of education.

Many institutions have tried to use traditional program reviews as a device for improving education quality, but they've often failed. For example, an assessment of the program review process at the University of Missouri found that such reviews tend to focus on research, departmental resources, governance opportunities for faculty, and curricula; they do not address educational purposes and methods or practices for improving scholarship. Moreover, the reviews' conclusions too often were predictable. Typically they cited examples of how the department was doing as well as could be expected and suggested the only way to get better results was to provide more operating funds, additional faculty lines, and better facilities. And because the extra funds were rarely forthcoming, the program reviews themselves were not well regarded.

The manner in which most traditional program reviews are conducted does not encourage departments to identify their weaknesses. Instead, departments seek evidence to support the argument that they are a good department and, unless additional money is forthcoming, would like to continue practicing business as usual. From the professors' vantage point, identifying weaknesses and problem areas only increases the likelihood that the department will receive fewer resources in the future. Instead, the case is made that more resources are required to improve the quality or breadth of departmental activities. With that mind-set, the general tendency is to suggest that there is no real way for departments to improve without meeting these requests.

Since program reviews rarely attract new resources for a department, subsequent reviews are met with faculty skepticism. Generally the buck gets passed back and forth between the administrators and the departments until even the most optimistic chairs come to see program review as an exercise in paper-shuffling. Using additional resources as the foundation for all improvement creates the wrong type of conversation—focusing on resources rather than the more basic question of what professors do with the resources they have and challenging basic assumptions.

A Systematic Process for Structured Conversation

Chapter 1 stated that one of the principal objectives of academic audit is to elicit thoughtful conversations about how to produce significant improvements in education quality without spending additional resources. Such audits require faculty members and academic administrators to think differently. Audits require professors to focus their attention on aspects of their work that have not received much attention and to ask questions that are not typically posed. And audits require faculty to be willing to drop their defenses, to see that the issues being addressed are important ones, and to accept that their units will likely not look very good the first time around.

One of the primary goals of the academic audit process is to bring professors together for structured, action-oriented conversations about academic quality (Massy, 2003a, 2003c, 2004, 2005). This provides opportunities for "academic soul-searching" and asking fundamental questions—for example, what should be the main focus of their attention, how they do their work, and how they might do it better. Though these sound like elementary, almost superficial, questions, they usually elicit deep thought. And most important, such questions trigger thinking about how departments might operate more purposefully and effectively. Randy Schulte, of the humanities department at Chattanooga State Technical Community College, talks about engaging faculty members in conversations. He explains, "At the heart of the Academic Audit evidence-gathering process is the conversation. To more fully engage not only faculty but all stakeholders . . . [you have to] create events that foster open and relaxed conversation" (personal communication, May 15, 2006). Creating a climate where people look differently at how they work can be a powerful tool in nurturing change. The practice of challenging basic assumptions can be contagious and dramatically shift the values and beliefs within an organization (Pascale & Sternin, 2005).

Although it sounds odd, one of the most challenging conversations for faculty involved in the academic audit process is to identify the critical purposes of their teaching programs, to think seriously about the learning outcomes of these programs, and to determine how well the programs align with the campus's larger strategic focus. Some of the most critical questions are: What should students know and be able to do when they complete the program? What knowledge and skills should they have acquired? Does the program build on students' previous knowledge or assume that all students start at the same place? What knowledge and skills do employers or graduate programs require, and does the existing program prepare them for the next step?

Professors typically don't think about how their courses link to other courses. Although they are collegial, share ideas and course materials, and debate critical disciplinary issues, they rarely sit down as a group and consider how their courses fit together, who is covering what key principles, and where there is overlap. Overlap might be fine—but it should be purposeful. Often when faculty members discuss these issues, sharing their syllabi with each other, they will find that there are gaps in some areas and double coverage in others. Too often the curriculum is based on individual professors' interests rather than well-thought-out educational purposes.

Academic audit creates a structured process to open up conversation in areas that should be addressed but are often overlooked. The focal areas of quality work that are addressed in the audit are not necessarily areas where professors traditionally focus their attention—particularly in research universities. Yet once one gets past some early objections, the audit process allows fundamental questions about teaching and learning to be addressed in a collegial format. A department chair who went through the academic audit process described how this can occur:

> Granted, when the department's audit team first met, no one seemed very competent at decoding terms such as *desired learning outcome* versus a *program objective*. But slowly, the strangeness of the questions we were asked to address began to provoke genuine discussion. . . .
>
> The exercise of writing the initial self-study provoked a dialogue about learning outcomes and program goals that forced us to ask tough questions that produced significant insights into both our successes and failures.
>
> *—Tom Poe, chair of the Department of Communications,*
> *University of Missouri–Kansas City*

Although educating students is one of university professors' most important jobs, faculty typically evaluate teaching and learning issues with less rigor than they use to judge scholarly research. Yet, even in research universities, education-related tasks account for 40% or more of a professor's time. Faculty members usually are drawn into EQW if they are willing to engage open-mindedly in the audit process. They find that an audit's commonsense questions cause them to think more deeply about their department's educational offerings and the consequences for students. Some of the questions turn out to be familiar and some are not, but few professors say the answers are not important. Indeed, most say the process begins to make them think differently.

Even if faculty members have not dealt with such issues before, they are more likely to focus on potential improvements than simply to dismiss the questions out of hand. We have found that starting with the important and intriguing questions is effective, and that faculty will quickly engage and start to question how they do their work—and why. Further, the structured format of the audit process ensures that key areas are covered and that conversations don't get stuck on one or two themes. Lastly, the starting questions we have developed (discussed in Chapter 5) are the kinds of questions likely to be asked by academic auditors during the site visit. A faculty member at the University of Missouri acknowledged that despite some initial awkwardness, the questions stimulate new ways of thinking:

> Participating in this audit process was an extraordinarily valuable experience. Both aspects, the self-study and the audit visit and report, proved useful. The self-study was useful because the questions required that members of a department think about the process of teaching and learning in novel ways. We asked ourselves questions we had not asked before, and the answers, or lack thereof, were very enlightening. We discovered strengths we had not realized and also noticed areas needing improvement. Please note that engaging in the self-study was a difficult and often frustrating experience. The quality assurance language is unfamiliar and does not always apply easily to an educational setting. Again, though, this is what made us think about teaching and learning in new ways.
>
> —*Alan Strathman, Department of Psychological Sciences,*
> *University of Missouri–Columbia*

The word *audit* suggests a judgmental evaluation often associated with financial matters and can be a bit offensive to most faculty members at first. The stated reason for conducting an audit is largely developmental, but that fact seems paradoxical for most faculty members. But with the right preparation, the appropriate questions, and the proper tone, audits allow a department to describe its strengths and weaknesses and identify plans for improvement. Once again, the words of an experienced faculty member and chair make this point clear:

> The audit team takes the point of view that in these circumstances we need to find independent sources of data that bear on the issues pointed out in the comments to assess the actual degree of the problem. In the end the committee concluded that each individual department is in the best position to

determine which of the suggestions offered in an audit report makes sense in the context of its own program, and that it is the enhancement of a department's commitment to its own processes and to its own continual improvement that is the real goal of the process review, not its specific compliance with all suggestions of the audit team.

—Paul Parris, chair, Department of Physics,
University of Missouri–Rolla

The most difficult aspects of audits are to get the departments to focus on the things that they don't do well and then identify areas for improvement. That is why structured conversations are so essential and why setting the appropriate tone for the audit becomes critically important. Our experience has shown that the conversations evolve in a developmental way, and once you get faculty members pondering some of the fundamental questions in a safe setting, their natural curiosity is aroused. The academic audit is a process, something that will not start off with a raging fire but will begin to help faculty members think about what they can do better. Dr. Parris describes this aspect of the academic audit very articulately:

From the department's point of view, the academic audit provided a unique opportunity to reflect on its activities at a level considerably different from that with which it had done so in the past. . . . The department's preparation and experience with the process provided a more coherent structure to the conversations on education than it had more informally engaged in previously, and stimulated its members to more thoroughly examine the ways that it organizes itself to design and implement its educational activities.

Furthermore, in preparing the audit self-study report the department identifies areas where its efforts are exemplary, where the faculty members see a need for improvement, and where they have not identified a problem but where recommendations can be helpful. Although pointing out areas for improvement inevitably seems judgmental, constructive criticism of a department's EQW is less likely to undermine the evaluation's developmental goals than criticizing a professor for poor teaching. As is becoming typical with academic audits conducted elsewhere, the University of Missouri decided that the developmental aspects should be paramount, and that identifying areas for improvement should not be viewed as a sign of poor performance but rather as recognition of where additional attention can fruitfully be focused.

As elsewhere, the initial focus of the academic audit at the University of Missouri was on departments' teaching and learning activities. It ignored the significant work faculty members do in the areas of research and service. In principle, however, audits do not need to be limited. As we conducted the initial round of an audit in Missouri, the limitation became a significant issue for the faculty and administrators alike. They felt we were only evaluating one portion of their work, and that to have a full review of the department we should extend the audit to address research and scholarship. As a result of this feedback, we extended the audit to include those topics and their synergy with teaching and learning. The extended process will be explained in detail in Chapter 7.

Another issue that came up in our early conversations was that faculty members find discussing the processes or strategies that a department uses to address education quality to be a rather odd experience. Their natural instinct is to evaluate the delivered quality of teaching itself, and they wonder how looking at processes can improve student learning.

Reflection on these views revealed what we consider to be an important truth: that the strategies or processes people use to accomplish tasks usually reflect the way they organize their work and the data (if any) that they use to make decisions. It's true that having good processes is not in and of itself sufficient. But the beauty of academic audit is that it requires professors to think about how they organize the tasks and data. In doing so they look at a great variety of issues that affect quality—not only resources, but how they use those resources and, most important, where the department focuses its attention and what activities are seen as most important.

It is probably safe to assume that most faculty members want to do a good job. They want to provide quality education, and they will do a better job when they use good processes to accomplish this goal. The audit structure also asks departments to address critical issues such as outcomes; assessment practices; and, most important, what they are doing, how they are doing it, and who is responsible. The role of an audit is to encourage departments to strengthen their techniques and processes to improve the quality of their work.

The Virtue of Peer Review

In addition to its structured format for questions, audits use faculty peers to review the self-study and to participate in the site visits. In addition to the obvious advantages of peer review, audits develop a cadre of thoughtful and introspective faculty members who are comfortable asking themselves and their colleagues puzzling questions. For example, in Missouri and Tennessee, the auditors were faculty members and administrators (mostly faculty) from other departments and campuses. But people from outside the institution could be used as well. Using faculty peers enhances the quality of the review and creates a meaningful dialogue with credibility.

Those being audited are faculty from within the department—all faculty in the case of small departments or those primarily responsible for leading the undergraduate education efforts and prominent researchers in large departments. Some of these same faculty members served as auditors for other departments. Such participation broadened their perspective and increased the pool of people with a commitment to EQW.

The audit visits in both Missouri and Tennessee lasted a day to one and a half days. The teams also got together for dinner the night before to discuss their early impressions and to divide up activities to focus their attention during the full day of the site visit. These site visits and dinners allow faculty members to talk about things they do not normally address and help establish a critical collegial tone. Due to the nature of the work, faculty members on the audit team strike up interesting conversations, and if those conversations revolve around the audit focal areas, they are meaningful for both sets of faculty.

The audit teams typically have eight to ten members and meet with faculty from the principle department in plenary sessions and then divide themselves into subgroups of two or three auditors to maximize the number of conversations. Auditors are encouraged to maintain a light and informal tone and to emphasize the collegiality of the visit—that is, they are peers getting together to discuss important issues in which they all have a shared sense of responsibility. In effect, the audits provide an antidote to the "hollowed collegiality" that plagues many departments where tough and important questions do not get asked (Massy, Wilger, & Colbeck, 1994).

Most, if not all, auditors are recruited internally from within the university or campus where the audit takes place. An academic audit focuses on commonsense questions about how a department conducts its work; so the process does not require expertise in the department's academic discipline. However, in most cases we've found it helpful to have at least one or two members from the principal discipline of the department being reviewed. These faculty members can often serve as interpreters and explain certain attributes of the field and why traditional approaches are used. However, one of the valuable aspects of using faculty members from outside the department's core discipline is that although they are familiar with the academy and many of its basic practices, they bring a very different mental model to the audit process. By challenging some of the basic tenets or beliefs of the department under review, these outside faculty members often ask the toughest questions.

Further, some of the disciplinary canons held sacred by those in the field are not necessarily viewed that way by professors from other departments. The audit visit provides an opportunity for challenging these basic beliefs—something that is not likely when all the review members are from the same discipline. For example, the open character and somewhat unstructured approach to course objectives found in humanities fields can appear odd to those in the basic sciences. But at the same time the anthropologist or the English faculty member might challenge the most rigidly accepted dogma from the scientific fields. Dr. Parris explains this unique feature:

> The site visit, initially anticipated with some anxiety by most of the members of the department, turned out to be a very pleasant experience, in large part due to the collegiality and professionalism of the audit team. One of the aspects that made the site visit particularly interesting was that the members of the audit team were generally drawn from fields outside the physical sciences. Consequently it was often necessary to explicitly explain to auditors some of the structures—for example, labs, recitations, etcetera—that we implicitly accept as axiomatic parts of a physics education. These conversations helped bring those unstated assumptions more clearly in focus, thereby allowing for the possibility of their critical examination.

Experience shows that faculty members in departments with good EQW will enthusiastically describe what they're doing to their peers—just as they would describe their research to an interested observer. However, those who have not engaged in any kind of process to improve their academic programs will find it hard to be specific about what they do and why. Departments with active discussions and procedures to improve their academic program will have produced a rich set of materials to address internal issues, whereas materials produced by departments that have not addressed these topics will be sketchy, generic, or nonexistent.

Another key point is that these materials will be department-specific, generated by the faculty members in the academic discipline. No externally created generic guidelines are used to assess the department; instead, the auditors assume that if a rigorous process has been followed, the faculty probably have made a prudent decision. In fact, the auditors are warned not to second-guess the judgments made by the faculty. But in the absence of any disciplined approach or thinking, auditors can feel comfortable asking critical "why" questions to challenge current practice. In such cases it usually turns out that the current practices have been adopted without serious questioning.

Using peers drawn mostly from within the university or system allows academic audits to be conducted without significant incremental expenses. Because out-of-pocket cost is not much of an issue, the major challenge is to encourage professors to take the time to discuss EQW. We have already noted that such discussions need not trigger the defensiveness inherent in direct quality evaluation. Using a group of experienced and sympathetic colleagues from within one's own institution, the audit process creates an atmosphere to discuss critical questions openly and coherently.

We emphasize again that the audit conversations do not require expertise in a particular discipline, and that audit teams with professors from a variety of fields produce interesting results. Since most faculty interact mainly with people in their own or related fields, the audit visits become a healthy place for viewing the world outside one's department. Further, the more faculty members become involved in the practices associated with this dialogue, the more they think about their own work in new ways. It is not at all uncommon for faculty members to comment as they leave a site visit on how they would like to apply these practices in their own department (Massy, 2003b).

Introduction to Academic Audit

The audit process shares certain attributes in common with regional or subject matter accreditation, especially as accreditation reviews have been evolving in recent years. In addition to the obvious similarity of the self-study and external visit, both types of reviews increasingly focus on quality improvement and assurance processes instead of resource levels, faculty governance, and scholarship. However, the elements of an academic audit are somewhat different than those used for regional accreditation or for accreditation by national professional organizations. These steps will be explained in more detail later.

The academic audit encourages departments to jump-start their quality process improvement. To obtain a sustained impact, the reviews should be repeated regularly—perhaps on a staggered five- or seven-year cycle. Successive rounds could replace the introductory workshops and preliminary events with other practices designed to sustain the quality process efforts. For example, the campus teaching development unit might convene regular seminars on education quality processes and an annual award event to celebrate good practices identified in the previous year's round of reviews.

First-time academic process reviews typically involve six key elements, which we'll describe briefly here: introductory workshops, departmental self-studies, auditor selection and training, audit visits, audit reports, and debriefing session and follow-up plans. Detailed descriptions, resource materials, and sample reports will be provided in Chapters 5 and 6.

Introductory Workshops

Certain activities that precede the audit visit have proved crucial. First, between six to twelve months before the site visit, members of the department being reviewed participate in a half- to full-day seminar on how to broaden quality improvement beyond curricular redesign. The seminars, conducted in a relaxed and informal style, provide a conceptual base for the forthcoming audit, address the faculty's questions, create the proper tone for the entire academic audit process, and generate some enthusiasm for the second activity: a self-study of the department's education quality processes.

These initial sessions introduce departments to quality processes in education and research as well as the review methodology itself. (Interviews in advance of the workshop may provide institution-specific discussion questions.) The agenda includes presentations, role-playing demonstrations, and breakout discussions. Comments from Dr. Karen Stephenson from Nashville State Community College (NSCC) illustrate the point that setting the context in the beginning is critical to the success of the audit process:

> To introduce this process to all faculty members, I asked faculty attending the workshops to share their thoughts about this process and how they thought their program could benefit from participating in this pilot. The role-playing portion of the workshops was mentioned several times in their comments, as this activity demonstrated the emphasis on quality

processes. Faculty members' comments were positive and supportive of our participating in this pilot. This meeting provided the positive energy needed to launch this initiative.

Administrative support is extremely important, and everyone at NSCC was very helpful. I attended as many weekly academic audit program meetings (especially at the beginning) as time allowed. I think my attendance at these meetings helped to emphasize the importance of this initiative and kept the lines of communication open between me and the faculty. Concerns or questions could be addressed quickly.

It's often effective to begin by reflecting on processes where performance is believed to be good. Celebrations of success build confidence about the application of the principles and provide a benchmark to think about other department activities. Further, comparing poorly aligned processes with the department's own best practices can help motivate improvement. Identifying exemplary practices that are currently being used makes it clear that in most cases improvements need not be earthshaking or require extra resources—that they may simply result from focusing energy on an identified problem.

Some find the list of focal areas and the quality principles (introduced in Chapters 2 and 3) a bit daunting at first. Although many of the ideas are familiar, others seem foreign. Because most departments are not used to thinking about quality issues, we have developed a series of commonsense questions that make the whole approach less daunting. It's easy to understand the academic audit process and the reason for conducting program reviews in this fashion once faculty members see the commonsense questions. These questions link closely to the seven quality principles discussed in Chapter 3.

What are we trying to do? Traditional thinking equates quality to inputs like faculty size and qualifications—for example, "Quality improvement requires more and better faculty." But inputs are means to an end and it's the end that ultimately matters. In education the end pertains to students' knowledge and skills, values, and quality of life. In research it's the publications, citations, and other outcomes that count. This leads to the first principle: Define quality in terms of outcomes.

How are we doing it? Quality experts insist that all work is process. In short, to do something you must engage in some sort of process, even if it's informal. It only makes sense that paying attention to processes can improve quality. The bottom line? Focus on how things get done.

Who is responsible for doing it? Tasks can be assigned to teams or left to individual initiative. Although individual initiatives are salutary, teams usually outperform lone wolves when it comes to sustaining and improving quality. Hence the principle: Work collaboratively.

How do we know we are succeeding? It's hard to consistently produce quality without feedback on how well you are accomplishing your goal. The feedback should be based on evidence rather than on anecdotes whenever possible, and evidence is important in applying the other quality principles. Consequently: Base decisions on evidence.

How can we do even better? Although focusing on outcomes, processes, responsibilities, and evidence gets the improvement ball rolling, the remaining three principles will help you move to the next level. Do your efforts "hang together," or are they in silos? A good way to escape this problem: Strive for coherence. Are you interested in how others solve the same problems you're working on, or does "not invented here" dominate? In other words: Learn from best practice. Do you work proactively on improvement or wait for problems to arise? To be proactive: Make continuous improvement a priority.

By using these basic commonsense questions the introductory sessions begin to make the academic audit process seem feasible and not just business- or education-related jargon that instigates negative initial reactions. Once these basic questions are internalized, attention can be focused on the five focal areas that compose the heart of the academic audit process.

Departmental Self-Studies

Departments start by reflecting on their education and research quality and—more important—the kinds of evidence they use in making quality judgments. Next they identify the practices they believe contribute most to quality and ask how the quality and evidentiary principles contributed to the success of these practices. Then they apply the lessons learned to a broader set of quality issues—using the focal areas as a checklist to ensure coverage. The final step is to consider a commitment to one or more of the initiatives.

The self-studies are short, action-oriented documents rather than long essays or lengthy descriptions. The self-study follows a pre-set format to ensure broad coverage of education quality issues, but there is wide flexibility within the format. It is not necessary to regurgitate facts and figures, and page length is limited to ensure that the project will not consume too much faculty time. The self-study provides an opportunity for in-depth reflection on the department's education quality—something that happens all too rarely in the course of daily activities.

However, through experience we have found that the audit team will need to see a reasonable profile of facts about the department—including the number of students, majors, courses and credit hours taught, annual graduates, and other basic information—to understand the department. Furthermore, in units where the research focal areas will be used, departments should provide background information about their research efforts, grants, doctoral programs, and other commonly accepted measures for viewing research productivity. The challenge is to obtain this information and present it in a reasonably succinct format, without overwhelming the report or the audit team with details that are not meaningful. The focus should be on providing an overall context for the department's activities and not in getting the team or the report bogged down in details.

The critical aspect of academic audit is to stimulate questions about how work gets done and where the department's energy and attention are focused. One other strategy that has proved beneficial is to allow the department to have a box for those documents they would like to make available to the team. The self-study and site visit discussions can refer to these materials without overwhelming the audit team with too much material. This can also be a place where a department can offer examples of student work, previous reports from accreditation teams, or anything that will help the auditors understand the department's activities in the campus or disciplinary context. But again, the objective is to provide examples of quality work and outcomes rather than to prove that the department's teaching and research meet certain standards. This simple distinction makes a huge difference in the amount of material a department feels it should provide.

As we approached the audit process we found that there are several basic questions that help faculty members spotlight the key issues in each of the focal areas. Creating the proper tone for the discussions and engaging in the structured conversations are critical in allowing the faculty to understand how their departments do their work.

Auditor Selection and Training

Audit teams, usually of five to seven members, are drawn from other departments on campus, other campuses in the system, and/or other universities. Because the reviewers look at quality processes rather than quality itself, they need not come from the discipline of the department being reviewed. (Drawing some reviewers from cognate disciplines is helpful, however.) The reviewers receive a day of training on AQW and the academic audit methodology.

Selection of the auditors is critical. Most need to be experienced faculty members who are familiar with the culture and idiosyncrasies of the academy. They need to be faculty members who can ask probing questions without putting an edge into the conversation. And they need to be faculty members who like to think deeply about their work and that of the university, and who share the big-picture goal of improving practices in higher education.

We found it is necessary to train an ample supply of auditors from a wide variety of fields. Scheduling audit visits around faculty calendars can be tricky because on any given visit you may have to contact twice as many auditors as you will eventually need to get a full team. Further, it's helpful to strike a good balance of team members, drawing from the humanities and the natural and social sciences, and to create a team that has gender and racial diversity whenever possible. Each reviewer brings a particular mental model to the audit process, and it's valuable to have a variety of perspectives present on each team.

The auditors must be familiar with education quality concepts, just like the people they will visit. In many cases auditors are members of departments that are being audited in the current round (by a different team, of course), and that dramatically helps the communication process and sets the conversational tone. Auditors also receive guidance, which includes a role-playing exercise, on how to facilitate conversations with the desired degree of structure.

Audit Visits

The length of the audit visit is about one day per department. (It may be somewhat longer if the department has many programs or shorter if, as might happen eventually, many departments on the campus are being reviewed.) The reviewers will meet with the department's leadership group, committees responsible for quality, ad hoc groups of faculty, and students. They will ask about matters raised in the self-studies and, at their discretion, other matters relating to AQW.

Auditors usually begin by asking about the department's philosophies and approaches to the five focal areas (i.e., learning outcomes, course and curriculum content, teaching and learning, student learning assessment, and QA). In some cases, exemplary departments may have developed notions of how the quality principles can be applied in the various focal areas. The auditors will be interested in such descriptions because they demonstrate forethought and commitment to quality work that is clearly absent in departments that have not systematically addressed quality issues or outcomes.

The auditors will also ask for examples of how these principles have been applied. For example: What have you learned from former students and employers? What changes have been made recently in your curriculum, what was the impetus for the changes, and what facts were used to make these decisions? What research went into designing the student assessment, and how do the assessments relate to what you are trying to accomplish? How do colleagues hold each other accountable for implementing these processes and improving the quality of students' education?

Because the review focuses on quality improvement rather than the justification of current practice, long-winded descriptions of proof are not required. Although an absence of backup material may trigger questions from the reviewers, there is no prescribed format to the questioning. It is more important that department members are able to engage the reviewers in well-informed discussions about a broad range of quality improvement issues and be able to back their assertions by citing meaningful evidence when asked.

Audit Reports

The report evaluates a department's approach to quality, highlights examples of exemplary practice, and indicates areas where improvement appears to be needed. (The department reviews the draft for factual errors.) Unless otherwise decided at the outset, the report is disseminated across the institution along with the self-study and any departmental response. The reports describe the impressions and assessments made by the audit team as it reviews the self-study, the background information provided at the site visit, and the information gleaned from the extensive interviews that are conducted at the site visit. Often the reports are written in a succinct format highlighting what the department does well (commendations), where the department has identified room for improvement (affirmations), and where the department needs to focus on improvements that were not previously identified by the department itself (recommendations).

Debriefing Session and Follow-Up Plans

Representatives from the departments and review teams get together with the project's sponsors to evaluate the methodology and results, discuss lessons learned, and share best practices. Hopefully the feedback will support a decision to mount additional audit rounds.

Improving performance in any focal area requires serious reflection followed by a commitment to improvement. Asking how well one's current activities are aligned with the quality principles is a good first step—but often it's not enough to effect change. As part of the academic audit we have instituted a process in which the departments write an action plan once they have had a chance to review the report prepared by the audit team. The department faculty should review the report and then discuss the areas where they received high marks. These areas will provide an opportunity for celebration and can serve as an example of good practice that can be applied in other areas of their department. The follow-up plan allows faculty to consider the recommendations of the site visit team, identify those issues where they agree improvements can be made, and then prepare a short action plan with specific steps and a suggested timeline. The action plans do not have to be long (two to three pages), but it is critical to reach consensus right after the visit and to capitalize on the mood to take action. Usually these action plans are written with a small subset of faculty members; the department chair takes the lead and helps the group reach consensus about where to focus attention. The action plan is reviewed by the faculty and then shared with the team leader of the audit visit.

To enhance the power of the action plan and to ensure the department's plans are in alignment with the larger academic school or college, we schedule a follow-up meeting or conference call with the team leaders of the site visit, the department chair, the college or school dean, and any additional campus or system administrators who are directly involved. The discussion during the meeting focuses on the key elements in the audit, attempts to reach consensus on the value of the proposed follow-up plan, and outlines specific steps the department will take to improve practices. In the best of situations the department chair and dean agree to meet at a specified time in the future to review the department's progress and see whether faculty members are responding to what they have learned in the process. Because we have followed up on some of the departments that we have reviewed, we often find the faculty members have taken action and are pleased that they are working on some of the issues that the site visit team identified.

Audit as a Force for Change

The primary purpose of an academic audit is to assess the quality practices used in a department (if any) and to help the faculty members and the chair think critically about the primary mission of their unit, how the unit aligns with the strategic goals of the campus, and how they can improve the quality of their work. Although the format is a systematic one—with structured questions, a self-study, a site visit, and a summary report—the primary goal is to engage the faculty in meaningful dialogues and to trigger academic soul-searching. Through the process the faculty members will have to address questions they are not used to asking and to avoid providing answers to questions that they have already answered. The audit's purpose is to shift the conversations from prestige or national rankings to the quality of what the department does and how to improve it in a systematic fashion.

There are a number of other critical elements that will help foster the use of academic audits as a force for institutional change. First, it is critical to get senior officers at the institution involved in the process and for them to emphasize the focus on improving quality—with no additional resources. Deans and provosts should be involved in discussions about the audit results and the resulting action plan. Another element is to spotlight the strategic goals of the institution that are connected to teaching and learning (and research and scholarship, if appropriate) and specifically address how the department's goals and activities align with the institution's overall mission. Concrete discussions about what the institution expects from the department as well as what the department can expect from the institution are helpful. Rewards should be matched with stated expectations and not with tacit objectives. After all, what is most important in the long run is what the department focuses its attention and energy on and what gets rewarded.

If an academic audit is done successfully, the practice of putting together an honest and revealing self-study can be very powerful—not only because the department inventories its strengths and weaknesses, but because the structured nature of the audit and the questions that it raises force faculty members to ask themselves questions that are not typically addressed. During this process departments must also articulate specific goals for their program and assess how they are meeting those goals. Most departments won't be effective at providing evidence or even at identifying reasonable outcomes in the initial phases of implementing academic audits. Consequently this type of review must be seen as an ongoing process that will improve over time—as faculty members become more comfortable with the format and begin to see the value of their efforts. That is also why the academic audit process should be repeated regularly over time and not just during budget-cutting times. Keeping a clear distinction between academic audit and budget-cutting is critical. If departments are to clearly articulate where they need to improve, they need to be reassured they will not be penalized for pointing out their weaknesses.

The action plans and the follow-up are critical in getting real results. Institutions where program reviews are most successful are those where, after the peer review, the chair, the dean, and the provost sit down and reach agreement on a specific follow-up plan. Taking action on the plan must be seen as essential; something that is not discarded after the audit is completed. Specific plans, timelines, the allocation of resources and faculty, and specific assignments are vital so that there is a clear indication of who is doing what and when it will be done.

In the initial audit round, most plans start from a base of relatively immature AQW. But there are exceptions. Alan Strathman, faculty member in the Division of Psychological Sciences at the University of Missouri–Columbia, described one such exception:

> The audit report for the Department of Psychological Sciences is quite comprehensive. As intended it details areas where the department excels as well as opportunities for improvement. . . . It would be impossible to list the many successes of the department noted in the report, but they include:
> - Our success in identifying learning outcomes and in creating coursework to help students achieve these outcomes
> - The clear sense students receive that our faculty are interested in the quality of their educational experience
> - The outstanding opportunities we provide for undergraduates to become involved in research
> - The importance the department places on the regular evaluation of teaching (e.g., midsemester feedback, end-of-semester evaluations, peer consultations)
> - The processes in place to ensure high-quality teaching by our faculty members and graduate instructors

Testimony From the Bellies of the Whales

Testimony from the deans, department chairs, and faculty members who have been through academic audits provides the most compelling evidence of the processes' efficacy. Often these comments come from faculty who were, at best, skeptical about the process. We conclude this chapter with more extended comments from the faculty we quoted earlier—faculty who were actively involved in the first round of audits at the University of Missouri.

If conducted with the right tone in a collegial fashion, the academic audit process can engage even the most jaded faculty members. The following comment shows how powerful the process can be:

> When the UMKC [University of Missouri–Kansas City] Department of Communication Studies was approached about taking part in a pilot program of academic self-assessment, the response was less than enthusiastic. Several faculty expressed the fear that maybe it was a ploy of the (always suspect) central administration to find a new way to blame departments for "not doing more with less." Other faculty took a more benign view, figuring it was simply a political move to respond to calls for increased accountability of tax-funded institutions. In any event, there was so much faculty dissatisfaction with past mandated program reviews that, as one faculty member put it, "anything would be better" than the inadequate assessment protocols we had in place. Even so, one senior faculty member loudly proclaimed that he wasn't about to waste his time in yet another program review that no one would read.
>
> A year later, when the faculty met to assess the usefulness of this new approach to program assessment, the mood in the room was markedly different. There was consensus that the process had produced a report that was fair and accurate, but even more, the process of assessment had proved invaluable in helping the department to identify strengths to build upon and, likewise, where weaknesses were uncovered, offered new perspectives that empowered us to find new solutions to old problems. All agreed that the process of academic audit had been eye opening. One of the most enthusiastic respondents was the faculty member who had first announced his unwillingness to participate in yet another review that no one would read. As he noted, even if no one beyond ourselves reads the final report, "we are a better department" for having stepped back to ask fundamental questions about how our too often merely implicit objectives matched up to our day-in-day-out operational methods and procedures. In turn, it had proved a good occasion to do an attitude check about our commitment

to maintaining a working relationship between the goals of teaching and our individual scholarly research interests. In other words, it engaged us in a meaningful conversation about why we had become educators in the first place.

—Tom Poe

One of the keys of achieving long-term success is to get the department faculty to think differently about how they do business. The audit process can do that, and the following comments from former participants help illustrate this notion as they look back on the audit process:

In sum, participating in this process has been a beneficial experience. The report provided validation to our beliefs that we are doing an excellent job educating our students. It also provided direction to our efforts at improvement. I believe every department could benefit by engaging in this process.

—Alan Strathman

As our faculty and students spent the day working with the visiting audit team to realign learning goals and educational methods and creating an ongoing plan of action, we found ourselves looking forward to opportunities to follow up with our visiting audit team, who had become genuine partners in reaching our goals. As one faculty member noted, our experience with this pilot program had offered the benefits of an annual physical check-up under something like a system-wide program of academic health maintenance and managed care. It felt good to be cared for.

—Tom Poe

As a result of its participation in the audit process, the UMR [University of Missouri–Rolla] physics department now has a clearer vision of the changes it needs to make in order to improve what is generally regarded on campus as an effective educational program serving the needs of a diverse body of physics students. It also has a broader understanding of the processes it has in place, and, more importantly, of processes it requires to be in a better position to judge and improve the effectiveness of its own programs. Given the broad departmental participation in the process, the process represented by this pilot program is a much better instrument for developing the academic resources of the UM [University of Missouri] system than the program review process currently in place.

—Paul Parris

To make the academic audit process successful over the long term, administrators and faculty members will have to follow up on their experience and integrate the new approaches. To change the nature of higher education institutions today we must change the way we think. We must question what we do, why we do it, and how to improve the quality of the manner in which it is done. Chris Argyris (1991) has long argued that "smart people" are often the least likely people to question their practices and to drop their defensive thinking. Because our institutions of higher education are filled with smart people, the task can seem overwhelming. The academic audit process, as a prime mover for change, is one way to get started.

5

Preparation and Departmental Self-Studies

A cademic audit, like more traditional program reviews, is a peer review process that includes a self-study and a site visit by peers from outside the department. However, the similarities end there. Unlike the traditional approach to program evaluation, this process emphasizes self-reflection and self-improvement rather than compliance with predetermined standards. The purpose of an academic audit is to encourage departments or programs to evaluate their education quality processes—the key faculty activities required to produce, assure, and regularly improve the quality of teaching and learning. An audit asks how faculty approach educational decision-making and how they organize their work, using the resources available to them and working collegially to provide a quality education in the best interests of the discipline and student learning.

This chapter builds on the previous one by elaborating how departments can approach the development of their self-studies. We shall use the Tennessee Board of Regents (TBR) as our primary source of examples, although similar examples can be found in Missouri and indeed in Hong Kong, where the concepts were first applied. The audit visit and report will similarly be elaborated in Chapter 6. The common theme in both chapters is that, although academic audit is a highly flexible instrument for eliciting change, certain principles need to be adhered to, to achieve success. The first of these is careful preparation.

Project Organization

Implementing the academic audit into a system of universities and community colleges is complex and must be well planned. The system office must provide planning and oversight as well as manage the process. Project implementation includes workshops for participating programs, auditor training and selection, planning for site visits, assignment of auditors and team leaders, and receipt and review of the final audit team reports. In Tennessee, this also includes ensuring that the auditor team completes additional assessment forms required for programs using the academic audit for performance funding purposes. The schedule in Figure 5.1 provides insight into the annual overall plan for the audit.

Orientation workshops held each spring provide an opportunity to introduce the concept of academic audit to campus administrators, department faculty, and others. At these orientation workshops, opportunities are created to introduce academic audit concepts and undergirding principles to build an understanding of the differences between an audit and a traditional program review or accreditation review.

It is important for chief academic officers and department heads to attend the orientation workshops. It also is essential to identify those programs that will participate in the audit for the academic year and make sure representatives from these programs attend as well. Because academic audit has been incorporated into the Tennessee Higher Education Commission's performance funding plan, programs may elect to be audited rather than conducting a traditional program review to fulfill performance funding requirements. A list of the programs being reviewed over a five-year period helps identify which programs will participate in the audit and in which years.

Figure 5.1 General Timeline for Academic Audit

Orientation session for next academic year's cohort	June
Work session for self-study teams	September
Recommendations of auditors and review date due to TBR	November 15
Self-study due to TBR	January 31
Chairs and audit teams formally appointed	January 31
Training for audit team members (regional sessions)	February
Audit team visit to campus	April
Audit team report due to TBR	May 15
Audit team report submitted to chief academic officer	June 1
Program response and follow-up report	Following Fall

Orientation Workshops

The June orientation workshops provide a first exposure to EQW for all interested parties on the campus—including but not limited to programs that will participate in the next audit cycle. It covers the five focal areas of EQW, the seven quality principles, and the audit process itself. We discussed the material covered in this session in earlier chapters, so only an outline, shown in Figure 5.2, is needed here.

The mechanics of writing the self-study report are deferred until the participant work session in September. This is because we've found that program faculty and administrators are not ready to digest the details of the report in the orientation session. Instead, the orientation focuses on EQW, the spirit of the self-assessment process, and how an audit differs from a traditional program review. It also discusses the purpose of the audit visit, the selection and training of auditors, and a typical site visit schedule—this positions the purpose of the site visit as holding improvement-oriented structured conversations between the auditors, faculty, administrators, and students.

Audit Work Sessions for Programs in Cycle

Once programs have been identified as participating in the audit for the year, the next step is a workshop to introduce the department chairs and representative faculty to the self-study process and the site visit. We have learned that it is important to help participants address the same questions posed in the orientation workshops: What are we trying to do? How are we doing it? Who is responsible? How do we know we are succeeding? How can we do better?

In discussing the organization of the self-study, topics such as these must be addressed: who has overall responsibility, who will participate, a timetable for program activity in the self-study process, and deadlines for drafts to be reviewed. This session also should outline the components of a self-study, including focal areas and quality principles, guidelines for writing the self-study, and what can constitute evidence that processes are occurring within a program's faculty and how to collect that evidence. We focus particularly on the means to collect evidence—for example, through conversations, electronic communications, sur-

Figure 5.2 **Orientation Workshop**

Part I: Areas Covered in Academic Audit
The orientation session introduces the focal areas that structure the self-assessment that program faculty will conduct. Those focal areas include:
- Learning objectives
- Curriculum and cocurriculum
- Teaching and learning methods
- Student learning assessment
- Quality assurance

Part II: Quality Principles Considered in the Audit
Although there is no hidden agenda and no right way to approach this process, the academic audit openly advocates the following principles as foundations of good educational practice:
- *Define quality in terms of outcomes.* Learning outcomes should pertain to what is or will become important for the department's students. Learning, not teaching per se, is what ultimately matters.
- *Focus on process.* Departments should analyze how teachers teach, how students learn, and how best to approach learning assessment. Departments should study their discipline's literature and collect data on what works well and what doesn't. Experimentation with active learning should be encouraged. Faculty should be urged to share and adopt their colleagues' successful teaching innovations.
- *Work collaboratively.* Teamwork and consensus lead to total faculty ownership of and responsibility for all aspects of the curriculum and make everyone accountable for the success of students. Dialogue and collaboration should be encouraged over territoriality and the lone-wolf approach.
- *Base decisions on evidence.* Departments should collect data to find out what students need. Data should be analyzed and findings incorporated in the design of curricula, learning processes, and assessment methods.
- *Strive for coherence.* Courses should build on one another to provide necessary breadth and depth. Assessment should be aligned with learning objectives.
- *Learn from best practice.* Faculty should seek out good practices in comparable departments and institutions and adapt the best to their own circumstances. Faculty should share best practices and help raise the bar for their department.
- *Make continuous improvement a priority.* Departments should continually and consciously strive to improve teaching and learning.

continued on next page

veys, literature reviews, individual and focus group interviews, and other sources. Often the participants add to this growing list. A key topic focuses on stakeholders in the academic audit process, including students, administrators, staff, faculty, and external stakeholders. Critical stakeholders to a system of universities and communities such as the

Figure 5.2 **Orientation Workshop (*continued*)**

Part III: Overview of Self-Study and Site Visit
The discussion of the self-study and site visit are more extensive and detailed in the work session held in the fall with those who will be in the current audit cycle. The orientation session, however, provides introduction to the self-study and the site visit to address expectations for whose who may be considering participating. We use the orientation session discussion of the self-study to reinforce the idea of program faculty's engagement in conversation and dialogue around a set of questions:
- What are we trying to do?
- How are we doing it?
- Who is responsible?
- How do we know we are succeeding?
- How can we do better?

TBR are coordinators who facilitate the transfer of students between institutions.

The work session should focus on the self-study process. We learned that if the participants felt comfortable with the self-study process and leave the work session with the tools to begin work within their units, the experience is much more positive, and moving forward is easier for first-time participants. Because this workshop session is so important, we discuss it in some detail here.

Part I: How to Organize the Self-Study

Focus of the self-study. To center the process on self-examination, we introduce the self-study by asking questions that program faculty typically raise in each focal area. Addressing the five areas in general terms can be overwhelming to most faculty members, and this is even truer for the seven quality principles. Starting with down-to-earth questions helped a great deal in both the Missouri and Tennessee audit initiatives.

In the beginning stages of the process in both states, the departments being audited and the auditors themselves struggled with the complicated matrix presented in the appendix to Chapter 3. To stimulate the early conversations, Missouri developed a list of starting audit questions—a simplified list designed to create the structured dialogues and prepare departments to assess their work and write the self-study. The questions, presented next, focus on the essential ingredients in each of the focal areas and provide an easy way for the department to begin its self-study. (Experienced departments "graduate" to the full set of questions presented in Chapter 4.) The University of Missouri and the TBR institutions found that the starting questions enhance the quality of initial faculty discussion and thus the self-study. These questions also serve as a jumping-off place for conversations during the audit visit itself.

Starting Questions

Learning objectives: What are the goals of the program, and how do they relate to student needs?

- *Define quality in terms of outcomes.* Have you consciously considered what students need to be successful in their chosen field and acquire meaningful values and social skills?
- *Are these decisions based on evidence?* Do you look beyond the standards of your discipline to seek input on goals? For example, do you use surveys or focus group interviews with employers or former students? Are the results documented so you can learn from their experiences?
- *Are you learning from best practice?* Do you evaluate student outcome goals of comparable departments at other institutions?

Curriculum and cocurriculum: What is to be taught, in what order, and from what perspective? What resources and resource materials will be used to deliver the content? How does the design connect to other courses students will take as part of their total program?

- *Are you working collaboratively?* Do you collaborate effectively with faculty on the curricular design? Are you able to reach agreement on the essential elements, or does the design represent a compromise?
- *Are you learning from best practice?* Do you evaluate the curricula of comparable departments at other institutions?
- *Do you make continuous improvement a priority?* Do you reconsider curricular decisions systematically and continue to check with students and employers to see whether the curriculum is still relevant?

Teaching and learning methods: How are teaching and learning organized? What methods are used to expose students to material, for answering questions and providing interpretation, for stimulating student interaction with the content, and for providing feedback on student work? What roles and responsibilities do various faculty members need to assume? What other resources are required?

- *Do you focus on how things get done?* Do you analyze the teaching and learning processes regularly to see whether your techniques are the best for your objectives (e.g., by debating what-if options)? Do you emphasize active learning? Do you ask whether the right people are doing the right things and address the trade-offs between resource utilization and outcomes? Do you act promptly on good ideas?
- *Do you work collaboratively?* Do you collaborate effectively on process design, or does the design represent a compromise just to get it done? Does the department achieve organizational learning from the experience of its members, or is process improvement a lone-wolf activity?
- *Are you striving for coherence?* Do the various process steps reinforce each other? Do teaching and learning processes appear coherent to students?

Student learning assessment: What measures and indicators are used to assess student learning? Do they assess the improvement observed in the students or only performance at the end of the program? How are the long-term outcomes of the educational experience determined? Are baseline and trend information available? Who is responsible for assessment?

- *Are you defining quality in terms of outcomes?* Have you defined key quality indicators based on your student outcomes goals? Do your assessment measures provide data needed to track the indicators? Do they measure learning that takes place solely in your courses, as opposed to measuring quality and preparation of students?
- *Are decisions based on evidence?* Are your assessment processes grounded in the literature wherever possible? Can you defend

your choices of assessment measures by some appropriate combination of theory, experience, and experimentation?

- *Are you learning from best practice?* Do you evaluate assessment
  practices of comparable departments in other institutions?

Quality assurance: How are you organized to carry out your designs
effectively, day in and day out, regardless of distractions? How can you
ensure that content is delivered as intended, that teaching and learning processes are implemented consistently, and that assessments are
utilized as planned and their results are evaluated and effectively used
to make changes?

- *Are you working collaboratively?* Do you collaborate effectively on
  the design of QA methods? Do you work with colleagues to interpret the results and take appropriate actions based on QA results?
- *Are you learning from best practice?* Do you evaluate the QA practices of comparable departments in other institutions?
- *Do you make continuous improvement a priority?* Do you reconsider your QA processes systematically and regularly?

Part II: Guidelines for Self-Studies

Our self-studies are organized into five sections: introduction, overall
performance, performance by focal areas, potential recommendations
and associated initiatives, and matrix of improvement initiatives. We
have set the length of the self-study at a maximum of 20 single-spaced
pages of 12-point type, plus up to 10 appendix pages. In addition to
making the auditors' task easier, the page limit places a premium on
crisp communication. Here we elaborate on what should be included
in each section and why. The guidelines we distribute to the campus
programs are as follows:

- *Introduction* (one-page summary). We suggest you begin this section with a few paragraphs to introduce the reader to your program.
  This might include such elements as an overview of current student
  demographics, the role and scope of the program, a very brief history (if applicable to an understanding of the program's current

status), and so forth. Not only will this introduction be helpful to the peer auditors, but it can also serve faculty team members as the first step in the process of widening their focal lens beyond the classroom toward a more holistic view of the program and its students.

- *Overall performance* (about three pages, not including any appendix tables). This section should include an overall assessment of your unit's education quality and how you work together as a faculty to improve quality. The audit team will ask about the logic and evidence behind your assessment, but it will not collect additional evidence nor substitute its judgment about education quality for yours. Your objective is to convince the auditors that the statement is insightful, not necessarily that you deliver exemplary education quality. For example, candid descriptions of weakness, buttressed by evidence, will be received better than unsupported or puffed-up claims of excellence.

- *Performance by focal area* (about two or three pages per focal area). Here you reflect on your performance in each of the five focal areas: 1) learning objectives; 2) curriculum and cocurriculum; 3) teaching and learning; 4) student learning assessment; and 5) quality assurance. We suggest that your team discussions move back and forth between the focal areas and subquestions as a means of gaining insight regarding the interconnectedness of the focal areas and your unit's strengths and weaknesses in applying the quality principles to these focal areas. This section represents the heart of your self-study report and provides groundwork for consideration of improvement initiatives. The following information should be provided for each focal area: 1) a short narrative that describes your department's quality processes as they pertain to the focal area, and 2) an evaluation of your quality processes in each focal area in light of the seven quality principles (wherever applicable). The quality principles should be integrated into your discussions of the focal areas, not treated as separate areas to address. If your exploration of a focal area reveals weaknesses or opportunities for improvement in that focal area, say so in your report. The purpose of the self-study is to identify successes and areas for improvement. You do not have to find that all is well in each focal area.

- *Potential recommendations and associated initiatives* (the description of each initiative should not exceed one page). Now the focus becomes strictly formative. Having assessed your overall performance and your education quality processes, you are asked to formulate some specific initiatives for improvement. If you have identified a specific, significant weakness in a focal area, you must indicate how you plan to correct the weakness. If you see an opportunity to improve on already good performance in a focal area, you may present an idea for achieving this improvement. The goal is to sketch out actions that would have a strong positive impact on education quality. As you describe initiatives:
  - Clearly state what needs to be accomplished and why.
  - Outline the tasks required to accomplish the objective(s).
  - Indicate how you will gauge whether the initiative is being implemented as planned.
  - Demonstrate that your unit is capable of carrying out the initiative, especially in light of other demands on your time and resources. If you need additional support to accomplish the initiative, say so.

  In short, you should provide enough information to demonstrate that the initiatives are well thought out and feasible. Above all, your plan should confirm the participants' enthusiastic commitment to move forward and the department's support of the effort.

- *Matrix of improvement initiatives* (about one page). Self-studies will conclude with detailed commitments for improvement and a structure for assessing progress. Provide a matrix that includes the following information for each initiative discussed in the fourth section (potential recommendations and associated initiatives) that is being put forward as a formal recommendation by the department/program:
  - Brief description of the recommended initiative and its result
  - Who will have overall responsibility for the initiative
  - Who will participate
  - When work on the initiative will begin
  - How long the work is expected to take

  It is important that the self-study be clear in this section because the review team will work from these details as they affirm the recommendations of the department and consider other recommendations that are merited.

Part III: Academic Audit Focal Areas and Questions for Faculty Discussion

You can use the list of starting questions presented in Part I as discussion stimuli for this section of the self-study. These questions were designed to help you examine the processes by which the faculty are pursuing their goals for student learning. Although most of these questions seem to call for yes or no answers, they are meant to prompt fuller discussions. If the answer is yes to a question, the self-study should briefly describe the who, what, when, where, and how of that answer, and faculty should be prepared to provide more details or examples when the audit team visits. If the answer is no, the self-study should discuss whether faculty wish to improve in this regard and how they plan to do so.

Part IV: Sources of Evidence

Essential to the academic audit site visit is the opportunity to review any sources of evidence provided by the audited program. At the TBR, we urged programs participating in the self-study to consider a variety of data sources that can provide insight into issues. Many programs use multiple surveys and focus group interviews to gain an understanding of how stakeholder groups view the program's effectiveness within the focal areas. Those same data, however, can serve as evidence to support areas of strength and those in need of improvement to the audit team during the site visit. Several of the Tennessee Super Dudes, a select group of 10 university and community college co-leaders for the TBR academic audit training, spent considerable time creating a set of suggested data sources that serve as sources of evidence. They are arrayed by focal area and summarized below.

Learning objectives
- Student demographics: major and/or educational objective, age, gender, and GPA and/or results of placement tests
- Enrolled student surveys (institutional or targeted) or interviews
- Alumni/graduate surveys (institutional or targeted) or interviews

- Employer surveys (institutional or targeted) or interviews
- Advisory board/committee meeting minutes
- Feedback from faculty teaching courses for which yours are prerequisites
- Peer feedback from senior/graduate institutions
- Competencies/outcomes (syllabi) of senior/graduate programs in your discipline
- National standards for your discipline: competencies, outcomes
- Syllabi

Curriculum and cocurriculum
- Departmental/institutional policies for curriculum development
- Minutes/notes from faculty meetings, curriculum development/textbook selection committees, and so forth
- Curricula from peer programs in the discipline and from senior/graduate programs
- National standards for curriculum in your discipline
- Feedback from stakeholders (students, graduates, employers, advisory boards)
- Documentation of curriculum revision (course inventory forms)
- Syllabi

Teaching and learning methods
- Current research/literature on effective teaching methodology in the discipline
- Minutes/notes from faculty meetings
- Feedback from stakeholders (students, graduates, employers, advisory boards)
- Learning styles inventory assessments
- Evaluations by students/supervisors
- End-of-course surveys
- Peer mentoring, classroom observations
- Annual personal goals and objectives
- Course analysis documents
- Assessments of student success in different instructional settings (web vs. traditional); other types of student success analysis (withdrawal rates, grade distribution, success in subsequent courses)

- Professional (internal or external), disciplinary, or pedagogical development
- Ongoing professional memberships

Student learning assessment
- Documentation of key learning quality indicators
- Feedback from stakeholders (students, graduates, employers, advisory boards)
- Minutes/notes from faculty meetings
- Pre- and post-tests
- Exit testing through departmental/programmatic final assessment (national, collaborative, or local instruments)
- Foundation testing such as Motivational Appraisal of Personal Potential (academic profile)
- Student portfolios, capstone course projects, co-op or internship supervisor evaluations
- Test item analysis
- Test/assessment bank or library
- Job placement rates
- Acceptance into senior/graduate programs
- Success (GPA/retention) in senior/graduate programs

Quality assurance
- Departmental/institutional policies that support collaboration, assessment, and professional development
- Assessment plans, review schedules, meeting calendars, and so forth
- Benchmarking for national comparison (National Survey of Student Engagement/Community College Survey of Student Engagement, National Community College Benchmark Project, etc.)
- Regularly published and shared information about progress on improvement initiatives, use of results[1]

Example of a Self-Study

Review of good examples of self-studies is helpful in developing a mental model for the substance and tone of the work of the program faculty. We include a self-study and its appendices, with permission from East Tennessee State University (ETSU), for a program completed in 2006.

Sociology BA, BS, and MA Programs
East Tennessee State University

1. Introduction

The Department of Sociology and Anthropology at East Tennessee State University offers an undergraduate major in sociology for BA and BS degree students; undergraduate minors in sociology, anthropology, and Appalachian studies; and two MA degree concentrations (general and applied).

For undergraduates majoring in sociology, the program of study is designed to provide students with 1) substantive knowledge about human society and culture; 2) an overview of theoretical orientations that have shaped the discipline; and 3) fundamental research skills (both qualitative and quantitative) that social scientists use to analyze various issues and problems confronting humans today (program requirements are listed in Appendix A). Our undergraduate program is also geared to prepare students for employment in the social services sector and for advanced study at the graduate level. We are in the process of proposing an undergraduate major in anthropology to the TBR for approval (see Appendix B).

The MA program is an important part of the department's educational mission. The MA program has two concentrations, each designed to meet a specific objective. The conventional thesis (General Sociology) concentration prepares students with the necessary knowledge and skills to continue their study in sociology at the PhD level. The Applied Sociology concentration provides students with the sociological knowledge and research skills useful for work in social services and other public sector areas of employment. ETSU's MA program in sociology serves the region and is the only such program available between Knoxville, Tennessee; Blacksburg, Virginia; and Charlotte, North Carolina. The majority of the department's graduate students have been recruited from eastern Tennessee, western North Carolina, and southwest Virginia. Many of our graduate students were first undergraduates at ETSU. (To view the program requirements for both MA concentrations, see Appendix C.)

For the fall semesters from 2002 to 2005, the population of undergraduate sociology majors was approximately 60% female and 40% male, with more than 90% of majors enrolled as in-state students (descriptive data are found in Appendix D). For that same time period, the average percentage of students who were members of minority groups was around 9%. For graduate students in the fall semesters from 2002 to 2005, the average was 69% female and 31% male, with about 80% of the students designated as in-state. On average, 7% of the graduate students during this period were members of minority groups.

Regarding the department's enrollments for undergraduate majors and graduate students for fall 2004 to spring 2005, 58 undergraduate students who declared sociology as their first major were enrolled in the fall and 69 who declared sociology as their first major were enrolled in the spring. In fall 2005, 68 students who declared sociology as their first major were enrolled. In addition, approximately 14 students who declared sociology as their *second major* were enrolled each semester as well (data on second majors were not included in the report prepared for sociology in Appendix D, but an update will be provided for the academic audit team on their site visit). The MA program headcount was 12 in fall 2004, 11 in spring 2005, and 14 in fall 2005. In general, although the department's student credit hour production has displayed steady growth over the past 10 years (regardless of major), the number of students in our undergraduate and graduate programs has fluctuated. For the past 3 years, the number of students in both degree programs has been increasing incrementally (see Appendix D).

To prepare the self-study that follows, the department faculty (sociologists and anthropologists) held four meetings in November and December 2005 and divided the workload for the different sections of the report. Because this academic audit has the fundamental charge of evaluating our sociology BA, BS, and MA programs, the six sociologists on the faculty (Beck, Cole, Copp, Hester, Kamolnick, and McCallister) each took notes and then drafted different sections of the report after we held our faculty discussions. Four anthropologists

(Blaustein, Cavender, Franklin, and King) participated in the discussions because future academic audits will likely include the anticipated BA program in anthropology. Once the anthropology major proposal is approved by the TBR, we can establish quality processes similar to those we are implementing in our sociology programs.

2. Overall Performance

As our discussion of the department's performance in each of the five focal areas will demonstrate, our faculty members routinely work collaboratively on a number of fronts to provide quality education to our undergraduate and graduate students. We believe that we offer students a thorough and rigorous program of study, and we expect as much of ourselves as we do our students. This level of performance is largely the product of a departmental culture in which we value quality teaching and seek ways to continuously improve our programs. As will become clear, though, we primarily rely on informal—rather than formal and systematic—methods for improving our programs. However, our faculty disagree with the description of "informal effort" provided in the TBR guidance notes on "maturity." In the guidance notes, informal effort is defined as this: "Individual professors experiment with the principles, but few colleagues pay much attention. Coverage of the focal areas remains spotty, and the department has yet to become a learning organization with respect to quality and the evidentiary principles." This definition *poorly* characterizes the department. Our mostly voluntary efforts to improve the quality of education in our undergraduate and graduate programs are fostered by a departmental norm of collegiality and the recognition that the different focal areas are relevant to our program quality (although we do not employ the terminology of "focal areas"). We consult with each other before we take action—to keep everyone informed, to ensure consistency, and to avoid decisions that might harm our programs. Thus, we pay attention to what we do individually and collectively.

In the narratives for the five focal areas that follow, we will discuss the mechanisms we currently have in place for promoting education quality, and we will describe our plans to implement new approaches for improving education quality in an organized and regular fashion.

3. Performance by Focal Area

Learning objectives. In 2000, the previous department chair (Beck) developed proposed learning objectives for the BA/BS and MA degrees in sociology as part of the SACS (Southern Association of Colleges and Schools) review process. The proposed objectives were distributed to faculty by memo for review and comment. The chair made revisions to the proposed learning objectives based on faculty responses. The revised objectives were presented in a faculty meeting and were also submitted as the departmental objectives for the SACS review. The objectives consisted of three quantifiable objectives with benchmarks for the BA/BS degree in sociology and three quantifiable objectives with benchmarks for the MA degree in sociology.

ETSU's internal SACS review team suggested revisions to the six objectives, recommending that we avoid simplistic quantifiable objectives (which, ironically, had been provided as models to guide us). In collaboration with the faculty, the chair then developed and submitted for SACS review five objectives for the BA, five objectives for the BS, three objectives for the MA in General Sociology, and four objectives for the MA in Applied Sociology. These revisions were accepted by SACS in the 2000–2001 accreditation review (see Appendix E). In developing the undergraduate and graduate program learning objectives, the logic was to develop objectives that captured the essence of what students should learn from the basic set of required courses and learning experiences for each degree. For undergraduates, this meant developing learning objectives that targeted what students should learn in Introduction to Sociology, Social Problems, Research Methods, Statistics, and Theory. For graduate students, the theory and methods courses were deemed essential, but faculty agreed that the learning objectives for each MA concentration should identify something unique that students gain from participating in either the thesis (General Sociology) or the internship and internship placement report experience (Applied Sociology).

The remainder of the narrative on learning objectives overlaps considerably with the focal area concerning student learning assessment, but it traces how we made further revisions in the undergraduate learning objectives that we have in place today.

At the fall 2001 faculty meeting, the Comprehensive Exit Exam Committee was formed. It was agreed that the committee would develop a comprehensive exit exam for graduating seniors as a means to assess what students had learned from their course of study in sociology. The faculty agreed that we would prefer to create our own comprehensive exit exam and replace ETS's major field test that had previously been used by the department for performance funding purposes. The exam was created collaboratively by the committee (Beck, Cole, Copp, Hester, and Kamolnick) and was designed to test students' knowledge from the following courses: Introduction to Sociology, Social Problems, Methods, Social Statistics, and Modern Social Theory. A pilot exam was administered to graduating seniors in December 2001 and again in April 2002.

Each spring and fall semester from 2002 through 2005, exit exams were administered, and results were reviewed by the Comprehensive Exit Exam Committee with minor revisions made to improve awkward or confusing exam questions for the subsequent year's graduating seniors. A study guide for the exit exam was instituted in 2004. After the April 2005 exit exam results were reviewed, with improving but consistently unimpressive results from 2001 to 2005, it was decided that a detailed review and complete overhaul of the exam should be conducted.

At the spring 2005 faculty meeting the ETSU Academic Quality Initiative (AQI) was discussed. The ETSU AQI is a voluntary three-year program in which faculty work together to set goals for student learning, measure attainment of these goals, and use the results to improve courses and teaching (see www.etsu.edu/aqi).

For Year 1 of the AQI each participating department agrees to:

- Select an option for participating in the AQI.
- Define expected learning outcomes.
- Propose measurement plans for selected learning outcomes.
- Submit an annual report for review by the AQI Advisory Committee (see www.etsu.edu/aqi).

Since the AQI focuses on learning objectives and their measurement, our participation was seen as an acceptable means to facilitate a review of both the exit exam and the BA/BS learning objectives, to identify reasons for our graduating seniors' performance deficiencies on the exit exam, and to propose teaching and learning improvements. A subset of the Comprehensive Exit Exam Committee (Beck, Cole, and Copp) agreed to participate as the AQI Advisory Committee. In collaboration with other sociology and anthropology faculty members and administrators, the department's AQI Advisory Committee selected a plan that offered the best fit for meeting the department's needs relating to learning objectives and their measurement—AQI Plan Option U1:

- Define a set of expected learning outcomes common to all undergraduate majors and concentrations in your department.
- Propose measurement plans for at least three of these outcomes, including one related to critical thinking or problem solving (see www.etsu.edu/aqi).

In April 2005 the department's Year 1 AQI draft proposal was submitted to the AQI Advisory Committee and the assistant vice president for academic affairs. The AQI Advisory Committee developed the AQI proposal by reviewing and revising both the five learning objectives for the BA/BS degrees that had been developed for the SACS review in 2000–2001 and the exit exam that had been used to measure these learning objectives. The goal of this revision was to ensure that learning objectives could actually be assessed using the exit exam.

The department's AQI proposal draft was reviewed by the ETSU AQI committee, headed by Dr. William Kirkwood (assistant vice president for academic quality initiatives and student learning), who recommended revisions to both the learning objectives and asked for further clarification on 1) how the exit exam would adequately serve as a data-gathering tool to assess students' performance on each learning objective, and 2) what the faculty's process would be for discussing results and implementing improvements. The department's AQI Advisory Committee discussed the suggested revisions and developed a revised AQI proposal that was submitted and accepted as the department's Year 1 AQI Plan (see Appendix F for the AQI proposal and Year 1 report). The following represent the revised learning objectives as developed for the AQI. At the completion of the BA and BS degree in sociology, students will be able to:

- Apply key concepts in sociology to a variety of societal processes.
- Understand, evaluate, and critique empirical research in the social sciences.
- Understand prominent social theories.
- Critically evaluate prominent social theories.
- Apply both relevant theories and research in the social sciences to problems facing individuals, groups, organizations, and societies.
- Use appropriate statistical analysis techniques on social science data for both descriptive and inferential purposes.

The exit exam has been revised according to our AQI plan. It now consists of four sections, each with 10 multiple-choice questions (with some questions in each section requiring in-depth understanding or problem solving) that relate to four learning objective topics: key concepts in sociology, research methods/statistical analysis, sociological theory, and social problems. The exam also has two required critical thinking essay questions that likewise relate to the learning objectives. The scores on each section of the multiple-choice questions and the scores from the essays are combined to form an assessment of students' ability to achieve the expected learning objectives.

It should be noted that the faculty discussion of the learning objectives in a fall 2005 meeting also resulted in further revision of the second learning objective to now read: "At the completion of the BA and BS degree in sociology, students will be able to understand and evaluate empirical research in the social sciences" ("critique" was considered too advanced an objective for undergraduates).

This change was jointly discussed and agreed on by the faculty, presented to the vice president for academic affairs for use in the AQI, and approved.

The AQI process will continue through 2006–2007. In Year 2 of the AQI (2005–2006), the department will:

- Collect data for each measurement plan proposed in Year 1.

- Review the data and propose plans to improve student learning to be implemented in Year 3.
- Submit an annual report for review by the AQI Advisory Committee (due September 1, 2006).

In Year 3 of the AQI, the department will:

- Implement the plans to improve student learning that were proposed in Year 2.
- Collect a second round of data for the measurement plans proposed in Year 1.
- Review data collected in Year 2 and Year 3 and decide whether to maintain or modify plans to improve student learning.
- Submit an annual report for the review by the AQI Advisory Committee (see www.etsu.edu/aqi).

We hope our participation in the AQI will result in developing a stronger understanding of students' strengths and weaknesses on the exit exam and in our undergraduate program, identifying what learning objectives need reinforcement/improvement in our program, and, ultimately, proposing and then implementing improvements in our teaching so that students will demonstrate a higher level of performance and learning in subsequent years.

In preparation for this self-study, the department's discussions of its learning objectives and the exit exam for the academic audit process have resulted in additional proposals:

- The department plans to assess the requirement for students to take an exit exam; the consequences for their performance on it; incentives for performing well; method and timing of administering the exam during the semester; and what, when, and how to communicate information regarding the exam to sociology majors. At the request of the faculty, the present department chair (Copp) polled arts and sciences department chairs on the use of an exit exam, how students seem to perform, and whether other departments offer incentives for students to perform well. A similar obstacle has

been found in some departments: Students have difficulty taking the exam seriously and do not push themselves to perform well.
- The department plans to develop a brief student survey to assess the program from the students' perspective.

Also in the process of preparing for this self-study, the faculty identified a departmental deficiency in the following area related to the learning objectives section in the academic audit guidance notes:

- *The department communicates program learning objectives to students and others.* Even though the department's learning objectives are listed online in the University Profile System database, along with other pertinent information about the department, the faculty agree that greater formal and informal dissemination of the department's undergraduate learning objectives is warranted. The department will increase access to and make a greater effort to disseminate information on the undergraduate program's learning objectives. For example, the department will include a list of the undergraduate objectives in the following ways:
  - On the department's web page (www.etsu.edu/cas/sociology/sociol.htm)
  - On the majors' checklist of courses
  - On the department's brochure that describes the sociology major and minor and the anthropology minor
  - In the letter to graduating seniors (implemented in fall 2005)
  - In activities where information about the department is presented to potential students

It is reasonable to assume that this deficiency in communication can be addressed as an integral part of the previously referenced proposal to assess aspects of the exit exam process and to develop a student assessment of the overall program.

Regarding the graduate program's learning objectives, our faculty have reviewed the set of learning objectives for each concentration (general and applied), and we have affirmed that they indeed fit the goals of our program. Moreover, our faculty agree that we *do* adequately communicate learning objectives to graduate students—both at the time of their initial one-on-one advisement with the graduate coordinator, and throughout the mentoring process that students receive from their committee chair and advisory committee members.

Curriculum and cocurriculum. The Department of Sociology and Anthropology collaborates effectively through an informal process regarding the undergraduate and graduate curricula. Collaboration occurs as a result of institutional requirements, program reviews, and a desire to improve course offerings, new course development, and students' timely progress through the program. Our department meets at the beginning of the fall and spring semesters to allow individuals to share what they are doing, their plans for the semester (such as new course offerings, starting an honor society, etc.), and any departmental issues or concerns. Although regular meetings are not scheduled beyond those two, our department maintains an open-door environment in which faculty informally seek out and utilize the ideas and experiences of other faculty, including those in anthropology. This process is active in that curriculum changes are made on an ongoing basis to improve our program for our students, and do not only occur as a result of an institutional mandate or as an attempt to "just get by" and do only the minimum required change. For instance, the university instituted changes in the general education requirements (1994–1995), requiring departments to incorporate oral-, writing-, and technology-intensive classes into their course offerings (these intensive requirements are now university requirements, not general education requirements). The Department of Sociology and Anthropology not only developed the intensive courses, but the faculty collaboratively decided to fold the intensives into our major requirements, ensuring that our students could efficiently complete their intensive and major requirements without having to enroll in additional courses outside the major.

Current curriculum changes have also occurred in response to previous program reviews. In 2001, the department participated in a program review, which specifically documented the need to recruit a new faculty member who would develop and regularly offer an undergraduate course in applied sociology. This course would not only introduce undergraduate students to applied sociology, but it would also generate interest in the department's Applied Sociology concentration in the graduate program. An applied sociologist was hired in August 2003 (McCallister), and her course, Community Sociology, became a required course for the major beginning in fall 2005 (the course was offered each semester before that as a special topics course).

Faculty are encouraged, both at the department and administration levels, to develop new courses. Our process for new course development reflects both a collaborative effort while still incorporating individual preferences and decisions. New course proposals are largely left up to the professor who will serve as the lead instructor for it; yet, leading up to the proposal stage, proposals are routinely discussed among the faculty to ensure that our courses complement rather than compete with each other and that we continue to offer a strong array of courses for our majors. Once a faculty member drafts a new course proposal, the course and its content must be submitted to and approved by the department chair, the college curriculum committee, the dean, and ultimately the undergraduate curriculum committee (and/or the graduate council). This process of open discussion and collaboration accurately fits how the department faculty proposed and obtained approval for 13 new courses and two nonsubstantive changes in the curriculum in the past academic year alone (see Appendix G for a complete list of the course and curriculum changes we have implemented since fall 2001). The majority of the new course proposals were for anthropology courses—as part of our process for developing the new major in anthropology—but other courses were in Appalachian studies and in the sociology major (SOAA 4057, Community Sociology).

Regarding analyzing the content and sequencing of our courses for the purpose of achieving program learning objectives, the sociology department currently employs an informal, ongoing process. This section of the narrative will explain the current process, including a description of cocurricular offerings at the undergraduate and graduate levels, and will also describe how the department will expand this process in the near future.

Currently the collaboration process in examining content and sequencing of courses includes those who are directly involved with the courses in question. For example, our department and the College of Arts and Sciences department chairs recently examined the college's requirements for the BS with a concentration in behavioral and social science. This is the most frequently chosen option for our sociology majors. Two social science department chairs—psychology and criminal justice—proposed dropping one of the categories for this concentration, data analysis, because the content of their courses in this category (PSYC 3444 and CJCR 3444) were, over time, absorbed by other courses offered in their departments. Sociology, on the other hand, still had a viable course with an outdated title (SOAA 3444 Microcomputers as a Research Tool) that was the only technology-intensive course for our majors to take. Students in other majors, namely political science, needed this course to fulfill their technology-intensive requirements as well. So although SOAA 3444 was not officially required for the major, it had virtually become a required course for sociology majors. To decide whether to keep this course, our department chair collaborated with the department faculty and an adjunct professor directly involved in teaching technology-intensive courses and potential technology-intensive courses. Together, a decision was made to make Social Statistics (SOAA 3350) technology intensive and to offer it every semester. This would provide all students in our major (BA and BS) with the opportunity to meet their technology-intensive requirement while simultaneously fulfilling a major course requirement. This group also decided to keep Microcomputers as a Research Tool (SOAA 3444) in the curriculum, changing the course name to Data Analysis and integrating it into a major requirement for the BS degree. The name change went into effect for spring 2006. The course remains technology intensive and will continue to teach descriptive and inferential data analysis using a hands-on, experiential approach that all faculty in the department agree to be valuable for BS students—whether in the workplace or in subsequent graduate study.

The design of cocurricular activities also reflects collaboration with an emphasis on faculty preferences or decisions. Individual professors develop activities centered on their areas of interest and expertise and then share the information with other faculty in the department, which results in a variety of offerings for our students. This variety of cocurricular offerings is a great strength of our department, at both the undergraduate and graduate levels.

At the undergraduate level, instructors offer regular opportunities to participate in cocurricular activities. For example, service-learning opportunities have been incorporated into some sections of our Introduction to Sociology and Social Problems courses (in fall 2005, a section of Social Problems was offered with a special service-learning designation; one instructor regularly awards extra credit opportunities to students that involve service-learning and coordinates her efforts with the campus service-learning director). Students are able to work directly with various community agencies, viewing firsthand many of the issues presented in their textbooks. In Community Sociology, an upper-level required course, students work directly with various community agencies, designing and conducting community-based research projects that assist the agencies. The instructor acts as a consultant, and the students are responsible for meeting regularly with the community members and collaborating with them to determine what information to collect and how to collect it. In addition to activities offered within individual classes, the sociology department provides opportunities for students to participate in Pi Gamma Mu and Alpha Kappa Delta (AKD), international social science honor societies housed in the sociology department. Over a year ago, the faculty collectively decided to renew the department's affiliation with AKD after the affiliation had lapsed for a decade. Students will begin meeting this spring semester to organize AKD activities.

Collaboration at the undergraduate level also occurs between departments on campus. For example, the sociology department regularly coordinates with other departments to bring in speakers and sponsors films. Most recently, the department took the lead in working with the women's studies program and the political science department to bring to campus two speakers who are involved with social programs in Chiapas, Mexico, regarding human rights, fair trade, and globalization. The campus event was well attended. We are currently collaborating with the International Student Health Interest Group (headed by an ETSU medical student) to cosponsor the visit of a prominent medical anthropologist to ETSU, who will give a talk later this semester on the topic of women's health and cultural anthropology in a global context. Our department also partners with other programs to introduce students to different perspectives on various social issues in our courses. For instance, Gender & Society (SOAA 3030) is a designated elective for the women's studies program, Minorities (SOAA 3110) is an elective for the African/African American studies program, Peoples & Cultures of Latin America (SOAA 3700) is a course in the global studies program, and Environmental Anthropology (SOAA 3250) is a designated elective in the environmental studies program. One special section of social problems every fall semester (and beginning in 2005–2006, both fall and spring semesters) is designated as having an emphasis on women's studies. In addition, the sociology department houses the minor for Appalachian studies. Finally, students can participate in various activities through the Center for Community Outreach. Headed by sociology professors Dr. Judith Hammond and Dr. Robert G. Leger, the center receives federal grants ranging from working with Families First to mentoring middle school and high school youths, and sociology students are encouraged to participate in volunteer opportunities provided through these grants.

At the graduate level, students are encouraged to participate in activities both inside and outside the department. Like the undergraduate students, graduate students can take Community Sociology; the primary difference is that graduate students take a leadership role in the class, facilitating contact between the students and community members and leading their group of students through the data collection process. Graduate students are also encouraged to attend professional meetings and to present their research. For instance, two students attended the 2004 Society for Applied Sociology annual meeting, and in 2005, one student presented research and another attended the meeting. All student travel was supported financially through our department. Students in our MA program in Applied Sociology are also required to complete an internship with an outside agency; students partner with an agency, work either 20 hours a week for one semester or 10 hours a week for two semesters, and incorporate their sociology skills into the internship. (For example, a current student in Applied Sociology is conducting a process evaluation of the Workforce Investment Act In-School Youth Evaluation, while another is set to begin working with a U.S. Department of Education GEAR UP grant.) In addition, graduate students can join AKD and the Graduate Student Association.

In conclusion, our departmental process for regularly updating the curriculum and maintaining a vibrant cocurriculum is informal, multifaceted, and routinely collaborative. The open and unregimented atmosphere of our department encourages the sharing of ideas and suggestions for improvements. We do recognize, however, that although the department is effective in collaborating on proposed changes, we do not systematically and formally evaluate our curriculum to ensure that course content and sequencing best meet the needs of our students. From our discussions in preparation for this self-study, we concluded that the curriculum needs to be reviewed on a continuous, scheduled basis. Beginning in fall 2006, the department will review the undergraduate and graduate curriculum every two years.

The goal of this review is to ensure that undergraduate students have the appropriate background courses to be successful as they continue through the major, and that graduate students possess the necessary knowledge and skills before beginning either their thesis or internship.

This review will consist of two elements. First, the sociology faculty will solicit student feedback regarding their levels of preparedness and background knowledge when taking courses in the major. At least two questions will be added to the Student Assessment of Instruction (SAI) instrument, asking students to indicate which courses in the major they have taken and whether they felt prepared for the specific course they took. This will provide the faculty with the appropriate feedback to begin assessing course sequencing.

The second element of the review involves a plan to conduct a multiphase, trilevel gap analysis, beginning in the fall 2006 semester, to determine the soundness of our curriculum and cocurriculum. This analysis will be conducted for both the undergraduate and graduate programs. The first phase will occur at the department level and will begin in September 2006. The sociology faculty will examine the course objectives of our required major courses to determine whether they dovetail with each program's learning objectives/outcomes. Course objectives should identify the key skills or abilities that will be taught/ enhanced, while also explaining how these skills/abilities tie into the program's learning outcomes. In addition, if the course contains a cocurricular element, faculty will examine that element to determine how it enhances the course objectives and thus the learning outcomes. This same process will also occur for both the thesis and Applied Sociology concentrations in our MA program.

The second phase will occur at the institutional level. Our department will compare its undergraduate sociology major/minor requirements to those of ETSU's peer institutions (East Carolina University, University of South Alabama, University of Arkansas at Little Rock, Florida A&M University, Florida Atlantic University, Eastern Kentucky University, Appalachian State University, University of North Carolina at Charlotte, University of North Carolina at Greensboro, University of Texas at Arlington, University of Texas at El Paso, and Old Dominion University). A sociology graduate assistant will compare peer institutions' course listings and requirements to those of our program. This graduate assistant will also conduct a similar comparison for our MA program. Not all peer institutions will have an MA program, especially an MA in Applied Sociology, so the faculty will identify additional programs of interest for comparison purposes. Once the graduate assistant compiles the data, the faculty will meet in February 2007 to assess whether there are gaps in the curriculum that should be filled. The faculty will examine the gaps, prioritize the need(s), and determine the feasibility and timetable of adding or revising classes (if necessary).

The third level of our curriculum and cocurriculum review will occur at the national level. The American Sociological Association (ASA) has publications available on the undergraduate sociology major and on graduate programs (*Liberal Learning and the Sociology Major Updated,* by Kathleen McKinney, Carla B. Howery, Kerry J. Strand, Edward L. Kain, and Catherine White Berheide, 2004). We will consult these ASA publications to determine whether there are any new steps we should be taking in the sociology curriculum that we offer to undergraduate and graduate students.

This multiphase, trilevel approach allows our department to gain a comprehensive look at its curriculum and major requirements. By examining our individual courses, the requirements of our peer institutions, and the benchmarks and best practices of sociology's national professional association, we will be better able to identify, prioritize, and close any gaps identified in our curriculum and cocurriculum. Once this detailed analysis is complete, improvements will be initiated. The department will continue to evaluate its curriculum every two years.

Teaching and learning methods. In this section we will share the results of our faculty discussions on the process of teaching and learning that we employ and the extent to which we focus on it, our use of instructional methods and materials, and our analysis of the extent to which we collaborate on our teaching and learning processes.

The department faculty have documented several mechanisms that focus on the process of teaching and learning throughout the program. The following are the most noteworthy. First, the Student Assessment of Instruction (SAI) process has been, and remains, an important data source that faculty and the department chair use in evaluating the effectiveness of teaching. Instructor use of SAI feedback is highly encouraged, and although all student comments may not be equally helpful, productive criticism and effective feedback regarding pedagogical style, evaluation format, and effectiveness of communication and delivery are quite important. SAIs are required of all faculty, no matter how senior, and are conducted each semester in at least two of the instructor's courses. For tenure-track faculty, we encourage that every course be evaluated by students. In addition, on their own initiative, our tenure-track faculty have established the practice of surveying their students at mid-semester so that they can make adjustments in teaching and learning processes while courses are in session—rather than waiting until the course is over to make improvements.

Second, the department is now in the process of implementing the TBR-mandated peer review of teaching. To date, peer review has been used to evaluate the most recent candidate seeking promotion, and the department intends to develop a plan for institutionalizing peer review for all faculty members. Early this spring semester we will be discussing our options and developing a workable department policy on peer review of teaching. Dr. Norma Macrae, dean of continuing studies, has offered to share ideas on how to conduct peer reviews. The chair has met with her and is bringing those ideas to the faculty discussion. We will be glad to share the details of the plan when the audit team visits our campus. A third mechanism that demonstrates our department's commitment to teaching is that teaching excellence is heavily weighted in the tenure and promotion process (it ranks over research and service). The expectation that our faculty be productive as researchers remains, but our responsibility to provide excellent instruction to our students is agreed on as fundamental.

Fourth, faculty are routinely encouraged to take advantage of university-sponsored workshops designed to improve teaching effectiveness and promote student learning. Over the past several years, the Writing and Communication Center has hosted workshops on best practices in teaching writing-intensive and oral-communication-intensive courses that some faculty and graduate students have either attended or have been asked to help lead. Our intensive course syllabi undergo a regular cycle of review by ETSU's writing-, oral-communication-, and technology-intensive committees. The office of Academic Technology Services (ATS, http://www.etsu.edu/oit/ats/) holds a variety of workshops every semester pertaining to using Blackboard and digital media technology. ATS also offers a two-year Faculty Technology Leadership (FTL) program to faculty selected from each college at ETSU. One of our faculty members (Franklin) was selected to enroll in graduate FTL courses. Although the primary purpose of the FTL program is developing online courses, another high priority is faculty mentoring. Dr. Franklin is expected to share his acquired skills and help the rest of the department's faculty in such activities as using Blackboard more effectively, interacting with students through Blackboard, assisting faculty in developing their own professional web pages, keeping the departmental web page current, and so forth.

A fifth example of our focus on teaching and learning involves graduate students. After graduate assistants have earned 18 graduate credit hours, they are eligible to teach their own course. The department faculty have instituted an annual workshop for graduate student instructors, in which we discuss approaches to teaching and offer comments on graduate students' course syllabi. We provide them with examples of assignments that we use and encourage them to modify them or create their own assignments. We have not yet instituted a policy of faculty observation of graduate student instruction; however, once we develop our plan for peer review of faculty instruction, we will adapt this to evaluating graduate student instruction as well.

Finally, a high level of collegiality exists among faculty that permits open dialogue regarding the department's teaching mission, teaching effectiveness, and concern for student outcomes.

The department has documented the use of instructional methods and materials designed to enhance student mastery of our program learning objectives. In summer 2003, the bulk of the classrooms in which we teach were retrofitted with multimedia technology that has enhanced our pedagogical flexibility. The majority of our faculty have taken full advantage of the opportunity to incorporate the classroom technology, as appropriate, into their teaching. Faculty vary in their use of these facilities—from fairly high-tech and web-intensive to fairly low-tech and traditional—but the opportunities exist and are emphasized and encouraged by administrators as well as other faculty who discuss the relative benefits of different instructional modalities. Familiarity, opportunity, access, and an institutional commitment exist to encourage every faculty member to use the most appropriate means to enhance student learning outcomes. In addition, faculty are encouraged to consider applying for Instructional Development Committee (IDC) grants to enhance their course offerings. For example, in the spring 2005 semester, one of our faculty members was awarded an IDC grant to purchase several skull casts that would enhance instruction in a number of anthropology courses.

Instructional methods and materials are also addressed by the SAI process, and faculty may use feedback offered by students to evaluate the methods and materials they use to instruct students. In fact, this is one of the more robust sections of the SAI, where students offer comments regarding course format, use of media, evaluation formats, and the difficulty and/or relevance of course materials. The department's implementation of peer review in teaching is expected to contribute significantly to the ongoing evaluation of pedagogical methods and materials. Faculty are in a position to thoughtfully judge the range of possible techniques that can be used to transmit and effectively reinforce information, as well as techniques for enhancing student ability to analyze, probe, and explore the dimensions of a complex topic. It is expected that productive and thoughtful comments from peers will rank highly among faculty for the purpose of enhancing teaching and learning strategies.

The department has documented the extent to which there is genuine ongoing collaboration in the design and delivery of the teaching and learning processes of the program. However, we respect and wish to preserve the autonomy that our professional status traditionally grants us in terms of deciding what, and how, we approach teaching and learning in our own classrooms. Unless faculty share an identical area of expertise and, within that area of expertise, a specific research and teaching agenda, it is highly unlikely that actual ongoing *collaboration* in the design and delivery of teaching and learning processes is occurring. General, department-level means and modalities can be addressed, and we do so. We have discussed this previously. We share teaching ideas and teaching materials at a subdepartment level according to the topics and interests that faculty have in common. Informal linkages exist between sociology and anthropology faculty, and within anthropology, between those who are primarily cultural anthropologists and those who focus on physical anthropology and archeology. Among sociology faculty, a high level of pluralism exists as to the type of courses taught (i.e., theory, research methods, substantive courses) level of courses taught (e.g., first-semester freshman to graduate students), type of courses taught (e.g., lecture-discussion, applied hands-on, small group, and writing-intensive vs. nonwriting-intensive classes). There exists, in short, a sense of community and a deep respect for our pluralism and our professional prerogative to choose our own instructional materials and implement our own pedagogical strategies.

In sum, collaboration in the design and delivery of teaching and learning naturally arises between professionals when their interests converge (those interests may be research driven as well). The department has determined that the present level of ongoing, genuine collaboration is a natural outcome of existing specializations, and that a formal, externally imposed mechanism is neither possible nor desirable. However, as mentioned earlier, we will be planning and then implementing a process of peer review of faculty teaching and learning—beginning this spring semester. In the course of a regular cycle of peer review, we will doubtless offer each other suggestions on enhancing our teaching methods.

We wish to add one department concern that our faculty share regarding our commitment to use the teaching methods that best support our program and course learning objectives. The computer lab that our department shares with the Department of Criminal Justice and Criminology (Rogers-Stout 320) has adequate computer equipment for students, but not for instructors. Student computers were replaced approximately two years ago by the Office of Information Technology (OIT), but now it seems OIT has deferred responsibility for the computer lab to the Department of Criminal Justice and Criminology. We need the computer lab—which, as a *classroom,* is a vital teaching facility in our program—to be equipped with a "smart board" or with a more effective projection system that can be controlled from an instructor's work station. Currently, the faculty member who teaches SOAA 3444 Data Analysis must haul a projector into the classroom that connects to her laptop (equipment the department has purchased from its own funds) and project it onto a wall. This is unwieldy and inconvenient. The projected image is small, and because of the current seating arrangement and location of available power outlets, students on the right side of the classroom cannot see what the instructor is doing. Teaching effectiveness would improve substantially if a centrally located projector and screen were installed in the classroom. For well over a year, the chair has discussed this problem with faculty and has brought it before the college's Council of Chairs. Together, department chairs in the College of Arts and Sciences have requested that our computer-based teaching labs receive the same updates in equipment as the "smart classrooms." The dean of arts and sciences shares our concern, and we hope to prevail in our efforts to offer quality instruction to our students.

Student learning assessment. As noted previously, the 2000–2001 academic year entailed both a SACS reaccreditation review for all programs at ETSU as well as the TBR academic program review for this department. Spurred by these administrative requirements, the faculty began to develop key indicators of the extent to which undergraduate majors and graduate students have learned the central concepts, theories, and methods used in sociology. The previous department chair, in collaboration with faculty, developed an exit exam for undergraduate majors, administered near the end of each fall and spring semester. Those faculty teaching required courses submitted both multiple-choice questions and ideas for short answer essays. Through a collaborative process of revision, an exit exam consisting of 70 multiple-choice items and three essay questions was finalized. From the beginning of the administration of this exit exam, the sociology department included a financial incentive for graduating majors to put forth an effort and attempt to maximize their score on the exam. Originally, the highest scoring student each semester received $25 for his or her achievement, and that has recently been increased to $50. However, it is the consensus among the faculty in this department that still the bulk of graduating seniors who major in sociology do not put forth an effort on the exit exam. Although the faculty are convinced that the exit exam's validity in measuring learning outcomes has been improved, the problems of student motivation and performance persist. Therefore, as we mentioned earlier, the faculty propose to undertake a process of investigating ways to increase investment and effort from graduating seniors in this main indicator of overall knowledge of sociology.

For graduate students, a written comprehensive exam requirement was instituted at approximately the same time as the undergraduate exit exam. Given the small number of graduate students in the program, it has been possible for the graduate coordinator to personalize the comprehensive exams for each student. There are required essays in methods and theory that each student must address, but additional essays are tailored to the specific courses completed by each graduate student. The process and practice of testing graduate students has been an ongoing collaboration between the department chair, graduate coordinator, and the faculty who teach graduate courses. Since graduate students cannot formally initiate either their thesis research or supervised internship before passing the comprehensive exam, motivation and effort by graduate students is not a problem.

How are our methods for assessing student learning grounded in best practice? The original process of developing the undergraduate exit exam and graduate comprehensive exam was collaborative. To some extent the exit exam we used from 2000 to 2005 was based on the major field exam in sociology (distributed by ETS). (The faculty agreed that ETS's major field exam was overly broad and tested students on some substantive areas that were not offered in the department's course electives.) We adapted many questions and the exam format from the ETS model to create our in-house exit exam. The written graduate comprehensive exam was developed based on the previous department practice of an oral exam administered to each graduate student.

In our effort to identify best practice that will help us improve our assessment of student learning, the faculty propose these steps:

- Review and evaluate a publication distributed by the ASA titled "Assessing Student Learning in Sociology," edited by Charles S. Hohm and William S. Johnson.
- Survey sociology departments at our peer institutions and in the region to ascertain other methods of evaluating student learning outcomes, both for undergraduate majors and graduate students.
- Examine the findings from the upcoming pilot review of assessment of student learning in the social and behavioral sciences section of the general education core.
- Sponsor the travel of a faculty member (McCallister) to attend a workshop on student learning assessment at Union College in Barbourville, Kentucky, on January 31, 2006.

We will pool the results of these efforts in the 2006–2007 academic year; any revisions in our assessment efforts will be incorporated by the 2007–2008 academic year. Revisions dealing with our undergraduate exit exam will aid us in Year 3 of our AQI and also after that project culminates. The review and possible revisions will be conducted collaboratively by the department faculty.

Currently, however, the faculty have informally used the results of both the undergraduate exit exam and graduate comprehensive exam to revise and refine the teaching of various subjects in some of the required courses. And, as previously mentioned, faculty have used these results to revise the content of the exit exam to better measure the expected learning outcomes.

An example of course revision based on performance of undergraduate students on the exit exam is Social Statistics (SOAA 3350), a required course. Poor performance of many students on questions concerning basic principles of descriptive and inferential statistical procedures led the instructor of this course to revise the presentation of material illustrating these basic principles. Also, there has been an effort to reinforce basic sociological concepts in Social Problems, another required course. At the graduate level, experience with incoming MA candidates who did not have extensive undergraduate sociology coursework and subsequently exhibited deficiencies in some graduate-level courses has led to the imposition of prerequisite undergraduate courses in some cases.

As explained in the section on learning outcomes, during the past academic year the chair of the department formed a faculty committee to review and revise both the exit exam and comprehensive exam as part of the AQI program. As a result, the undergraduate exit exam has been shortened to 40 multiple-choice items (for 80% of the exam grade), and the essay questions have been changed in content and weight (2 questions, each worth 10%). Just as important is the new practice of providing graduating seniors with a study guide for the exit exam a few weeks before they take it. In regard to the comprehensive exam for graduate students, although no specific content revisions have been made at this point, a more specific grading scale on which to judge the performance of each graduate student has been instituted. This allows faculty to critically assess the knowledge of the students and provide appropriate feedback both to the student and the graduate coordinator.

The department faculty propose to use an annual review of students' performance on the exit exam and comprehensive exam to evaluate the connection between course content, teaching methods, and learning outcomes. This process will enable faculty to reevaluate and improve course content and/or methods of delivering that content. This proposed yearly review will also facilitate regular review of the exit and comprehensive exams.

The academic audit emphasizes the need for multiple measures to assess student learning and program effectiveness. Upon review, department faculty stress that the current assessments of student learning do employ multiple measures of knowledge of key concepts and abilities. In regard to the undergraduate exit exam, the multiple-choice section is split into four sections: key sociological concepts, methods and statistics, theory, and social problems. Each section contains 10 questions. The individual items in each section can be considered measures of basic sociologically relevant concepts and facts. Furthermore, the essays represent additional measures of applications of knowledge in methodology and theory that require some problem solving and critical thinking on the part of students.

The required sections of the graduate comprehensive exam, methods and theory, instruct the student to answer two essays within each section, and these constitute multiple measures. Students must also answer essays that pertain to elective courses in their graduate program of study. Furthermore, the oral defense of the graduate student's thesis or internship report involves answering questions about the applicability and appropriateness of certain methods and theories relevant to the student's thesis or internship experience.

Quality assurance. The BS, BA, and MA programs in our department exhibit multiple indicators of our commitment to quality. The department focuses its programs on positive growth. This is evidenced in our development of new courses, our review of existing courses and monitoring the sequence of courses, and our proposed departmental major in anthropology. We also see progress in our acquisition and use of a broad spectrum of technology by faculty and students. Indeed, the advance of technology in education is a positive factor in assuring quality in teaching and learning.

For the different focal areas discussed in our self-study, we have documented or proposed ways that we will improve education quality systematically and regularly. Presently our programs promote quality through undergraduate exit exams and the department's related participation in the AQI, MA written exams and oral defenses, teaching evaluations (SAIs), training sessions for our graduate student instructors, and the department's ranking of teaching quality above research and service in the tenure and promotion process. In addition, we propose to promote quality of education through peer review of faculty instruction and a stronger evaluation of graduate student instruction, a formal and systematic review of peer institutions' sociology curricula, a biennial curriculum review (of course learning outcomes in light of overall program objectives), and a plan for reviewing and implementing best practices concerning student learning assessment.

To ensure that these efforts will take place as planned, please refer to the matrix of improvement initiatives in Section 5 of this report. The matrix indicates departmental faculty members' responsibilities and the timetable we will follow to carry out each initiative. Also,

ETSU has an annual follow-up process for ascertaining the disposition of program review and academic audit recommendations.

The following section summarizes the proposed initiatives that have been described in preceding sections.

4. Potential Initiatives

Having assessed our overall performance and our quality processes for the five focal areas, we have determined the following specific initiatives for improvement that have the potential to positively impact education quality in our programs:

- Make a concerted effort to communicate learning objectives to undergraduates; sustain this communication with graduate students.
- Develop and administer a brief student survey to assess the program from the students' perspective.
- Ensure that course content and sequencing best meet the needs of our students by identifying, prioritizing, and closing any gaps identified in our curriculum and cocurriculum:
  - Examine the course objectives of our required major courses to determine whether they dovetail with each program's learning objectives/outcomes (at the undergraduate and graduate levels); review the undergraduate and graduate curriculum every two years.
  - Compare peer institutions' course listings and requirements to ours at the undergraduate and graduate levels (carried out by a graduate assistant in fall 2006). Faculty will meet in February 2007 to assess whether there are gaps in the curriculum that should be filled; prioritize the need(s) and determine feasibility and timetable of adding or revising courses.
  - Consult ASA publications on the sociology curriculum to determine whether we should offer different courses and/or experiences to undergraduate and graduate students.
- Solicit feedback from students regarding their levels of preparedness and background knowledge when taking courses in the major (collect through additional SAI questions); this also relates to the curriculum/cocurriculum focal area.

- Develop a policy and plan for peer review of faculty instruction; adapt the policy for assessing graduate student instruction.
- Improve instructional technology in computer lab/classroom shared with Department of Criminal Justice and Criminology.
- Assess the requirement for students to take the exit exam; the consequences for their performance on it; incentives for performing well; method and timing of administering the exam during the semester; and what, when, and how to communicate information regarding the exam to sociology majors. Incorporate the results of the AQI.
- Evaluate student learning assessment methods used elsewhere. Possibly modify current practices for assessment, in addition to our documented plan to incorporate any assessment modifications as per the AQI plan. Sources for information:
  - Consult ASA publication "Assessing Student Learning in Sociology" for recommendations.
  - Survey peer institutions' sociology departments on their methods for assessing student learning and evaluating student learning outcomes for undergraduate and graduate students.
  - Consult the general education core pilot assessment for possible best practices to adopt.
  - Use the information gained from Dr. McCallister's participation in workshop on student learning assessment.

For each initiative, through either our AQI process or our biennial review process, we will be able to gauge how we are implementing improvements. We have settled on initiatives that can be accomplished within the department.

5. Matrix of Improvement Initiatives

Initiative	Responsibility	Participation	Begins	Duration of Cycle
1a. Communicate learning objectives to undergrads	Cole (Introduction to Sociology coordinator). Hester	Sociology faculty	Fall 2007	Ongoing
1b. Sustain communication of learning objectives to grad students	Graduate studies coordinatory and all advisory committee chairs	All graduate faculty in department	N/A	Ongoing
2. Develop and administer brief survey of students' perspectives on program	McCallister, Beck	Sociology and anthropology faculty	December 2006 or early spring 2007	Administer annually for a few years and then biennially
3a. Compare required course objectives with undergraduate and graduate program learning objectives; close gaps	Kamolnick, Hester	Sociology and anthropology faculty	Gather information fall 2006; faculty discussion February 2007	Every two years
3b. Compare peer institutions' course listings and requirements	McCallister, Kamolnick, graduate assistant	Sociology faculty	September–December 2006; faculty discussion February 2007	Every two years
5. Develop peer teaching evaluation policy	Copp	Sociology and anthropology faculty	Pilot spring 2006	Ongoing
6. Improve instructional technology in computer lab/classroom	Copp	Arts and Sciences department chairs	Spring 2006	TBA

continued on next page

Initiative	Responsibility	Participation	Begins	Duration of Cycle
7. Assess best practices for administering major exit exam	Copp, Cole	Sociology faculty	Fall 2006	One year; periodically review to improve
8a. Consult ASA publication on assessing student learning	Beck	Sociology faculty	Fall 2006	One year
8b. Survey peer institutions' student learning assessment practices	Beck	Sociology and anthropology faculty	Spring 2007	One year
8c. Consult general education core assessment for possible best practices	Copp	Sociology and anthropology faculty	Fall 2006	September 2006
8d. Incorporate information from student learning assessment workshop	McCallister	Sociology and anthropology faculty	Spring 2006	One semester

Appendix A: Sociology Major Requirements

SOAA 1020 Introduction to Sociology 3
SOAA 2020 Social Problems 3
SOAA 3210 Sociological Research 3
SOAA 3350 Social Statistics 3
SOAA 3444 Data Analysis (BS students only*) 3
SOAA 4057 Community Sociology 3
SOAA 4807 Modern Social Theory 3
*beginning fall 2006

Sociology Electives 9 (BS students) 12 (BA students)
Total 30 credit hours

Intensive Courses

The university requires that students who enter ETSU as freshmen or with fewer than 60 transfer credits must take two oral-communication-intensive (OCI) courses, of which one must be in the major or the minor (SOAA 4057 Community Sociology); one technology-intensive (TI) course in the major or minor (either SOAA 3350 Social Statistics or SOAA 3444 Data Analysis); four writing-intensive (WI) courses, at least two of which must be in the major or the minor (choose from SOAA 2020 Social Problems, SOAA 3030 Gender and Society, SOAA 4627 Ethnographic Fieldwork Techniques, or SOAA 4807 Modern Social Theory), and at least two of which must be at the 3000–4000 level. Students who transfer with 60 or more credits or an associate's degree are required to take one OCI course, one TI course, and two WI courses. Students must meet proficiency-intensive requirements through courses taken at ETSU (intensive status for a course does not transfer from other schools).

Expected Learning Outcomes for BA/BS students (revised December 2005)

At the completion of the BA and BS degree in sociology, students will be able to:

- Apply key concepts in sociology to a variety of societal processes.
- Understand and evaluate empirical research in the social sciences.

- – Understand prominent social theories.
- – Critically evaluate prominent social theories.
- ▪ Apply both relevant theories and research in the social sciences to problems facing individuals, groups, organizations, and societies.
- ▪ Use appropriate statistical analysis techniques on social science data for both descriptive and inferential purposes.

Appendix B: Anthropology Major Proposal

Institution: East Tennessee State University
Proposal: Anthropology Major
Effective date: Fall 2007

Purpose

The primary purpose of the proposed anthropology major is to provide students with an understanding of anthropology's unique perspective on the study of humankind. To fulfill this goal, the following educational objectives will be met:

1. To enhance students' understanding of the concept of culture
2. To provide students with an understanding of cultural diversity through a holistic, cross-cultural examination of subsistence systems, economic organization, social organization, political systems, family, law, artistic expression, and religion
3. To engage students in critical thinking about the origins and evolution of culture through the analysis of the material remains of prehistoric and historic cultures
4. To develop students' understanding of the application of the basic principles of evolutionary theory with specific reference to the genetic and fossil evidence of human biological evolution
5. To promote students' understanding of human behavior and culture patterning in the context of the complex relationship between biology, culture, and environment
6. To develop students' understanding of human biological variation in terms of genetic patterning and adaptation

Curriculum

The proposed program requires completion of 33 semester credit hours distributed as follows:

Curriculum Component	Hours Required
General Education	41/42
Major Field Core	33
Concentration	NA
Electives (free)	13–28
Other (minor)	18–26
Total	120

Number of new courses: 2 with 3 credit hours each

Need

The anthropology major has been in development for several years. Student interest in anthropology prompted the department to move beyond a concentration and establish an anthropology minor in 1998. From the date of its inception to the present, the number of students electing to minor in anthropology has grown steadily from 1 the first year, to 14 the second year, and an average of 29 each year thereafter. To date, 55 students have graduated with an anthropology minor. Though impossible to quantify accurately, several students over the years have transferred to other universities, both within and outside the state, because they could not obtain an anthropology major at ETSU. The situation is more problematic for the so-called nontraditional students who desire to obtain a major in anthropology at ETSU but cannot transfer due to family and employment obligations. Furthermore, students with a BA degree in anthropology would be far more competitive than those with a minor in gaining admission into graduate programs in anthropology and associated financial support.

An undergraduate with a BA in anthropology would be competitive with undergraduate majors in sociology and psychology for many jobs in the social services, including state and nongovernmental organizations. They would also qualify for employment with public and private organizations concerned with cultural resource management and educational programs connected to museums and state and federal park services.

Impact

An anthropology major will have a positive impact on the Department of Sociology and Anthropology. Historically, the sociology and anthropology programs have complemented each other, and there is no reason to anticipate that this will change with the installation of an anthropology major. Looking ahead, the department will need to offer additional sections of Social Statistics (SOAA 3350) since this course is currently required of all sociology majors and will be required for the anthropology major as well. As discussed in detail in the section "Program Performance and Justification" (see subsection "Evidence of Demand and Need"), an anthropology major will also have a positive impact on the College of Arts and Sciences as well.

PROGRAM STRUCTURE

A. Total credits required for graduation: 120

B. Residency requirement: Not applicable

C. General education: Total credits: 41–42
ENGL 1010 Critical Reading and Expository Writing............3
ENGL 1020 Critical Thinking and Argumentation 3
Mathematics 3–4
Communication: Oral Communication........................3
Natural Science 8
HIST 2010 The United States to 1877 3
HIST 2020 The United States Since 1877 3
Literature...3
Fine Arts 3
Social/Behavioral Sciences 6
Humanities Elective 3
Total 41–42

BA Requirement: 2 courses of a single foreign
    language at or above 2000 level................................6
1 course non–United States history 3

D. Major field core: Total credits: 15
ANTH1240 Introduction to Cultural Anthropology.............3
ANTH1260 Introduction to Archaeology.......................3
ANTH1280 Introduction to Physical Anthropology.............3
SOAA 3350 Social Statistics 3
ANTH4830 Studies in Anthropological Theory (proposed) 3

E. Concentration(s): NA

F. Electives: Total Credits: 18
Guided electives: Students must choose one course from each of the four focus areas:

Archaeology
ANTH4007 Archaeology of the Southeastern United States......3
ANTH4017 Historic Native American Cultures
                    of the Southeastern U.S. 3
ANTH4037 Old World Archaeology..........................3
ANTH4400 Archaeological Field School 4

Biology and Culture
ANTH3400 Human Osteology and Paleontology 3
ANTH4240 Primatology (proposed)..........................3
ANTH4260 Biosociology (proposed) 3

Culture Studies
ANTH2150 American Folk Music 3
ANTH3070 Peoples and Cultures of Latin America..............3
ANTH4630 Native American Cultures in Contemporary Society 3
ANTH4567 Scottish Ethnology...............................3

Health and Culture
ANTH3070 Medical Anthropology............................3
ANTH3080 Nutritional Anthropology.........................3
ANTH3250 Environmental Anthropology......................3
ANTH3500 Appalachian Folk Medicine.......................3

Aside from the five required core courses (15 credit hours) and the four required focus area course electives (12 hours), students must take two other elective courses (6 credit hours) in the focus areas listed above, one of the elective courses listed below, or a special topics course if it is anthropological in content.

ANTH2040 Folk Culture in the Modern World.................3
ANTH3260 Visual Anthropology..............................3
ANTH3800 Religion, Society, and Culture 3
ENGL 3100 Introduction to Linguistics 3
ANTH4627 Ethnographic Field Work Techniques...............3

G. Other credits: Minor program of 18–24 credit hours required

H. Admission, retention, and graduation requirements: In addition to maintaining an overall grade point average of 2.0 in the major, a student must earn a minimum grade of C in each major core course.

I. Describe any unique features such as interdepartmental cooperation, collaboration with other institutions, articulation, industry partnerships, etc.: Not applicable

J. Description of new courses:
ANTH4240 Primatology, 3 credit hours
Prerequisites: ANTH 1240 or SOAA 1020. A survey of the biology and behavior of nonhuman primates focusing on selected species of monkeys and all the great apes. Topics examined include morphology, ecology, subsistence, social organization, play, sexual behavior, intelligence, communication, tool use, and protoculture.

ANTH 4260 Biosociology, 3 credit hours
Prerequisites: ANTH 1240 or SOAA 1020. A critical examination of theories concerning the biological and evolutionary foundation of human behavior with regard to such topics as gender, social stratification, reproduction, and violence.

ANTH 4830 Studies in Anthropological Theory, 3 credit hours
Prerequisites: ANTH 1240, 1260, and 1280. The historical development of anthropological theory from the 19th century to the present,
focusing on how macro and mid-range theoretic orientations have
defined the nature of anthropology and its perspective on understanding human behavior.

PROGRAM PERFORMANCE AND JUSTIFICATION

Institution: East Tennessee State University
Program name: Anthropology Major
Date: February 28, 2006

Accreditation

The anthropology major requires no formal certification from any
accrediting agency. It is, however, conventional in that it is similar
in format and content to other anthropology majors throughout the
United States.

Evaluation Plans

The six objectives of the anthropology major listed earlier in this proposal will be evaluated through four modalities. First, all anthropology
courses will be evaluated through the Student Assessment of Instruction (SAI). The SAIs are presently administered by the university each
semester. At the end of each semester, data obtained by the SAIs will
be reviewed by the chair of the Department of Sociology and Anthropology and the coordinator of the anthropology program. At the end
of each semester, any concerns identified by the SAIs with regard to
course content and instructional methods will be shared with the
anthropology faculty and, if necessary, a plan of remediation will be
devised. Second, following current university policy, the Department
of Sociology and Anthropology is externally evaluated every five years.
This usually entails having an external review team consisting of two
members from other universities and two members from other departments at ETSU. The addition of the anthropology major will require
that in the future at least one of the non-ETSU team members be an

anthropologist, or that a non-ETSU anthropologist be added to the review team. Third, in accord with current university policy, a student exit exam will be developed and administered to all graduating anthropology majors to assess the program's success in fulfilling its six learning objectives. The anthropology faculty will consult with members of the sociology faculty, the American Anthropological Association, and anthropologists at other universities to develop an exam that effectively measures a student's knowledge of basic anthropological concepts, theory, and research methods. Student performance on the exam will enable the identification of weaknesses and strengths in the anthropology program and outcomes will be used by the anthropology faculty to make necessary modifications in course content and instructional methods and techniques. Fourth, to fully evaluate the strengths and weakness of the program with respect to program content, instruction, and clarification of learning goals and objectives, a survey instrument will be administered to all graduating anthropology majors to obtain information about the strengths and weaknesses of the program, their suggestions for modification, and new courses and extracurricular activities they would like to be offered. Lastly, the Department of Sociology and Anthropology is presently undergoing an academic audit, a new evaluation process that actively engages faculty in the process of critically examining learning objectives, curriculum, teaching methods and techniques, student learning assessment, and quality assurance. A lot of what has been learned from the academic audit will be applied to the anthropology major in the future.

Evidence of Demand and Need

Educational need. The anthropology major will broaden and deepen the Department of Sociology and Anthropology's curriculum. Both sociology and anthropology are concerned with understanding human behavior. Anthropology, however, is unique in comparison to sociology in its emphases on 1) cultural variation, 2) the cultural and biological evolution of humans, and 3) the relationship between biology and culture. An anthropology major will also enhance the educational mission of other academic departments, particularly but not exclusively those in the College of Arts and Sciences, as illustrated by the following examples. Both biology and anthropology are concerned with scientific evolution, but anthropology more than biology applies the principles of scientific evolution to understanding the evolution of humankind. Anthropology is historical in perspective, but anthropology is unique in comparison to the discipline of history in its emphasis on the study of prehistory (anthropological archaeology) and the history of nonliterate societies. Anthropology shares with political science an interest in political organization and law, but anthropology is more concerned with how nonstate societies (i.e., bands, tribes, and chiefdoms) govern and regulate themselves. With respect to psychology, anthropology provides an understanding of how culture in its various manifestations shapes personality, perception, and cognition.

Student interest/demand. As noted earlier, student interest in an anthropology major has increased steadily since the inception of an anthropology minor program in 1998 from 1 student in 1998 to 6 in 1999 to an average of 25 students each year since. To date, 116 students have declared a minor in anthropology and 69 students have graduated with a minor. Many of these students minoring in anthropology have informally reported to the anthropology faculty that they would have elected for a major.

Labor market evidence. There is no labor market evidence available defining a need for people with an anthropology major. As noted earlier, however, graduates with an anthropology major would be competitive with other social science majors for employment in the social services sectors and humanities majors for positions in educational programs attached to state and federal parks, historic sites, and museums.

Societal need evidence. Aside from offering a conventional program of study, the proposed anthropology program will address some areas of enduring interest to ETSU's service population in upper east Tennessee, southwestern Virginia, and western North Carolina through course offerings and faculty/student research. These areas include 1) the study and preservation of the region's rich prehistoric and historic sites, many of which are under threat of destruction; 2) Native American ethnology, particularly indigenous inhabitants of the southeastern U.S.; 3) the history and biology of mixed racial populations in the southeastern U.S. (e.g., the Melungeons); 4) the folk culture of southern Appalachia;

5) the study of southern Appalachia's increasingly diverse cultural landscape; and 6) the cultural context of health and health care delivery in
southern Appalachia which ties in with ETSU's growing prominence
as a major health care resource in the region. This programmatic focus
and public interest in anthropology was partially captured in an edito-
rial that appeared in the *Kingsport Times-News* on October 14, 1998,
shortly after the anthropology minor was approved by the TBR. It
should be noted that the newspaper mistakenly thought that ETSU
had installed an anthropology major at the time:

> With a region as rich in prehistoric and Native American
> archaeological sites as ours, it only makes sense that East
> Tennessee State University is pursuing the establishment of
> a new program in archaeology. It stands to reason that the
> emphasis and energy that a major university can bring to areas
> would improve the knowledge base and presentation of such
> historic sites and artifacts. Taken together with ETSU's already
> well-known reputation for preserving what is, in many ways,
> a fast-disappearing Appalachian culture, and you have the
> foundation of what could one day soon be a truly comprehensive
> regional repository of the record of this region's people, their
> culture and customs, from the Stone Age to the present day. To
> have that effort spearheaded by an academic institution, rather
> than a commercial enterprise, will, among other things, help
> set a tone for on-going and future historically-based projects.
> To have the imprimatur of a university associated with, say, the
> excavation of a period site immediately increases its relative
> importance and the public's interest. Having that expertise
> "next door" is something many localities would love to have.
> Congratulations to ETSU—and the Tennessee Board of
> Regents—for recognizing the importance of this program.

Program duplication. The University of Tennessee at Knoxville, University of Tennessee at Chattanooga, University of Memphis, Middle
Tennessee State University, University of the South, Rhodes University,
and Vanderbilt University offer an anthropology major. The three private universities can be eliminated from discussion because their tuition

and other expenses are more than many Tennesseeans can afford. One of ETSU's peer institutions located not far from Johnson City, Appalachian State University, also offers an anthropology major, but the cost of out-of-state tuition also makes it an unreasonable option.

Though the proposed anthropology major duplicates existing programs at other state universities, it will nonetheless address the specific need of some students residing in ETSU's service area. As previously noted, many students attending ETSU, especially the increasing number of nontraditional students, who desire to study anthropology cannot transfer to another state institution due to their family and employment situations. Some students report that they do not want to transfer to a large institution like the University of Tennessee at Knoxville, Middle Tennessee State University, or the University of Memphis, or that they do not want to live far away from home.

Similar to the anthropology programs at the other state universities, ETSU's program, as discussed earlier, is designed to address the specific needs of its service area with regard to the six programmatic foci mentioned in the section "Societal Need" above.

Human Resource Needs

Faculty. The four full-time tenured or tenure-track and one full-time lecturer on the anthropology faculty, plus one adjunct faculty member in the Department of Public Health, are enough to sustain and ensure students' timely progress through the program. It is hoped, however, that the department can add a tenure-track position in physical anthropology in the near future to strengthen the biological component of the curriculum.

Administrative needs. There is no need for additional administrative personnel.

Clerical and support personnel. There is no need for additional clerical and support personnel.

Other Needs for Support

Library. Library holdings are more than adequate to support an anthropology major (see Appendix A). Mainline anthropology journals have been under subscription for many years, and the library has favorably responded to the Department of Sociology and Anthropology's request to add books to its anthropology collection since the inception of the anthropology minor in 1998. In 1999, the department invested $2,000 for the purchase of books (ethnographies) to improve the library's anthropology collection. An additional $500 is requested to add two or three other journals or an anthropology database to move beyond an "adequate" designation.

Instructional facilities. The classrooms at ETSU are first-rate in terms of technology support.

Instructional equipment. Additional investments must be made in archaeological and osteological instructional materials to support instruction in selected courses. Over the past eight years, the Department of Sociology and Anthropology devoted several thousand dollars of indirect fund monies obtained through grant activities to purchase anthropology books and films, fossil casts, and archaeological equipment and supplies. Recently, the Office of Research and Sponsored Programs generously provided additional funds to purchase equipment for a recently established archaeology lab.

Appendix C: Sociology Master of Arts Degree Concentrations

General Sociology (Thesis) Concentration
All students selecting the General Sociology, or thesis, concentration must complete a minimum of 30 credit hours, 21 of which must be in sociology.

SOAA 5110 Contemporary Social Theory 3
SOAA 5210 Sociological Research 3
SOAA 5960 Thesis 3–6
Electives 18–21
Total . . . . 30 credit hours

Students enrolled in the General Sociology concentration may take 18–21 credit hours of electives. This offers a high degree of choice and personalized study, culminating in a thesis that can be oriented toward the student's special area of interest. Other than the courses offered by the department, students may consult with the graduate coordinator and take up to nine hours of graduate study outside sociology/anthropology to gain knowledge and expertise in related fields of study (psychology, public health, management, criminal justice, etc.). Students may enroll in up to three independent study courses (9 credit hours maximum), although the department recommends that students take no more than two (6 credit hours total). Those students who are deemed to have had insufficient coursework in sociology at the undergraduate level may be required to take between one and three "5xx7" courses before enrolling in the required courses.

Students, in consultation with the graduate coordinator, shall select an advisory committee (a chair and two other members) by the time they have completed 18 credit hours. Students must formally submit a committee form to the graduate school. Before students actually begin work on their thesis research, they must prepare and present to the department's graduate faculty a thesis prospectus. Students will defend the prospectus before their chosen committee; after gaining approval, they may enroll in SOAA 5960 Thesis. Once a student has completed the thesis to the satisfaction of his or her committee, a thesis defense will be scheduled.

A written comprehensive exam is also required to successfully complete the degree program. The exam includes questions regarding knowledge of sociological theory, research methods, and other areas of primary knowledge in sociology.

Applied Sociology (Nonthesis) Concentration
All students selecting the Applied Sociology concentration must complete a minimum of 36 credit hours, 27 of which must be in sociology.
SOAA 5110 Contemporary Social Theory 3
SOAA 5210 Sociological Research 3
SOAA 5820 Skills in Applied Sociology & Anthropology 3
SOAA 5320 Program Evaluation 3
SOAA 5850 Supervised Internship 6
SOAA 5870 Internship Placement Report 3

and one of the following:

SOAA 5627 Ethnographic Fieldwork Techniques 3
SOAA 5444 Applied Data Analysis for Social Sciences 3

Electives 12
Total . . . . 36 credit hours

    Any exceptions to these core courses must be approved by the graduate coordinator and the student's advisory committee chair. As with the General Sociology (thesis) concentration, those students deemed to have had insufficient coursework in sociology at the undergraduate level may be required to enroll in one to three "5xx7" courses.

    The special feature of the Applied Sociology concentration is SOAA 5850 Supervised Internship (6 credit hours). Students, in conjunction with the graduate coordinator and their advisory committee, will select an appropriate placement in an agency or organization in which they will work, under supervision, for a total of 280–300 hours (approximately 20 hours per week over one semester or 10 hours per week over two semesters). The culmination of the Applied Sociology concentration is an analytical report based on the students' internship experience and knowledge gained from previous coursework, for which they receive 3 credits by taking SOAA 5870 Internship Placement Report. Students interested in the Applied Sociology concentration should indicate so in their first semester of study, and a screening interview will be conducted by the second semester. And, as with the General Sociology concentration, a written comprehensive exam is required to successfully complete the degree program.

Appendix D: SOAA Program Data

ETSU Performance Funding
Program Review Information

Enrollment (Majors)
Headcount

Term	Undergraduate	Graduate	Total
Fall 2002	50	9	59
Fall 2003	53	16	69
Fall 2004	58	12	70
Fall 2005	68	14	82

Term	Undergraduate	Graduate	Total
Spring 2003	14	12	59
Spring 2004	55	10	65
Spring 2005	69	11	80

Term	Undergraduate	Graduate	Total
Summer 2003	18	10	28
Summer 2004	25	2	27
Summer 2005	20	6	26

Full-Time Equivalency

Term	Undergraduate	Graduate	Total
Fall 2002	45.00	6.42	51.42
Fall 2003	45.67	8.33	54.00
Fall 2004	55.00	7.75	62.75

Term	Undergraduate	Graduate	Total
Spring 2003	41.73	8.33	50.06
Spring 2004	49.80	5.00	54.80
Spring 2005	63.80	7.75	71.55

Term	Undergraduate	Graduate	Total
Summer 2003	12.13	3.50	15.63
Summer 2004	15.00	0.92	15.92
Summer 2005	11.20	2.42	13.62

Test Score Means

Term	ACT (U)	GRE (G)
Fall 2002	20.1	964.4
Fall 2003	21.1	907.1
Fall 2004	22.2	894.4

Term	ACT (U)	GRE (G)
Spring 2003	21.2	939.1
Spring 2004	21.4	905.0
Spring 2005	22.5	821.4

Term	ACT (U)	GRE (G)
Summer 2003	21.3	903.3
Summer 2004	21.1	980.0
Summer 2005	22.3	810.0

Aggregate Grade Point Average

Term	Undergraduate	Graduate
Fall 2002	2.866	3.681
Fall 2003	2.889	3.636
Fall 2004	3.029	3.648

Term	Undergraduate	Graduate
Spring 2003	2.937	3.595
Spring 2004	2.902	3.664
Spring 2005	2.998	3.749

Term	Undergraduate	Graduate
Summer 2003	2.805	3.574
Summer 2004	3.112	3.605
Summer 2005	2,904	3.773

Degrees Awarded

Term	Undergraduate	Graduate
Fall 2002	9	0
Fall 2003	8	2
Fall 2004	8	1

Term	Undergraduate	Graduate
Spring 2003	6	0
Spring 2004	7	3
Spring 2005	8	1

Term	Undergraduate	Graduate
Summer 2003	2	0
Summer 2004	2	1
Summer 2005	1	0

Year	Undergraduate	Graduate	Total
2002–2003	17	0	17
2003–2004	17	6	23
2004–2005	17	2	19

Curriculum (Course Enrollment Regardless of Major)

Courses Offered	2002–2003		
	Courses	Sections	Headcount
Total # of 1000 courses offered	4	37	1879
Total # of 2000 courses offered	5	20	527
Total # of 3000 courses offered	12	14	369
Total # of 4000 courses offered	3	17	26
Total # of 5000 courses offered	11	30	89
Total # of 4xx7/5xx7 dual-listed	10	17	280

Courses Offered	2003–2004		
	Courses	Sections	Headcount
Total # of 1000 courses offered	4	38	2113
Total # of 2000 courses offered	5	19	480
Total # of 3000 courses offered	13	16	420
Total # of 4000 courses offered	3	20	45
Total # of 5000 courses offered	11	23	53
Total # of 4xx7/5xx7 dual-listed	11	21	313

Courses Offered	2004–2005		
	Courses	Sections	Headcount
Total # of 1000 courses offered	5	39	1987
Total # of 2000 courses offered	5	21	522
Total # of 3000 courses offered	13	16	450
Total # of 4000 courses offered	3	19	45
Total # of 5000 courses offered	12	30	58
Total # of 4xx7/5xx7 dual-listed	10	22	319

Diversity of Majors

	2002–2003		
Enrollment	Undergraduate	Graduate	Total
Out-of-State	3	0	3
International	2	1	3
Minority	6	0	6
Male	14	5	19
Female	36	4	40
Total	50	9	59

	2003–2004		
Enrollment	Undergraduate	Graduate	Total
Out-of-State	2	0	3
International	2	1	3
Minority	6	0	6
Male	14	5	19
Female	36	4	40
Total	50	9	59

	2004–2005		
Enrollment	Undergraduate	Graduate	Total
Out-of-State	3	4	7
International	2	0	2
Minority	5	2	7
Male	29	4	33
Female	39	10	49
Total	68	14	82

Appendix E: Learning Objectives Approved in 2000–2001 SACS Review

Learning Objectives for Both the BA and BS Degrees
  (revised further in 2005)
At the completion of the BA degree in sociology students will be expected to:

- Understand and communicate well the sociological perspective on various societal processes and issues in contemporary societies.
- Evaluate and critique empirical research in the social sciences.
- Understand and critically evaluate prominent social theories.
- Apply both relevant theories and research in the social sciences to problems facing individuals, groups, organizations, and societies.
- Use appropriate statistical analysis techniques on social science data for both descriptive and inferential purposes.

Learning Objectives for the MA Concentration
  in General Sociology (2001–)
At the completion of the MA degree in General Sociology students will be expected to:

- Understand and critically assess specific theories relevant to the subject matter contained in the thesis research of each student.
- Understand and apply appropriate methods of research to issues and problems that are sociologically relevant.
- Apply analytical and problem-solving skills to specific issues facing families, groups, organizations, and/or communities.

Learning Objectives for the MA Concentration
  in Applied Sociology (2001–)
At the completion of the MA degree in Applied Sociology students will be expected to:

- Understand and critically assess specific theories relevant to the issues and problems addressed in the internship experience of each student.

- Understand and apply appropriate methods of research to issues and problems that are sociologically relevant.
- Design, execute, and write the results of an evaluation study of a specific program or services offered through an organization.
- Apply analytical and problem-solving skills to specific issues facing families, groups, organizations, and/or communities.

Appendix F: AQI Proposal/Year 1 Report

Academic Quality Initiative, Year 1
Measurement Plans Report

Departmental Information

Department	Sociology & Anthropology
Contact Person	Dr. Martha Copp
Phone	439-7056
Email	coppm@etsu.edu

1. Which option for participating in the AQI is your department following? Type an *X* in the appropriate box. (Note: Options G1 and G2 are available only to departments that do not offer undergraduate degrees.)

X	U1:	List a set of expected learning outcomes common to all undergraduate majors and concentrations in your department. The set must include at least three outcomes, one of which is related to critical thinking or problem solving. Propose measurement plans for at least three of these outcomes, one of which must be related to critical thinking or problem solving.
	U2:	List a set of expected learning outcomes for each undergraduate major and concentration in your department. The set for each major/concentration must include at least three outcomes, one of which is related to critical thinking or problem solving. *Go to Questions 2 and 3 regarding measurement plans.*

U3:	List a set of expected learning outcomes for a general education core course enrolling at least 200 students annually and taught by at least three different instructors over a two-year cycle. At least one outcome must be related to critical thinking or problem solving. Propose measurement plans for at least three of these outcomes, one of which must be related to critical thinking or problem solving.
G1:	List a set of expected learning outcomes common to all graduate majors and concentrations in your department. The set must include at least three outcomes, one of which is related to critical thinking or problem solving. Propose measurement plans for at least three of these outcomes, one of which must be related to critical thinking or problem solving.
G2:	List a set of expected learning outcomes for each graduate major and concentration in your department. The set for each major/concentration must include at least three outcomes, one of which is related to critical thinking or problem solving. *Go to Questions 2 and 3 regarding measurement plans.*

2. Departments following option **U2** or **G2** have two choices regarding measurement plans. Which have you chosen?

A:	Propose measurement plans for at least three expected learning outcomes common to all undergraduate (U2) or graduate (G2) majors and concentrations. One outcome measured must be related to critical thinking or problem solving.
B:	Propose measurement plans for at least three expected learning outcomes in each undergraduate (U2) or graduate (G2) major and concentration. One outcome measured in each major or concentration must be related to critical thinking or problem solving.

3. If you checked **B**, what is the official name of the major or concentration discussed in this report?

Measurement Plans

Major/Concentration	

In the tables provided please describe how you plan to measure student attainment of expected learning outcomes.

- Type the measurement plan for each learning outcome in a separate table.
- Three tables are provided. If you need more, use copy and paste to create additional ones.

Each measurement plan should describe:
1. The expected learning outcome to be measured.
   - At least one of the measurement plans must assess an expected learning outcome related to critical thinking or problem solving. Indicate which plan this is by typing **CT/PS** after the learning outcome the plan measures.
   - If wished, you may define the attainment of a learning outcome by setting a target level for student performance on some measure (e.g., "Successful completion of the spreadsheets unit in COSC 1400 is defined as a score of at least 80% on the Microsoft Excel portion of the final exam.") A row is provided for this optional step.
2. The student work you will observe and/or collect to measure attainment of the learning outcome.
   - Student work includes performance on selected items on tests given in courses or on national standardized tests (e.g., licensure exams), written assignments, oral presentations, other class projects, and internships and similar practicums. It may also include student responses to questions in interviews or surveys.
   - Describe the test items or subscores, class assignments, or other samples of student work that you plan to observe and/or collect to determine whether a learning outcome is attained. Please be as specific as possible. The AQI Advisory Committee will look for sufficient detail to be convinced that you are ready to conduct the assessment in 2005–2006.
3. Who will evaluate the student work with respect to attainment of the learning outcome and the process by which that person(s) will evaluate it.
   - Describe how faculty or others (e.g., professionals in the community) will assess or critique the student work described in Step 2 to determine the degree to which a learning outcome is met.
   - If faculty or others will use scoring rubrics or other rating forms to evaluate student work, please describe these.
4. How faculty will discuss the results of the assessment and develop plans for improving student learning.

5. When your department will perform Steps 2, 3, and 4 in 2005–2006 and again in 2006–2007.
   - Your AQI report for Year 2 (due April, 2006) will present findings of the measurement plan and your department's plans for improvement based on the results. Please plan your calendar for carrying out the measurement plan in 2005–2006 accordingly.
   - In the third year of the AQI you will repeat the measurement plan, and you will also implement improvement plans proposed in Year 2.

Guidelines for Creating Measurement Plans

Measurement Plan 1

1a. Learning outcome to be measured	At the completion of the BA and BS degree in sociology, students will be able to apply key concepts in sociology to a variety of societal processes.
1b. Target level for student performance (optional)	At the end of Year 2 we anticipate setting a target level for evaluation in Year 3.
2. Student work to be observed/collected	A major exam will be administered to graduating seniors. One portion of this exam will contain 10 multiple-choice questions on how key concepts in sociology are applied to different societal processes (e.g., socialization and stratification). In the essay portion of the exit exam, students will be asked to explain how key concepts in sociology relate to the different problems posed for them in the questions. A grading rubric for the essays will be used to identify students' ability to successfully relate those concepts. Both the score on the multiple-choice questions and the score from the essays will be combined to form an index of students' ability to achieve this expected learning outcome. a. Are 10 multiple-choice questions sufficient to measure this outcome, especially given its breadth? Even with the essay question it seems you would need more questions to evaluate this fully. Please explain or add more items. The exit exam we offered previously was too long and must be revised to achieve a reasonable length. Each section of the exam tackles a different learning outcome, but because there is a natural overlap between concepts and theory, for example—or concepts and methods, or theory and methods with social problems (a learning outcome not involved in this AQI plan)— we feel confident that we can evaluate how students

		perform on this learning outcome and the others as well. Regarding the key concepts for the first learning outcome, early in fall 2005, faculty will meet to review and revise the list of key concepts to be covered in the exit exam. b. Please send us a copy of the grading rubic. The grading rubric will be provided in the AQI Year 2 report.
3.	Who will evaluate the student work and how that person(s) will do so	A faculty team consisting of Dr. Martha Copp, Dr. Scott Beck, and Ms. Betsie Cole will create and edit the exam, with assistance from Dr. Paul Kamolnick and Dr. Leslie McCallister. The multiple-choice questions will be graded electronically. Faculty will share the grading of the essays using a jointly created rubric.
4.	How faculty will discuss assessment results and develop improvement plans	Faculty will meet to review and discuss students' index scores. Key concepts are targeted in SOAA 1020 Introduction to Sociology and are reinforced in subsequent courses in the major. If students' scores reveal patterned deficiencies, faculty will discuss the deficiencies and recommend improvements in how we teach key concepts. Areas of deficiency and recommendations will be shared with all of our faculty and adjuncts. When will faculty meet to review the findings and plan improvement actions? Indicate here or in Item 5 below. Please see Item 5.
5.	Calendar for Steps 2, 3, and 4 in 2005–2006 and 2006–2007	The department intends to use this exam format each year for the next five-year performance funding cycle. In a faculty meeting in early fall 2005 we will discuss the exit exam and the AQI goals. The fall term's graduating seniors will take the major exit exam in late November or early December 2005. The fall exams will be graded and evaluated, and then faculty will meet to discuss the results and propose improvements in early January 2006. Seniors graduating in May 2006 will take the major exit exam in mid to late April 2006. (It is not advisable to require students to take the exit exam earlier in the semester; hence, our Year 2 AQI report will be based on fall 2005 data, but we will incorporate spring 2006 data as soon as the exam results are available.) In the summer of 2006, faculty will review and discuss the 2005–2006 exam results and plan improvement actions. Note: Year 2 report deadlines were changed to September 1, 2006, so our Year 2 AQI report will be based on both fall 2005 and spring 2006 data.

	The faculty team of Copp, Beck, and Cole will meet again in summer 2006 to make minor changes to the exam if we discover that any questions need editing. The 2006–2007 exit exam will have the same format, however, and the department will meet to discuss results according to the same schedule as in 2005–2006.
Comments on Measurement Plan 1 (optional)	This comment pertains to the measurement instrument we will use for all measurement plans: the major exit exam. The exit exam format will contain four sections, each with 10 multiple-choice questions (with some questions in each section requiring in-depth understanding or problem solving) that relate to four learning outcome areas: key concepts in sociology, research methods/statistical analysis, sociological theory, and social problems. The exam will also have a section of required critical thinking essay questions that likewise relate to these learning outcomes. Overall the exit exam must have a manageable length so that students will give each answer adequate time.

Measurement Plan 2

All comments on Measurement Plan 1 apply here as well. Our response to the comments received on Item 2 of Measurement Plan 1 also applies to Measurement Plans 2 and 3. It seemed unnecessary to repeat the justification in each measurement plan.

1a. Learning outcome to be measured.	At the completion of the BA and BS degree in sociology, students will be able to understand, evaluate, and critique empirical research in the social sciences. **CT/PS**
1b. Target level for student performance (optional)	At the end of Year 2 we anticipate setting a target level for evaluation in Year 3.
2. Student work to be observed/collected	A major exit exam will be administered to graduating seniors. One portion of this exam will contain 10 multiple-choice questions to gauge students' understanding and ability to evaluate both sociological research methods and statistical analysis techniques. Students will also be required to answer an essay question that requires them to demonstrate their ability to understand, interpret, and critique statistical data (and simultaneously apply appropriate key concepts in sociology). A grading rubric will be used to grade the essay. Both the score on the multiple-choice questions and the score from the essay will be combined to form an index of students' ability to achieve this expected learning outcome.

3.	Who will evaluate the student work and how that person(s) will do so	A faculty team consisting of Dr. Martha Copp, Dr. Scott Beck, and Ms. Betsie Cole will create and edit the exam, with assistance from Dr. Paul Kamolnick and Dr. Leslie McCallister. The multiple-choice questions will be graded electronically. The essay question will be graded by either Beck or McCallister using a jointly created rubric.
4.	How faculty will discuss assessment results and develop improvement plans	Faculty will meet to review and discuss students' index scores for this expected learning outcome. The main courses that target this learning outcome are SOAA 3210 Sociological Research, SOAA 3350 Social Statistics, and SOAA 3444 Microcomputers as a Research Tool. If students' scores reveal patterned deficiencies, faculty will discuss the deficiencies and recommend improvements to the faculty who teach in the areas of research methods and statistics.
5.	Calendar for Steps 2, 3, and 4 in 2005–2006 and 2006–2007	The department intends to use this exam format each year for the next five-year performance funding cycle. In a faculty meeting in early fall 2005 we will discuss the exit exam and the AQI goals. The fall term's graduating seniors will take the major exit exam in late November or early December 2005. The fall exams will be graded and evaluated, and then faculty will meet to discuss the results and propose improvements in early January 2006. Seniors graduating in May 2006 will take the major exit exam in mid to late April 2006. (It is not advisable to require students to take the exit exam earlier in the semester; hence, our Year 2 AQI report will be based on fall 2005 data, but we will incorporate spring 2006 data as soon as the exam results are available.) In the summer of 2006, faculty will review and discuss the 2005–2006 exam results and plan improvement actions. Note: Year 2 report deadlines were changed to September 1, 2006, so our Year 2 AQI report will be based on both fall 2005 and spring 2006 data. The faculty team of Copp, Beck, and Cole will meet again in summer 2006 to make minor changes to the exam if we discover that any questions need editing. The 2006–2007 exit exam will have the same format, however, and the department will meet to discuss results according to the same schedule as in 2005–2006.
Comments on Measurement Plan 2 (optional)		

Measurement Plan 3

1a. Learning outcome to be measured	a. At the completion of the BA and BS degree in sociology, students will be able to understand and critically evaluate prominent social theories. **CT/PS** b. At the completion of the BA and BS degree in sociology, students will be able to critically evaluate prominent social theories. **CT/PS**
1b. Target level for student performance (optional)	At the end of Year 2 we anticipate setting a target level for evaluation in Year 3.
2. Student work to be observed/collected	A major exit exam will be administered to graduating seniors. One portion of this exam will contain 10 multiple-choice questions that assess students' ability to understand and apply major social theories. The 10 multiple-choice questions will help us evaulate students' ability to achieve the first expected learning outcome in this measurement plan. To gather information regarding the second expected learning outcome in this measurement plan, students will also be required to answer an essay question that requires them to demonstrate their ability to understand and critically evaluate sociological theories (and simultaneously apply appropriate key concepts in sociology). A grading rubric will be used to grade the essay. Both the score on the multiple-choice questions and the score from the essay will be combined to form an index of students' ability to achieve this expected learning outcome.
3. Who will evaluate the student work	A faculty team consisting of Dr. Martha Copp, Dr. Scott Beck, and Ms. Betsie Cole will create and edit the exam, with assistance from Dr. Paul Kamolnick and Dr. Leslie McCallister. The multiple-choice questions will be graded electronically. The essay question will be graded by Kamolnick, Cole, Copp, or Beck using a jointly created rubric.
4. How faculty will discuss assessment results and develop improvement plans	Faculty will meet to review and discuss students' index scores for both expected learning outcomes in this measurement plan. The main courses that target the learning outcomes are SOAA 1020 Introduction to Sociology, SOAA 2020 Social Problems, and SOAA 4807 Modern Sociological Theory. If students' scores reveal patterned deficiencies, faculty will discuss the deficiencies and recommend improvements in teaching students about social theories. Areas of deficiency and recommendations will be shared with all our faculty and adjuncts.

| 5. Calendar for Steps 2, 3, and 4 in 2005–2006 and 2006–2007 | The department intends to use this exam format each year for the next five-year performance funding cycle. In a faculty meeting in early fall 2005 we will discuss the exit exam and the AQI goals. The fall term's graduating seniors will take the major exit exam in late November or early December 2005. The fall exams will be graded and evaluated, and then faculty will meet to discuss the results and propose improvements in early January 2006. (It is not advisable to require students to take the exit exam earlier in the semester; hence, our Year 2 AQI report will be based on fall 2005 data, but we will incorporate spring 2006 data as soon as the exam results are available.) In the summer of 2006, faculty will review and discuss the 2005–2006 exam results and plan improvement actions.

Note: Year 2 report deadlines were changed to September 1, 2006, so our Year 2 AQI report will be based on both fall 2005 and spring 2006 data.

The faculty team of Copp, Beck, and Cole will meet again in summer 2006 to make minor changes to the exam if we discover that any questions need editing. The 2006–2007 exit exam will have the same format, however, and the department will meet to discuss results according to the same schedule as in 2005–2006. |
| Comments on Measurement Plan 3 (optional) | |

Faculty Participation in Creating Measurement Plans

The AQI seeks to promote dialogue and collaboration among faculty regarding student learning. Please describe how faculty in your department participated in creating the measurement plans present in this report.

| Faculty participation in creating measurement plans | Dr. Martha Copp, Ms. Betsie Cole, and Dr. Scott Beck worked on the measurement plan presented in this report. Faculty met in person on three occasions and also communicated via email about the structure and logic of the measurement plan and instrument. |

Faculty Commitment to Measurement Plans

How would you describe the current level of faculty commitment to these measurement plans? What challenges, if any, remain in building this commitment?

Faculty commitment to measurement plans	The measurement plan has been added to a departmental procedure for evaluating students that was already in place. It is anticipated that faculty will be strongly committed to the procedure, as it will give them feedback on courses they teach in the major.

Submission of Report

The department chair should submit this report as an email attachment to Bill Kirkwood in the Office of Academic Affairs. This submission constitutes the chair's electronic signature and indicates that he or she has read the report and is submitting it on behalf of the department.

Deadlines for Submission of Report

The deadline for submitting departmental AQI reports is April 1, 2005. Departments wishing to receive early feedback on their reports should submit draft reports by February 15, 2005.

Appendix G: New Courses and Minor Curriculum Revisions (Fall 2001–Spring 2006)

New Courses

Anthropology

SOAA 1260   Introduction to Archaeology
SOAA 1280   Introduction to Physical Anthropology
SOAA 3028   Honors Cultural Anthropology
SOAA 3080   Nutritional Anthropology
SOAA 3250   Environmental Anthropology
SOAA 3260   Visual Anthropology
SOAA 3400   Human Osteology and Paleontology
SOAA 4007/5007   Archaeology of the Southeastern United States
SOAA 4017/5017   Historic Native American Cultures in the Southeastern United States
SOAA 4037/5037   Old World Archaeology

SOAA 4400 Archaeological Field School
SOAA 4567/5567 Scottish Ethnology (also APST)
SOAA 4630 Native American Culture in Contemporary Society
SOAA 4907/5907 Foodways of Appalachia (also APST)

Sociology
SOAA 4057/5057 Community Sociology (Oral Communication
                Intensive)
replaces 4027/5027 Advanced Principles of Sociology

Appalachian Studies
APST 3530 Religion in Appalachia
APST 4237/5237 Scots-Irish in Appalachia
APST 4337/5337 Appalachia in Scotland
APST 4567/5567 Scottish Ethnology (also SOAA)
APST 4907/5907 Foodways of Appalachia (also SOAA)

Nonsubstantive Course or Curriculum Changes
SOAA 3350 approved as Using Information Technology Intensive
course
Course name change: SOAA 3444 Data Analysis (old title: Microcomputers as a Research Tool), required for BS degree (effective fall
2006)

[1] *Developed by Randy Schulte at Chattanooga State Technical Community
College and Karen Brunner at Roane State Community College in the
Tennessee Board of Regents.*

6

The Audit and Audit Report

The site visit by the audit team sets in motion the peer review process. The audit team uses the visit to focus on the quality processes and triangulates the self-study review carried out by the program faculty with dialogue between faculty, students, administrators, and other stakeholder groups. Auditors may ask questions similar to the self-study questions addressed in Chapter 5. The role of the audit team is to set the tone for a collegial, supportive dialogue. Let's look over the shoulder of an audit team meeting under way with the site faculty and administrators:

> The audit team for the psychology program at the community college gathers the night before the audit visit to make last-minute plans. The three-member team is conducting its first-ever audit. Although already trained by the TBR system personnel, team members are struck by the potential complexity of their work. The team leader says it well: "It seems overwhelming to think that we will be covering an entire program in a single day. We have to cover a lot of ground in a short time tomorrow." The team, however, decides to focus on the task as outlined in their training sessions—to respond to the written self-study report and explore areas that were unclear in the report. Second, they decide to compare what was written in the self-study report to descriptions of what actually goes on in the program. One team member goes on to say, "We need to remember the importance of the fact that the program faculty have their own objectives and explored where they agree that they are meeting those objectives. Our task is to appraise their conceptualization of their goals and their status in

relation to what actually is happening in the program." The team is comfortable with the approach and spends time talking through the report and identifying areas where team members have questions and concerns. They decide to use this to assign areas to lead the exploration with the program the next day. The team is ready.

Putting Together the Audit Team

At the TBR, auditors are chosen for a particular site visit from the pool of trained auditors. We have discovered that there are fundamental guidelines that make the peer review process work well. For the TBR's academic audit process, we use the following as guidelines:

- Auditors are volunteers (primarily faculty) who receive training on education quality processes and audit methodology.
- Audit teams (three to four members) will most likely come from other TBR institutions.
- Because the auditors will be focusing on quality *processes,* they do not have to come from the academic discipline of the department being audited, though TBR strives to have faculty from the discipline on the team.
- Audit visits are typically one day per department.
- Auditors meet with departmental leadership, faculty, and students.
- Auditors ask questions similar to the self-study questions.
- Auditors write a report highlighting examples of exemplary practice, noting areas for improvement, and evaluating a department's approach to education quality processes.

Auditor Training

We have found the best practice is to present the basic concepts of the academic audit, describe why these types of reviews are beneficial, talk at length about academic soul-searching, and discuss the value of looking at quality processes to improve how work gets done. Since these concepts often are foreign to most faculty members, training sessions should include lots of time for questions and answers and for faculty members to experiment with the ideas. They need to be able to challenge some of the concepts in a nondefensive manner—being open to new ways of conducting the audits. Some of the best ideas about how to structure the audits have come from the training sessions, especially if the participants have been on site visit teams for their professional areas.

Another practice that is successful is to have experienced auditors at the training session to serve as mentors for any new members. We have found that much of the practice of conducting academic audits is so unfamiliar to most faculty members that they have to experience an audit before they can fully believe it will work as described. Further, these experienced auditors can convey stories and examples of conversations and conditions they found in previous site visits to clarify the illustrations and make examples. Those selected for auditor training participate in a training session with a follow-up refresher session each year. We work to help auditors push for answers during meetings with faculty, students, administrators, and other stakeholders—but do so with a soft touch. Strategies used during training to help auditors understand their special role include case studies, role-play, practice exercises, and debriefing sessions. The Missouri program often has auditors from prior years role-play a dialogue between an auditor and a faculty member to demonstrate the types of questions and follow-up questions that work effectively to solicit information. The following is a sample role-play used in Tennessee:

> An auditor and faculty member in engineering technology are in a site visit session. The program self-study has indicated that the graduates of the program do well in the workplace. At the start of the role-play, the auditor asks the faculty member whether the program does a good job preparing students for employment. The faculty member responds that they do and that she is very proud of the graduates. The auditor asks the faculty member to describe how the program faculty know that graduates are doing well and are competitive for positions upon graduation. She pauses and stares for a moment, stumbling a bit before she replies that she just feels that they do a good job because faculty work hard and spend time with the students. The auditor asks about any use of employer or alumni surveys or interviews as well as data on job placement rates. Again, the auditor gets a blank stare and a weak response: "Those sound like good ideas. We should look into it."

The role-play should be debriefed with the auditor trainees to illustrate how the probing/clarifying questioning can provide insight into current program practices and whether the strengths cited can be supported via evidence and quality practices.

Auditor Assignment

Building a cadre of trained auditors is an important activity. In Tennessee we require that each campus submit the names of faculty members from TBR institutions that would be particularly suited to serve on the onsite audit review team(s) in April. Each program may select up to two faculty in the discipline whom they would like to have on the audit team. These nominations are submitted no later than November 15 with a brief description of the nominees' academic credentials. They are asked also to provide contact information (email and phone number) so that they can be included in auditor training sessions in January and early February. At this same time each program/department that is being audited proposes its date in April for the on-site visit.

Each campus submits a tentative academic audit schedule when the self-study document is submitted to TBR. The due date usually falls around January 31. In addition to the date for the campus visit and the planned agenda, this tentative schedule includes information about hotel accommodations and contact information for the designated campus contact.

The self-study document is provided to the audit team at least four weeks before the scheduled visit. This document is emailed to the chair and team members by the TBR Office of Academic Affairs. Included in this email is the tentative schedule for the visit and a copy of the academic audit handbook

The chair of the visiting team makes contact with the designated campus contact at least three weeks before the scheduled visit. This conversation assures that both parties are aware of local arrangements, meeting rooms, tentatively scheduled meetings with faculty and students, and available work space/materials for the visiting team.

Many of the audit team members from previous years have advised that all teams should assign a specific focal area to each team member. This allows team members to focus on that area in their reading of the self-study document as well as their planning for questions and exploration during the site visit.

It is ideal for the team to be able to get together the evening before the visit. If this is not possible, the schedule for the site visit should remain flexible to allow a breakfast meeting at the hotel before the team goes to the campus for the initial meeting with campus officials. Table 6.1 presents a schedule for a typical audit day.

Table 6.1 Typical Audit Day

Session	Time/Attendees	Location
Breakfast and team meeting at hotel	7:30 a.m.–8:15 a.m. Audit team	Hotel, room/location
Opening session and introductions	8:30 a.m.–9:00 a.m. Audit team Faculty and administrators	ABC bldg, room 1
Small group meeting #1	9:00 a.m.–10:00 a.m. Audit team Faculty and administrators	ABC bldg, room 2
Small group meeting #2	10:15 a.m.–11:00 a.m. Audit team Students	ABC bldg, room 2
Small group meeting #3	11:15 a.m.–12:15 p.m. Audit team Faculty members	ABC bldg, room 2
Working lunch	12:15 p.m.–1:30 p.m.	ABC bldg, room 1
Flexible meeting and work time	1:30 p.m.–3:30 p.m. Audit team	ABC bldg, room 2
• *Possible time for materials review, tours, or additional meetings with faculty or students* • *Time for group to discuss observations and work on reports*		
Exit session	3:30 p.m.–4:00 p.m. Audit team Faculty and administrators	ABC bldg, room 1
• *Brief report of initial commendations, affirmations, and recommendations* • *If the performance funding summary sheet is required, a copy of that sheet must be left with the campus contact before departure* • *Department and campus will get opportunity to respond to the written report*		
Logistics information: Campus contact for the academic audit—name, position, phone, email Hotel accommodations—hotel name, address, phone		

Tone and Process of Questioning

As mentioned earlier, the interactions of the site audit team with those being audited are grounded in a context of collegial and supportive dialogue. The peer auditors are to encourage reflection and self-examination in the conversations conducted with faculty, students, and others. The auditor team will want to ask faculty clarifying questions to confirm that they are following the quality processes within the focal areas as cited in the self-study report. This is the time to see whether they are doing what they say they are doing. In Tennessee auditors ask questions designed to help the team better understand how faculty and other stakeholders see their strengths and weaknesses. This supportive, reflective environment is essential for the audit process to work. Let's look again to see how this works:

> *At the local community college, two site teams for two programs being audited arrive early in the morning. With the two audit teams together, the chief academic officer, the site visit coordinator, and program faculty review the two programs with the site teams. The two teams receive the final schedule for the day. At that point the two teams move to separate rooms, and each audit team meets with all program faculty from their respective programs.*
>
> *The audit team leader compliments the faculty on the creation of the self-study and expresses confidence that the process has been helpful to them. The team leader indicates that each team member appreciates the opportunity to read the self-study and looks forward to talking about it. He lets them know that it is often hard to put in writing a full explanation of what is happening, so this time with them will allow the team to ask clarifying questions and to make sure that they understand the self-study. The team leader invites the faculty to make any opening comments they wish, and two or three faculty speak about their views of the process.*
>
> *At this point the conversation becomes much more specific with audit team members asking clarifying questions.*

Because the team members have assigned areas of concern for further exploration, one team member asks, "Tell me about the method you use to know whether your students are meeting course objectives." The conversation is productive, and the program faculty hand the team member a sample course syllabus with an accompanying example of an online assessment used for the sixth course objective: "Students will identify two theories of motivation and develop two scenarios illustrating each using a sports context." The team has a particularly interesting session with students because of the diversity of students in attendance. The same probing questions asked by the team of the previous groups are asked of the students. They talk about processes used in the various classes to allow students to demonstrate mastery and understanding. The tone of the meeting is positive yet probing with participants freely expressing viewpoints and responding openly to the clarifying questions put forth by the audit team members. The day is quickly over, and the faculty and administrators eagerly await any feedback from the audit team.

The primary objective of the site visit is to verify and confirm what is in the self-study report. The self-study process leads to a set of areas in which the faculty believe they can improve. It also identifies areas of strength and facilitates the consensus of the faculty regarding quality processes that should improve or be initiated. The exit session focuses on affirmations, commendations, and recommendations (discussed in greater detail later). These are brief and presented in bullet form.

Audit Report-Writing Guidelines

In writing the audit report, it is essential to collect key points from reviewers within one week of the visit. If you can outline your primary points before the team leaves the day of the audit, all the better. The team leader should write the final report based on the consensus of the team about findings. The template in Figure 6.1 is useful in writing the report. Note that the report must be limited to 10 pages.

Figure 6.1 **Template for Academic Audit Team's Narrative Report**

---

1. *Introduction.* Briefly describe the unit/program evaluated, the date of the audit, the protocol observed by the auditors, and other relevant information.

2. *Overall performance.* What is the team's overall summary conclusion about the state of the unit/program?

3. *Performance in the focal areas.* How does the unit's/program's work in each focal area measure up against the quality and evidentiary principles?

   - Learning objectives
   - Curriculum and cocurriculum
   - Teaching and learning methods
   - Student learning assessment
   - Quality assurance

4. *Conclusions.* Briefly indicate the team's conclusions regarding the following by providing each in bulleted or numbered sequence:

   - *Commendations.* What processes, practices, initiatives, and commitments are particularly commendable and merit recognition?
   - *Affirmations.* What processes, practices, or plans warrant the team's affirmation and encouragement?
   - *Recommendations.* What are some areas for improvement identified by the team on the basis of the unit's/program's self-study and site visit?

In Tennessee we use the recommendations set forth in the initial site visit as a guide for the three-year follow-up site visit with the program. Programs are responsible for assessing how well they are advancing toward implementation. This three-year review of recommendations ensures the institutionalization of the continuous quality improvement process within TBR. Many programs participating for the first time in the academic audit report that collaborative faculty meetings are continuing regularly as they establish action steps and benchmarks derived from the recommendations. The process of self-

Figure 6.2 **Key Themes and Tips for Writing Audit Reports**

It is important for respondents to observe the following suggestions when developing the audit report:

- The purpose of the report is to summarize findings from the self-study report and the visit.
- Keep the tone of the report developmental—focus on how the department can improve on its own. Address what it will work on as a result of the review.
- The report is the synthesis of the teaching and research focal areas pulled together by the team leader.
- Provide feedback on all five themes in focal areas in summary form and give overview perceptions.
- Reports are written by the audit team, assignments are made at the visit, and members provide bullet-type comments.
- Use the debriefing time to gather ideas from members and create an overview of the report.
- At the visit agree on a report format and how long each section should be. Find some consensus from the group, and develop a strategy for the report (e.g., bulleted comments only).
- At the visit there is an oral debriefing with the department/unit before the team arrives. The team decides on overall points. Use these themes to provide the context for the report and the executive summary.
- Ask for evidence as you gather impressions. Don't build summary points around comments from one faculty member or one small group of students—look for confirming evidence.
- Keep it simple, and tell them what the program/unit did well and what they can do to improve. Point out what they can do in other areas to use the same strategies to improve other areas. Write the report so that it is helpful for the department, but also write it as if others will read it (i.e., be sensitive to language and tone of comments).

reflection and self-review becomes codified within the institution. Thus the quality of the written audit report is critical to its acceptance and use by program faculty. There are important tips to remember, outlined in Figure 6.2.

Performance Funding Checklist

Tennessee was one of the earliest states to adopt a form of higher education funding for performance in determined areas. In accordance with the 2005–2010 Performance Funding guidelines of the Tennessee Higher Education Commission (THEC), each nonaccreditable undergraduate program undergoes either an academic audit or external peer review according to a preapproved review cycle

Although programs, both graduate and undergraduate, in TBR institutions have chosen to participate in the audit, the audit team must prepare an additional report if the program is also conducting the audit visit for performance funding purposes. TBR, in collaboration with the THEC, developed a reporting template that would not violate the spirit of self-examination and continuous quality improvement reflected in the academic audit process while meeting the THEC reporting requirements for performance funding. The template currently being used appears in Figure 6.3 (related information appears in Figure 6.4 and Table 6.2).

Tips to Make the Process Work

Both the University of Missouri and the TBR have acquired significant experience with the audit process. We have learned what works and what does not work. The Missouri experience led the participants to build a list of helpful hints that are worth noting:

- The team must be prepared and have a plan.
- The chair should have a list of topics and clear plans for how long to discuss each.
- The team should make time before the audit meeting to discuss logistics and set a plan.
- The leaders of both parties should clearly communicate expectations.
- Everyone should have a copy of the self-study at least two weeks before the onsite visit.
- The chair and audit team should discuss questions regarding the self-study.

Figure 6.3. **Academic Audit Onsite Evaluation Checklist for Audit Teams Conducting Performance Funding Review**

Institution _____

Program _____

CIP Code _____

Degree Level: ☐Certificate   ☐ Associate   ☐ Baccalaureate
                   ☐ Master's   ☐ Doctoral

Instructions for Audit Chairs and Teams

Part I: Academic Audit Summary Sheet (only for performance funding purposes)
Using the attached Academic Audit Summary Sheet, complete the 25 elements on the evaluation results checklist (marking "met" or "not met"). This exercise must be completed and signed by the team before the exit session. A copy should be provided to the campus contact.

Part II: Narrative Evaluation
The audit chair and team will use their evaluations indicated on the audit checklist and their summarized findings from the self-study report and onsite visit to write a narrative report of the team's conclusions. The template for completing this report (limited to 10 pages) is attached. This report is due to TBR on May 15.

The audit evaluation will become part of the record of the academic program review and will be shared with the academic department/ unit, the college, and the central administration, as well as the Tennessee Higher Education Commission. Each department/campus will be provided an opportunity to respond and comment on the written report.

Audit chair's name, title, and institution _____

Audit chair's signature _____ **Date** _____

Names, titles, institutions, and signatures
of other audit team members

_____

_____

Figure 6.4 **Academic Audit Summary Sheet Effective Fall Semester 2005 and Required for Performance Funding Excesses**

Institution _____

_____

Program _____

Instructions for External Reviewers

In accordance with the 2005–2010 Performance Funding guidelines of the Tennessee Higher Education Commission (THEC), each non-accreditable undergraduate program undergoes either an academic audit or external peer review according to a preapproved review cycle.

The criteria used to evaluate a program appear in the attached Academic Audit Summary Sheet. The Summary Sheet lists 25 items grouped into eight categories. THEC will use the items designated with an asterisk (*) to assess Standard 1C when the academic audit process is used. The criteria in the eighth category (support) may be used by the institution and submitted as part of the performance funding report. If the academic audit process did not include information about items 8.1–8.3, they should be marked "N/A." These items will not be included in the THEC performance funding points.

These summary items have been selected based on the academic audit focal areas to be consistent with the spirit and process of the academic audit. The program faculty has provided a self-study document that includes information for each item within the focal areas. Support-

---

continued on next page

- The team leader should have a template for use (as shown earlier in Figure 6.1).
- Planners should establish team leaders (some options suggested: a leader for each track and an overall leader; one overall leader, etc.).
- The team should determine what they want to know before meetings; this will dictate the level of questioning.
- Everyone should know that the purpose of the report is to summarize findings from the self-study report and the visit.

Figure 6.4 **Academic Audit Summary Sheet** (*continued*)

ing documents will be available as specified in the self-study. As the academic audit team leader, you should assess this and other evidence observed during the site visit to determine whether the process has met each item within a category. A checkmark should be placed in the appropriate box to indicate whether you believe that a program has "met" or "not met" each item in the table. If a particular item is inappropriate or not applicable to the program, the item should be marked "N/A."

This Academic Audit Summary Sheet will be sent to the appropriate campus official for inclusion in the Annual Performance Funding Report. When combined with the self-study and the written report prepared by the visiting team, the summary sheet will facilitate institutional development of a program action plan to ensure continuous quality improvement.

Your judgment of the criteria designated by an asterisk on this form (see categories 1–6) will be used in allocating state funds for the community college or university's budget.

Name, title, and institutional affiliation of visiting team chair

_____

_____

- The team should keep the tone of the report developmental—focus on how the department can improve on its own. Address what it will work on as a result of the review.
- The report is written as a synthesis of the teaching and research focal areas.
- The written report should provide feedback on all five themes in focal areas in summary form and give overview perceptions.
- The audit team writes the reports with assignments made at the visit, and members provide bullet-type comments.

Table 6.2 **Academic Audit Summary Sheet**

Summary Items for			Evaluation Results	
1. Learning objectives			Met	Not met
*	1.1	The faculty completed an honest analysis of their process for developing learning objectives for the program, considering measurability, clarity, and what students need to know.		
*	1.2	The faculty have documented or proposed a process for developing learning objectives that are based on realistic and appropriate evidence.		
*	1.3	The faculty have documented or proposed specific plans to take best practices and appropriate benchmarks into account in the analysis of learning objectives.		
2. Curriculum and cocurriculum			Met	Not met
*	2.1	The faculty completed an honest analysis of the extent to which they collaborate effectively on the design of curriculum and planned improvements.		
*	2.2	The faculty have documented or proposed a plan for analyzing the content and sequencing of courses in terms of achieving program learning objectives.		
*	2.3	The faculty have documented or proposed a plan for determining the soundness of curriculum and cocurriculum based on appropriate evidence, including comparison with best practices where appropriate.		
3. Teaching and learning processes			Met	Not met
*	3.1	The faculty examined the extent to which there is focus on the actual process of teaching and learning throughout the program.		
*	3.2	The faculty have documented or proposed a plan that ensures the use of instructional methods and materials for achieving student mastery of learning objectives.		
*	3.3	The faculty have analyzed the extent to which there is true, ongoing collaboration in the design and delivery of the teaching and learning process of the program.		

continued on next page

Table 6.2 **Academic Audit Summary Sheet** (*continued*)

Summary Items for			Evaluation Results	
4. Student learning assessments			Met	Not met
*	4.1	The faculty have documented or proposed key quality indicators that are based on the learning objectives of the program.		
*	4.2	The faculty have documented or proposed assessments of student learning that are grounded in best practices and appropriate comparisons.		
*	4.3	The faculty have documented or proposed a plan for using student learning assessments that lead to continuous improvements in the program.		
*	4.4	The program plan for improvement will use multiple measures to assess student learning and program effectiveness.		
5. Quality assurance			Met	Not met
*	5.1	There is an evident commitment to making continuous quality improvements in the program a top priority.		
*	5.2	The faculty have documented or proposed ways to ensure that QA will be a systematic and regular process.		
6. Overall assessment			Met	Not met
*	6.1	The academic audit process was faculty driven.		
*	6.2	The academic audit process (self-study and visit) included descriptions of the program's quality processes, including all five domains.		
*	6.3	The faculty accurately identified the program's level of quality process maturity as a result of the academic audit process.		
*	6.4	The process resulted in a candid description of weaknesses in program processes and suggestions for improvements.		
*	6.5	Overall, the visiting team *affirms* the honest and thoroughness of the program faculty in completing the academic audit of this program.		

continued on next page

Table 6.2 Academic Audit Summary Sheet (*continued*)

Summary Items for			Evaluation Results	
			Yes	No
7. Follow-up of previous academic audit			Yes	No
	7.1	An action plan was developed as a result of the previous academic audit.		
	7.2	Recommendations from the previous academic audit have been completed.		
8. Support			Yes	No
	8.1	The program regularly evaluates its equipment and facilities, encouraging necessary improvements within the context of overall college resources.		
	8.2	The program's operating budget is consistent with the needs of the program.		
	8.3	The program has a history of enrollment and graduation rates sufficient to sustain high quality and cost-effectiveness.		

- The team should use the debriefing time to gather ideas from members and create an overview of the report.
- At the visit the team should agree on a report format and how long each section should be. The team should find consensus and develop a strategy for the report (e.g., present bulleted comments).
- At the visit there is an oral debriefing with the department/unit before the team leaves. The team decides on overall points. The team should use these themes to provide context for the report and the executive summary.
- The team should ask for evidence as it gathers impressions. Don't build summary points around comments from one faculty member or one small group of students—look for confirming evidence.
- The team should keep it simple and tell the program faculty what they did well and what they can do to improve. Point out how they can use similar strategies to improve other areas.
- Write the report so it is helpful for the department itself. But also write it as if others will read it.

Follow-Up to Process Is Important

The academic audit process requires a clear plan for follow-up. The site visit results in a set of commendations, affirmations, and recommendations. The TBR will hold informal site visits in Year 3 to review how the program is moving to address the recommended steps in the self-study. This feedback becomes part of the continuous improvement cycle of the audit process. At ETSU, audit leader Cynthia Burnley has developed a specific process that is used on campus to ensure the work continues and is monitored. The ETSU process is outlined in Figure 6.5, and a sample timeline is provided in Figure 6.6.

Figure 6.5 **ETSU Academic Audit Follow-Up Process**

The effectiveness of academic audits is dependent on follow-up procedures that are timely and meaningful. These steps constitute the ETSU follow-up process:

- *Department response.* Within approximately one month of receiving the narrative report (excluding summer months), faculty in the unit prepare a written response to each recommendation in the report and set priorities for making improvements.
- *College dean response.* The college dean meets with the chair and coordinator and prepares a written response within three weeks of receiving the department response. The coordinator prepares a summary document of the department's and dean's responses.
- *Graduate dean response* (if applicable). The summary document is sent to the graduate dean if a graduate program was audited. The graduate dean prepares a response within the next three weeks and discusses it in a meeting with the chair, college dean, and coordinator. The graduate dean's responses are incorporated in the summary document, and it is sent to the provost.
- *Vice president/provost response.* Within two weeks, the summary document is finalized in a meeting with the provost, graduate dean, college dean, chair, and coordinator. All parties sign the summary document, which indicates their support of all responses and plans for implementation.

Figure 6.6 **Audit Report and Follow-Up Timeline**

Activity	Schedule
1. Audit team submits narrative report	Four weeks after site visit
2. Department prepares response	Four weeks after report received (excluding summer months)
3. College dean's response	Three weeks after department's response
4. Graduate dean's response (if applicable)	Three weeks after college dean's response
5. Provost's response	Two weeks after graduate dean's response
6. Signed summary document distributed	One week after provost's response
7. Annual follow-up	Yearly, until closure is reached on all recommendations or another audit occurs.

The discussions outlined in Figure 6.5 provide opportunities for administrators to support program improvements, separate from annual budget hearings. Academic units will later use the summary document in subsequent planning and budget hearings (if applicable). Progress toward addressing goals is assessed annually until closure is reached on each recommendation or a subsequent audit is conducted.

Getting Feedback on the Process

At the TBR, we distribute a feedback survey to faculty leadership in each participating program and the auditors at the end of the annual cycle. We use the feedback gleaned to fine-tune and change processes and materials. Sample questions from the survey are included in Table 6.3.

Surveys completed as a follow-up to the first year of the audit at the TBR indicate strong agreement among the participating programs that the process was fair (90.9%). In addition, a large percentage of participants believe that time spent preparing the self-study and the information gleaned in that process was worthwhile (87%). Program participants saw the audit process as helping identify program strengths (92.3%) and areas in need of improvement (87%) relative to the quality principles and the focal areas. We learned from the first-year survey results that we should improve the handbook used in the audit process because more than half (52%) of the respondents were either neutral or disagreed with the statement that the audit handbook and other resource materials were clear and helpful. We have since

Table 6.3 **Audited Program Feedback**

Question	Strongly Agree	Agree	Neutral	Disagree	Strongly Disagree
1. The audit process appropriately identified areas of strength of the department or discipline being audited.					
2. The audit process appropriately identified areas in which the department or discipline being audited needed to improve.					
3. There was sufficient time to interact with the visiting audit team.					
4. The audit handbook and other resource materials were clear and helpful.					
5. Although faculty spent time preparing a self-study for the audit, the information gleaned was worthwhile.					
6. The process did not intimidate the faculty members of the department or program being audited.					
7. The team auditing the department/program was well prepared.					
8. The audit process was reasonable in terms of fairness.					

revised all materials based on their feedback. We highly recommend a mechanism to gather feedback at each cycle, whether it is a survey, focus group interviews, or other combination of strategies to learn how auditors and program/institutional participants perceive the impact and benefit of the audit process.

Examples of Audit Reports

Examples of good audit reports are helpful in understanding both the structure and tone of the reports. Two examples are included here. We presented the self-study from the ETSU BA/BS and MA programs in sociology in Chapter 5. The report of the audit team site visit for the same program is included in this chapter as a way of illustrating the connectedness of the entire process. Also included is the audit report from a community college program.

Audit Report 1

ETSU Academic Audit Team's Narrative Report
BA/BS and Master of Arts in Sociology

1. Introduction

On April 21, 2006, three academic audit team members—Dr. Dixie Dennis (Austin Peay State University), Dr. Walter Boles (Middle Tennessee State University), and Dr. William Badley (Middle Tennessee State University)—conducted the audit on the campus of ETSU for the sociology department's BA/BS and MA degrees. The team members had read the academic audit self-study submitted by the sociology department, and met early that morning to discuss strategy and to assign specific focal areas for team members to address in questioning and in the narrative report. As a result of the exit discussion, ETSU's chair of sociology, Dr. Martha Copp, sent additional information on the department's plan for biennial review, which is included in this report.

2. Overall Performance

The overall impression of the sociology department is that the faculty members are concerned, conscientious, informally collaborative, and honest. The student interviewees expressed their affection, respect, and gratitude for the faculty's open-door policy for helping them and for the individualization of instruction. The student feedback provided clear evidence of a department that has its students' welfare in clear sight. In addition, the audit team agrees with the department's objection to the imputation of the phrase *informal effort* to its performance. More apt would be the phrase *informal emergent effort.* This does not have the implication that department members do not pay attention to each other or to the development of the department as a learning community. The implication of the addition of the word *emergent* provides the acknowledgment by the audit team that the department is in the process of starting and implementing methods for establishing and assessing learning outcomes with future plans to incorporate what is learned in teaching and learning methods. The informality (the lack of formal structures for collaboration) does not imply that the department faculty did not communicate regularly about course development and the department's issues—for example, the exit exam for undergraduates. Although informal collaboration provides the department with open and frequent collaboration on proposed changes (e.g., the exit exam, cooperation with other departments), the self-study honestly portrays a lack: "We do not systematically and formally evaluate our curriculum to ensure that course content and sequencing best meet the needs of our students." Thus the biennial review is planned and will address these issues. The audit team concluded that the informality of collaboration could mean that some could opt out of participation or could unwittingly be excluded; and if the department continues to expand as it plans, then the precariousness of informal discussion for consistent collegial communication would increase.

3. Performance in Focal Areas

Learning objectives. The faculty in the Department of Sociology and Anthropology at ETSU began developing and refining program learning objectives in 2000. This task is an arduous one, a task that much of the nation is currently grappling with. Faculty members, with the help of the 2005 ETSU Academic Quality Initiative, have made tremendous strides. They explained to the academic audit team that they will continue to expand their program learning objectives to course learning objectives and to measurement of course assignments/ activities, as outlined in the biennial review. Although faculty reported that "the goal of this [learning objectives] revision was to ensure that learning objectives could actually be assessed using the exit exam," the academic audit team believes that the exit exam should be one of several indicators for revision. For example, there should be clear links between the sociology department's goals/mission, the program objectives, the individual course objectives, class assignments/activities, and the original departmental goals and program objectives. These goals and learning outcomes links should appear on students' syllabi related to student activities or tasks. Linking student learning objectives to class activities is an important element, for it clearly communicates to students the purposes of instruction and expectations about what will be assessed, an important evidentiary indicator of the program's success. The course syllabus becomes a method of communication for students to have a context for the course activities; students are becoming lifelong learners, and the sociology faculty members further their aim of becoming a learning community through the evidence of student success, or lack thereof, provided by assessed learning outcomes.

The sociology self-study mentions the addition of two questions to be added to the student assessment of instruction, seeking students' "feedback regarding their levels of preparedness and background knowledge when taking courses in the major." This supports the praiseworthy major focus to "assess the program from the students' perspective." The audit team is suggesting that a qualitative section may be added at the end of the exit exam. This qualitative exam section could include open-ended questions such as, "What course do you believe needs to be included in the curriculum?" or "What was the best part of being a student in this program?" or "What was the worst part of being a student in this program?" and so forth. This inclusion would help faculty who obviously are concerned that their students learn and how their students perceive the major experience. In addition, the audit team suggests that the undergraduate exit exam could be used as a pretest to assess new MA students, a baseline of sociological knowledge the department considers important.

Curriculum and cocurriculum. In an important sense, ETSU sociology faculty members are commended for their informality (in-the-hall communication) regarding curriculum changes and course-sequencing decisions. Obviously faculty members enjoy collaborating to help the department and students. The academic audit team members wondered, though, if adding a few formal faculty meetings (with announced agendas) could ensure that all faculty members are involved from the beginning of discussions. Academic audit team members believe that it is difficult to justify *how* informal processes elicit collaboration among all faculty or show documentation of plans/accomplishments. In other words, some documented formal processes may strengthen the informal collaboration process. Faculty reported also extending their informal processes to "achieving program learning objectives." Although that process, again, is a "good" one, additional formal faculty meetings may speed that difficult process.

The academic audit team members were greatly impressed by the sociology faculty's collaboration between departments on the ETSU campus. Their stance on valuing diversity should be a model across ETSU as well as other TBR institutions.

Faculty members are commended, again, for informal plans to conduct their multilevel analysis of the soundness of the curriculum and cocurriculum. Also admirable is that the faculty "will continue to evaluate its curriculum every two years." That process could be extended to occur annually in a formal full-faculty meeting or an afternoon retreat.

Teaching and learning methods. The department is quite aware that this is one area that needs improvement. With that recognition, mentioned in the self-study, the department has committed itself to a biennial review. Specifically, the department has had two members who were involved in peer faculty review for purposes of tenure and promotion; these faculty members were observed by a departmental colleague and a representative from their college. The faculty members were given written feedback on teaching and classroom procedures. The academic audit team understands that this procedure will be expanded throughout the department. It was also indicative of the department's use of evidence to improve teaching and learning that the undergraduate exit exam was reviewed to determine why student performance was not what was expected. The department's conclusion was that students were not motivated to try hard and that results should also be discussed in the context of course content and course sequencing at various levels (introduction of content, reiteration of content, and then content assessment).

Student learning assessment. It is commendable that the department is participating in the university-wide academic quality initiative with its emphasis on clearly stated learning outcomes; however, the audit team believes there should be several methods of assessment of student learning. Mentioned above is the suggestion that open-ended questions be added (along with the two proposed by the department) to the student assessment of faculty. In addition, it is suggested that the alumni association be approached again to see whether it is possible to collect indirect evidence (i.e., surveys) of graduates. Another possibility is to use the undergraduate exit exam as an incoming exam for the MA program; as a pretest, it could provide baseline information for improvement of the MA program. Other institutions have established advisory boards of local supervised learning sites where students serve to provide input; a formalized survey from these supervised learning sites is also a possibility.

Quality assurance. Because of the size of the department, informal collaboration has been the mode of procedure. It is suggested, however, that as the department increases in size, with the addition of the anthropology major, it should make formal a meetings calendar to create the necessary discussions of assessment plans and review schedules. The department has committed itself to a biennial review of its curriculum and to analyze peer institutions for purposes of improvements; there should be a formal mechanism for conveying and discussing the results of these important innovations and ensuring that all department members are aware of these results.

4. Conclusions

Commendations. Foremost in commendations is the students' appreciation for their helpful and understanding faculty members, especially in the faculty's accessibility for advice and individualization of instruction. Also commendable is the extent of collaboration despite the lack of formal mechanisms for communication. The audit team applauds the honesty of the self-study and its spirit to move to an evidentiary learning community. The collaborative efforts across campus in cocurricular events and the supervised internships are also laudable efforts.

Affirmations. The audit team encourages the establishment of the biennial review and the institutionalization of faculty peer review of teaching and learning. The audit team tried to make clear that the process to create a collaborative, evidence-driven unit—a journey the sociology department has begun—is a process that most of us in higher education are beginning. It is a cultural change epitomized by the shift in emphasis from teaching (what professors do) to learning (what students do and know).

Recommendations. Although the department is beginning to do much to create a collaborative, evidence-driven unit, the audit team recommends these actions: attach departmental learning outcomes to all course syllabi, create an advisory board of stakeholders, provide open-ended questions on the student assessment of faculty forms, survey graduates through the alumni office, and continue to examine the undergraduate exit exam with consequent adaptations of curriculum, teaching, and the instrument. Also, the undergraduate exit exam could be used as a pretest for incoming MA students to provide evidence for adapting the graduate curriculum. There was one recommendation from the undergraduate student interviews: offer an introductory theories course early in the major. At the graduate level the student group thought that because of the length of the supervised internship report, they were writing a thesis, although they were in the applied sociology MA program, not the thesis program. The audit team recommends that from the beginning of the master's degree, student advising makes clear the distinctions between the programs and that the faculty perhaps reexamine the internship report requirements.

Overall. As stated earlier, the audit team prefers the phrase *informal emergent effort* to describe the sociology department. In other words, this is not a pejorative phrase. It acknowledges that the department (as many other institutions and departments) is beginning the process and is doing so in an exemplary open and earnest attitude. The audit team appreciates the honesty, professionalism, and hospitality of the members of the sociology department and the representative.

Audit Report 2

Division of Social and Behavioral Sciences
Chattanooga State Technical Community College

1. Introduction

On March 22, 2005, the audit team visited Chattanooga State Technical Community College to review four programs in the Division of Social and Behavioral Sciences. Those programs were history, economics, geography, and political science. (This report uses the term *Division of Social and Behavioral Sciences* to refer to the entire division and/or its representatives and the terms *social sciences division* or *division* to refer

to the collection of units directly involved in this audit: history, economics, geography, and political science.) All the programs reviewed
are relatively small. History is the largest, with a total of three full-time
faculty; economics has one full-time faculty member; geography is
taught by a full-time history faculty member with credentials in geography; and political science is taught by adjunct faculty. There are plans
to hire a new full-time political science faculty member this year.

The social sciences faculty had conducted and submitted a self-
study in fall 2004. Members of the audit team reviewed the self-study
before the visit, developed follow-up questions for the interviews, and
held a meeting on the evening before the visit to focus the direction of
interviews during the visit itself. After reading the self-study, the audit
team chose four primary areas of focus for the interviews: 1) the depth
and breadth of involvement of faculty in the self-study; 2) the origin and
review of the "central competencies"; 3) assessment of student learning,
both at the individual student level and in a broader, department sense;
4) assessment techniques and variation from discipline to discipline.

Onsite interviews were conducted on March 22, 2005. These were
attended by the chair of the Division of Social and Behavioral Sciences, the curriculum coordinator for programs described in the self-
study, one additional history faculty member, the full-time economics
instructor, and roughly ten students. The exit session was also attended
by the dean of arts and sciences.

2. Overall Performance

The division's primary strengths lie in its individual teachers. Both the
self-study and the interviews revealed a faculty that is concerned about
student learning, knowledgeable about learning styles, and dedicated
to the profession. Faculty members' use of technology is commendable, and the division leadership seems truly interested in addressing
weaknesses pointed out in the self-study and interviews.

The division's primary weaknesses lie in a lack of collaboration
between faculty, both formally and informally. A number of statements
in the self-study and interviews indicated faculty are given extreme latitude in focusing their courses, approaching subjects, and assessing student learning. Although academic freedom is certainly an important

component of any college course, there is also a need for accountability and some consistency. These two characteristics seem somewhat lacking in the division. Another weakness lies in the use of data to ensure that the learning objectives are appropriate, teaching methods are effective, and student achievement of the outcomes is consistent between different sections of a course.

Although the self-study was not as polished or thorough as it might have been, especially in terms of analysis, it was very honest and forthright in representing the current state of the disciplines involved. The content of the self-study was confirmed by onsite interviews, which were excellent. Administrators, faculty, and students were open and honest, knowledgeable about their self-study and departmental processes, cooperative with the audit team, and cordial and pleasant to work with. It became apparent during the interview process that the new departmental and divisional administrators, as well as some faculty, embrace the audit process as a means to institute positive change in the division.

3. Performance in the Focal Areas

Learning objectives. Based on the self-study report, social sciences faculty appear confident that learning objectives are clearly defined. All course syllabi list the competencies, so faculty and students alike can clearly understand the learning objectives. Faculty also have the inherent belief that the competencies address students' needs. In addition, faculty believe they exceed the course competencies as they work their magic in the classroom; students increase their understanding of the world and gain a deeper appreciation of the world's complexity. Furthermore, the increase in understanding implies that students leave classes with a greater awareness of how they can more effectively navigate their way through their lives. In other words, students can make practical applications of the principles they have learned. Chattanooga State appears to be blessed with a competent, dedicated, and professional group of teachers in the Division of Social and Behavioral Sciences.

Although divisional syllabi link specific course objectives to the clearly labeled central competencies, audit interviews imply a weakness regarding consistency of expectations. Faculty are given free rein in interpreting the relative importance of the learning objectives and in determining their expectations of students. This latitude may easily result in such an extensive range of educational experiences for students that consistency of content suffers. The competencies and objectives have been reviewed in light of the recent TBR emphasis on general education competencies, but more discussion and perhaps compromise from faculty members might lead to a common set of objectives that most instructors could embrace. The desirable result would be greater consistency within the various courses. Also, the discussion process would reflect the logic behind the objectives as opposed to a simple adoption of an existing set of objectives.

In regard to the focal area of learning objectives, status quo seems to be the predominant element. Ad hoc adjustments have been made, but there has been little emphasis on implementing quality principles. Therefore, the division appears to be at a firefighting level.

Curriculum and cocurriculum. Review of the self-study and onsite interviews indicated that the content of the courses is clearly defined in the instructional objectives of the department syllabi. However, due to the length and scope of the syllabi, which average 10 pages, it is not possible for a faculty member to cover every item on them. Each instructor, therefore, is given latitude to focus on those areas listed in the syllabi that he or she judges to best meet student needs, with the caveat that the entire time period and geographic scope of each course should be addressed as noted in the learning objectives. The self-study recommended that cross-departmental faculty committees be established to communicate and coordinate the identified applications of the foundational course material in various major coursework. The self-study also identified the need for a systematic method in making decisions about course content. There is a need for consistency and consensus in what is being taught.

In regard to the focal areas of curriculum and cocurriculum, both the self-study and the interviews note concerns about collaboration and basing decisions on evidence; the division, however, has instituted various means to address these issues, including regular department meetings and more contact with adjunct faculty. Therefore, the division appears to be at the emergent level.

Teaching and learning methods. The self-study stated that instructors use a variety of methods to reach the different learning styles of students in their classes. The study gave examples of various methods used in the courses, including lectures, classroom discussions, films, and online support and assignments. The study also stated faculty employed teaching methods that helped students transfer information from one class into other classes. An example of this is the economics class that encourages students to select their topics for a speech from what they are learning in other classes in the division, such as history, geography, and political science. Overall the self-study implies that faculty are aware of various student learning styles and accordingly use a variety of teaching methods. Onsite interviews confirmed this awareness and provided the audit team with a more in-depth look at the different teaching methods used to reach the different learning styles. The following are some examples of the learning methods used with the students: maps to complete for geography, discussions online regarding a structured paper, and critical thinking questions.

There is some informal discussion among full-time faculty, and the program coordinator does correspond with adjuncts. However, until recently there has not been a formal mechanism for faculty to share teaching and learning methods. The disciplines have now begun monthly meetings at which some of these issues may be addressed. In addition, the division plans to hire four new faculty this year, and there are plans to mentor them on different teaching methods that help meet the needs of students with different learning styles.

Ten students attended one of the interview sessions. The students' majors varied from undecided to prelaw. The overall sense from the students was that they felt their different learning styles were being met. The students stated that if they needed further help, the faculty were more than willing to assist with their learning needs. The students told the auditors that several different teaching methods were used both in the classroom and outside the classroom. Some examples were peer tutors, web sites, and class participation. One student stated the class participation helped "massage in the information." A few students expressed a concern regarding getting more students aware of the different resources available to assist with teaching and learning. The students explained that posters were used and information was shared via word of mouth, but they felt more needed to be done to better communicate the availability of resources to the general student body.

The disciplines use a variety of teaching methods and are successful in addressing different student learning styles and needs. However, faculty members do not consistently or systematically share their teaching methods with each other or appear to have time to brainstorm and develop new ideas. Therefore, the division appears to be at the emergent level.

Student assessment. The self-study described how current measures of assessment are primarily based on student performance on a variety of activities, including multiple-choice exams, writing assignments, and critical thinking activities. Onsite interviews confirmed that a number of student learning assessment tools are used in different classrooms, but that faculty do not systematically share assessment tools with other faculty. Interviews indicated that only the instructor was aware of the material covered on the test and the types of questions used. The self-study and interviews indicated that a formal mechanism to assess student learning is not available at this time. Each instructor develops his or her own exams, and the disciplines do not have a mechanism to assess whether testing practices are grounded in sound educational research. The division did acknowledge that this would be a plan for the future, especially with the hiring of new faculty.

The self-study also presented the idea of developing pre- and post-tests to assess student learning, and the faculty expressed an interest in developing a common assessment tool for evaluating papers. In addition, interviews indicated there is not currently a common test bank for all faculty to draw from in developing exams. Such a test bank might help faculty both develop exams and achieve greater consistency across the department in covering material.

The disciplines do not currently have a student learning assessment guideline to identify whether students have learned what is necessary to progress to higher education or the workplace. The division is aware that student learning assessment needs to be evaluated beyond the current semester to assess whether changes need to be made in programs, and they are working on learning from other degree programs and advisory committee partners to assess whether there are any areas for improvement.

Interviews with students indicated that they felt prepared to progress to the next level—whether that was proceeding to the next sequence of classes, transferring to a four-year college, or starting a job.

In summary, a variety of appropriate student assessment methods are used by individual instructors. Both the self-study and the interviews indicated concerns about collaboration and basing decisions on evidence; members of the faculty, however, have recognized these needs and are instituting various means to address them. Therefore, the division appears to be at the emergent level.

Quality assurance. The faculty are quite proud of their technological expertise and believe that their knowledge in this area contributes to the quality of their division. They cite, for instance, the continuity that exists when a professor gives PowerPoint presentations to multiple sections of the same course. Their skills in perusing the Internet allow them to upgrade their lectures from the mundane to the exciting. Furthermore, these skills are not limited to full-time faculty; the atmosphere within the division encourages sharing this knowledge between full-time faculty and adjunct faculty. On the other hand, faculty did not express strong opinions in other areas of quality assessment, an omission indicating that QA has not been a strong priority.

Quality principles appear to have been compromised due to frequent organizational changes. The resultant turmoil inherent within persistent leadership changes virtually guarantees firefighting responses rather than a mature system of effective processes that lead to QA. There is, however, an expressed desire for change as evidenced in the self-study and interviews. The new leadership in place, coupled with plans to hire new faculty in the near future, offers an exciting opportunity for faculty to work together to set a shared agenda that could lead to significant improvement over the next few years.

More structured measures of quality appear to be needed. Little external data was provided to the auditors to confirm that quality processes are producing positive benefits in student learning. For example, the link between the learning objectives and student mastery appears tenuous. Other than the typical assessment measures for individual

students—such as test grades, written and oral reports, and participation in class discussion—assessment measures in a wider context
appear limited. In addition, specific evidence to show that the needs of
external stakeholders are being met is lacking. Implementing a process
to determine how students from the division fare at four-year institutions or in the work world would yield important data. Creating a
process to allow faculty to compare students' performance and faculty
assessment measures could also nurture quality improvement both at
the individual level and at the division level. For example, a review of
student portfolios or an "essay-grading" workshop could be instituted
as a way to share best practice and to promote self-reflection. Furthermore, processes to actually use data to effect positive changes in each of
the focal areas should be implemented.

In addition, interviews revealed that data from student evaluations
of faculty is currently underutilized. Written comments from student
evaluations are not being reviewed by the division head due to a mis-
understanding about privacy. Reading those comments and discussing
them with faculty members during evaluation periods could have a significant impact on the quality of the student experience.

Interviews also revealed the need for revising the supervisor's faculty evaluation form. Adding a "needs improvement" option would
provide the flexibility to document specific areas that should be focused
on in an effort to bring about improvement.

In regard to the QA focal area, the division ranges from its firefighting history to emergent effort. The audit team clearly recognizes
the desire of the division to experiment with quality principles and
encourages faculty to do so.

4. Application of Principles

Defining quality in terms of outcomes. Student focus groups con-
veyed the definite impression that Chattanooga State ranks high in
terms of quality outcomes. Themes emerging from the focus sessions
include an understanding of the course objectives, the existence of
challenging course content, an emphasis on critical thinking, a nurturing teaching environment, and practical applications that prepare
students for the real world. Discussions with the faculty members cor-

roborated the desire of the faculty to continue, and even improve, the framework for excellence. This conclusion, however, is weakened by the actual self-study report that indicates a general malaise within the division about documenting the outcomes of the learning objectives. Instituting a few simple processes to substantiate the validity of the existing assumptions about students' needs could provide illuminating data that would serve as a motivating force to build greater cohesion and purpose. In addition, such processes could inspire individuals within the division to reflect on their strengths and weaknesses, resulting in subtle changes that would lead to small individual improvements and would cumulatively result in major improvements for the overall division. The natural byproduct of an improved division is an increase in student success, both in the collegiate environment and in the working environment.

Focusing on how things get done. How things get done is one of the weaker areas for many institutions. Being caught up in the actual doing of things often takes precedence over thinking about how those things are done. This is perfectly natural in the academic arena when, for faculty, what they do—teaching—exists in the format of specific class deadlines. One must "do" at 10:00, 11:00, and 2:00, so class preparation becomes the priority. Finding the mechanism(s) to bring attention to how things get done, however, is a valuable goal. Currently, faculty in the Division of Social and Behavioral Sciences are empowered to make individual decisions that may detract from the quality of the division. A process to build teamwork and to provide a platform to exchange ideas could be invaluable. The recently introduced schedule of meetings for faculty and coordinators provides an effective vehicle to bring about improvement in how things get done in each of the focal areas. A new cohesion between group members could also help ensure long-term institutional support.

Working collaboratively. Historically the social sciences division has not been strong in terms of working collaboratively. Evidence from the self-study and interviews indicates that although faculty are dedicated to their students and innovative in their teaching methods, they have not developed effective means of working together to develop learning objectives and curriculum, to share teaching methods, to devise appropriate assessment mechanisms, and to ensure continuous improvement.

The division, however, has gone through a number of changes recently, and these changes may lead in a more positive direction in terms of working collaboratively. The current division chair has only been in her position for the past year and a half. She is leading the division in an effort to pull together as a team to identify long-term goals, to work with adjunct faculty to keep them current, and to share different teaching methods. Interviews indicate that division faculty understand that collaboration within the department will increase student learning. In addition, the division has instituted a series of weekly meetings with various coordinators, directors, and faculty. The meetings provide an excellent opportunity for faculty, coordinators, and the chair to discuss common issues related to all aspects of teaching and learning, and if continued, they will provide an excellent means of improving collaboration.

The audit team feels the division is beginning to work collaboratively and strongly encourages its faculty to continue this work. The collaboration needs to include but not be limited to sharing teaching methods, consensus about learning objectives for each class, and measures of evaluation of student assessment of learning outcomes.

Basing decisions on evidence. The division does not currently have tools to assess how well students are equipped to continue in a four-year program and/or on the job once they leave the college. The division chair indicated that plans are in the works to learn from other degree programs and to work with an advisory committee to provide a tool to gather evidence of what the students need to know to progress successfully.

The division incorporates peer evaluations of faculty by tenured faculty until a faculty member is fully tenured. Student evaluations are done on each faculty member. The faculty member is allowed to choose which class will evaluate him or her. The dean evaluates the numerical information, and only the faculty member reads the comments. The newly appointed division chair was unaware that she should read the student comments as well. The dean is planning to read the comments and advise faculty members as necessary based on the findings. The audit team encourages the division to continue peer evaluations of all faculty, even if they are tenured.

Striving for coherence. Representatives from the division who were interviewed by the audit team recognize that there is a need for the faculty to come to consensus about course content and expected student outcomes. Assessment methods should be aligned with expected student outcomes. Efforts are being made to provide the faculty with opportunities to work together to make decisions and strive for coherence and consistency in what is being taught in the division. More opportunities for collaboration will be a focus as new faculty are hired and given opportunities to provide input. The audit team encourages the division to continue efforts in making sure that there is consistency in delivery of course content and student assessment.

Learning from best practice. Representatives from the social sciences division, as well as students who were interviewed by the audit team, indicated that a variety of teaching methods are being used by the faculty. Examples include critical thinking assignments, use of technology in research, and study groups. The audit team recommends that a process be instituted to ensure that best practices within and without the institution are shared, including a follow-up reflecting application of best practices.

Making continuous improvement a priority. Representatives from the social sciences division who were interviewed by the audit team indicated that efforts are being made to improve quality by broadening classroom methodology, adapting to a wide variety of student learning styles, and defining assessment processes that reflect positive student outcomes. The audit team encourages a more team-oriented approach to setting departmental goals, developing curriculum, sharing teaching methods, and developing student assessment methods.

5. Overall Maturity Assessment and Rationale

Rating: emergent. Both the self-study and the audit visit indicated that quality principles have been compromised in recent years due to changes in leadership and faculty turnover, resulting in frequent firefighting processes, a general lack of collaboration, and weak assessment and improvement strategies. There is a recognized need for the division to become more team oriented and to develop procedures for such activities as setting divisional goals, developing curriculum, sharing teaching methods, and developing student assessment methods. Recently, however, there has been a significant effort to address these issues, including closer mentoring and monitoring of adjunct faculty and establishing regular division and discipline meetings.

There is also evidence of excellent teaching and learning going on at all levels of the division. Although not all the faculty consistently work as a team, they appear to work well as individuals. There is also an expressed desire for more teamwork and collaboration, as evidenced in the self-study and in the interviews. The new leadership in place and the prospect of four new hires in the near future offer the opportunity for the faculty to work together to set a shared agenda that could lead to significant improvement over the next few years.

6. Conclusions

The auditors *commend* the social sciences division for the following:

- Listing the central competencies in the master syllabi for each course and linking them to specific instructional objectives
- Using technology in the classroom and training adjunct faculty to incorporate technology into their classrooms
- Employing a combination of teaching methods that appeal to a wide variety of student learning styles
- Employing a portfolio approach to faculty evaluation
- Initiating improvement in communication through the common reading of *Are We Communicating Yet?* and discussing the application of its principles to the division
- Implementing regular division/department meetings for faculty and coordinators at which instructional issues can be discussed

The auditors *affirm* the division's efforts in the following:

- Working to achieve consistency in course content and developing regular processes (such as department meetings and other opportunities for collaboration) to attain that goal

- More effectively using student comments on instructional evaluation forms as a tool for both individual faculty improvement and divisional improvement

The auditors *recommend* that the division investigate or implement the following:

- Instituting a process to review competencies with the goal of creating clear, measurable learning outcomes
- Seeking consensus regarding what areas within the learning outcomes are most important and making them a priority in all sections of a course, regardless of instructor or delivery mode (the auditors agree that instructors should have academic freedom, but greater concern for consistency in course content, delivery, and assessment would help ensure quality among multiple sections of courses)
- Developing a core group of questions to be included on final exams or preparing departmental test banks to help ensure that all priority content is covered
- Asking faculty to submit tests as a way to document the material that is being covered
- Developing more ways for faculty to share ideas regarding best practices (the faculty should share their techniques during regularly scheduled meetings and be given an opportunity to network, brainstorm, and develop new ideas as a team)
- Developing methods to measure how well students are equipped to function in four-year programs and/or the work world once they leave the college
- Altering the faculty evaluation forms to include a "needs improvement" choice
- Using student evaluations of instruction as a more integral part of the annual evaluation process for faculty, with the goal of continual improvement within the satisfactory range
- Including external measures, such as national exams and reviews of graduate performance in four-year colleges, that would aid in reviewing and documenting quality

- Establishing advisory boards for appropriate disciplines as a way to maintain contact with external stakeholders
- Utilizing more structured peer evaluations, especially for tenured, fully promoted faculty

7

Auditing Quality Work
for Research and Scholarship

A cademic audit as originally developed by William Massy (2003c) focused exclusively on teaching and learning. Massy's notion was that the academy had developed peer review processes to evaluate research and scholarship but that there was no real systematic counterpart used to examine the teaching component of higher education. Further, given the inclination of many faculty members toward research, there was a need to spotlight additional attention on teaching and learning activities.

When the first round of academic audits at the University of Missouri excluded research and scholarship, however, faculty members were concerned that the audits only addressed a portion of their work. All four of the University of Missouri campuses are research-oriented, and all offer doctoral and professional degrees. As a consequence, approximately 40% or more of most University of Missouri faculty members' time is allocated to research. So although the audits were successful in helping the departments see where their strengths and weaknesses were in the teaching and learning domains, many participants finished the process feeling that the reviews were incomplete. Several faculty members asked why almost half of their work at the institution was being ignored. Further, faculty members recognized the importance of the interaction between their teaching and their research and the value of students interacting with faculty members who have active research agendas. Consequently, we decided to extend the audit process to include an assessment of the quality processes associated with research and scholarship.

The decision to include research was consistent with Massy's notion of academic quality improvement. The absence of a research component came up frequently during the introductory workshops and early meetings with faculty members. Massy's response was that although the beginning audits would focus on teaching and learning, the same practices could be modified later to help faculty learn how to be more effective with their scholarship. Why, for example, couldn't the seven quality principles be applied to scholarly and research activities?

Research Focal Areas

Our first step was to create focal areas for scholarship and research that would mirror those already defined for teaching and learning. To do so, we convened a group of experienced researchers and scholars. Many of these faculty members had been involved in the first round of academic audits or other quality-oriented processes. Using a focus group format with open discussions, these faculty members helped us define the core areas that would need to be in place for a successful department research program. They talked about clarifying the definition of scholarship and research as well as how one can gather evidence and measure the success of a unit's efforts. Further, they discussed the seven principles for promoting quality processes and debated the value of each of those principles as applied to research. These discussions produced a long list of ideas, many suggestions for good practice, and a variety of questions that would need to be asked to evaluate a department's research environment.

The following focal areas evolved after much deliberation. They follow the same line of reasoning as the focal areas for teaching and learning, but of course their content focuses on quality work as applied to research and scholarship. Pursuant to an audit's focus on academic quality work (AQW), the focal areas address the department's research goals and metrics, what the department can do to improve its members' research and scholarship, how the quality of doctoral training can be assured and improved over time, and the potential synergies between research and teaching.

Research Outcomes

What measures are being used to gauge performance in the department, and how do the department's research and scholarship efforts compare to its peer departments? Departments should articulate research outcomes that are consistent with their mission and identified goals and not automatically adopt national standards if such standards are incompatible with the departments' role on campus.

Research Environment

Does the department have a vibrant research environment, and what specific steps are taken to create an environment that supports senior faculty members' efforts, mentors junior faculty, and adapts to the changing nature of scholarship in the field?

Sponsored Projects

How does the department's sponsored research, if there is any, compare to that of its peer departments? Does the climate support its investigators and the grant application and administration processes?

Doctoral Training

How does the department's doctoral program, if there is one, compare to those of its national peers (e.g., in terms of graduation rates, success of graduates, mentoring effectively in both research and teaching, and providing students with the skills for different types of positions, including those in industry or public service)?

Synergy With Education

How does the department's research and scholarship contribute to its educational programs? Are undergraduates involved in research, and are there checks and balances in place to ensure that research does not undermine teaching effectiveness?

Quality Principles Applied to Research and Scholarship

Once the five focal areas were determined, questions were developed to support the seven principles associated with successful quality practices. The focus groups had generated questions that the faculty members felt were relevant in evaluating quality, so whenever possible these questions were mapped into the seven quality principles presented originally in Chapter 3. Careful attention was given to ensure that the research questions would be comparable to those for teaching and learning. The seven areas are articulated below.

Define Quality in Terms of Outcomes

The quality of research outcomes, not the reputation of the faculty, is what ultimately matters. Desired outcomes should relate to the department's mission, not some abstract notion based on disciplinary canons.

Focus on How Things Get Done

Departments should think carefully about how research is done in the discipline and how it is fostered within the department. They should identify the elements that create impediments to achieving their research goals and eliminate them whenever possible.

Work Collaboratively

Departments should encourage faculty members to share information and help one another solve difficult problems because such teamwork makes the department a learning organization.

Base Decisions on Evidence

Departments should review the literature and consult with outside experts to identify how emerging trends affect their research efforts. They should gather concrete evidence on their performance relative to peers and develop realistic goals and strategies.

Strive for Coherence

Although departments may view their research programs as aggregations of individual initiatives, exemplary departments take a holistic view (e.g., do new hires complement existing expertise or break new ground in newly identified strategic areas for the department?).

Learn From Best Practice

Departments and professors should compare excellent versus average or poor-performing environments, assess the reasons for the differences, and look for ways to improve the research environments within their unit.

Make Continuous Improvement a Priority

Departments should have a regular plan to improve individual faculty scholarship efforts and to create a culture that cultivates scholarship, sponsored research initiatives, faculty mentoring, and doctoral programs.

Some Comments About the Process

It's helpful to review the process we used to develop the focal areas, principle-based questions, and other elements of the audit's research component. These same strategies would likely be helpful for other universities that adopt a structure to evaluate their research efforts and prefer to tailor some elements to their institutions. Furthermore, it seems likely that similar processes could be used to extend audit to other arenas like academic/professional service or service-learning programs.

We first gathered faculty members together who had been through the audit process as auditors or department chairs and discussed the general nature of a quality audit and its value. We felt it was important to address this element early in the deliberations to set the stage for thinking about research and asking faculty to step outside the traditional modes of viewing research and scholarship. We also invited a small number of other "good thinkers" who had not been through the process but who were successful researchers and had demonstrated the ability to create successful research programs. Having a few outsiders in the discussions was useful to challenge our thinking and to remain healthily skeptical about the audit process in general and its value in examining research.

We began by asking the group to think about the processes being used to support research rather than just focusing solely on the research outcomes. Then we asked participants to engage in soul-searching similar to what was described earlier in relation to the teaching and learning audits. Open-ended brainstorming sessions helped get the participants to think aloud about the thought patterns and behavioral regimens that produce high-quality scholarly efforts within a department, including nontraditional views of scholarship, how to create a good research climate, how to mentor junior faculty, how research is or should be integrated into formal and informal instruction, and how all these factors are tied together to produce a fully functioning department.

We talked a lot about how each unit should compare itself to its peers and how such benchmarking can produce improvements that are authentic to the specific academic department or campus. For example, faculty members should not try to turn their current department into one just like the department where they did their doctoral work. Because faculty members often come from prestigious research universities, they may unconsciously try to reconstitute their current department in ways that are infeasible or inappropriate. They may try to earn their departments a national ranking when in reality there is little chance of succeeding with current or prospective resources—or, indeed, when that might be inappropriate given their campus's mission.

Professors need to honestly examine the proper role for research in their department and ensure it matches the department and campus goals. Faculty should consider this question not just from their personal point of view but also from research and scholarship's role in engaging students in learning and discovery and in determining the proper mix of activities for the campus and the specific department.

For example, we have seen small academic units within large research campuses that do not offer graduate degrees. In some cases these units adopted the wider research culture of the campus in its entirety and by doing so created a mismatch between their role on campus and the local research climate. On the other hand, departments with similar characteristics have adopted a culture like that found in prestigious liberal arts colleges (e.g., Grinnell or Oberlin), where the focus is on undergraduate students but faculty are expected to be active scholars. The latter departments have looked for ways to truly engage undergraduate students in the research culture because that is such a critical part of the student experience—a task that is made easier because faculty do not turn to graduate students for help with research.

During these discussions we talked extensively about the appropriate measures for assessing research, how to identify realistic peer departments, how to benchmark with the best among the peer group, how to foster a comparable environment, and how to set reasonable goals with limited resources. The groups developed probing questions based on the seven quality principles, questions that invite faculty to examine their research and scholarly efforts in the same terms as the original audit format successfully accomplished for teaching and learning activities.

At the end of the day, the research component of the expanded academic audit came to look much like the educational component. The seven quality principles are used to stimulate reflection and determine improvement strategies in each of the five research focal areas. As before, the challenge was to develop questions that would detect a lack of focus on outcomes, inadequate attention to best practice, failure to adopt coherent strategies, and lack of clarity about what constitutes quality. Collegiality is just as important in the research arena as in teaching, as is continuous improvement of those things the department can affect. It became clear that faculty who were focused on improving research quality were able to distinguish between good and bad practices. It also became clear that by adopting a systematic and disciplined approach, a department could improve its research and scholarly environment in ways that showed high promise for improving research outcomes.

Once we had created the framework and the materials needed to carry it into practice, it was critical to validate those materials with the original group. We asked questions like these: Do the materials make sense, and are they well formatted? Do they reflect the earlier group discussion? Do they provide a comprehensive view, or did we miss something? We also approached some thoughtful researchers who had not been part of the original conversations and asked them to review the materials: Were we asking all the hard questions about the research and scholarly environment? For instance, how can we make the research component of an audit work from a practical standpoint? How do we know good research environments when we see them?

The result, after taking account of all the feedback, was the list of concept-defining questions presented in the appendix to this chapter. These questions define what is meant by *academic quality work* in the research realm, just as the list of teaching-related questions in the appendix to Chapter 3 defines AQW in the educational realm.

Starting Questions for Research and Scholarship

We also developed a set of starting questions, as we did for teaching, that focus on what we and our advisors considered to be the key issues in research. We noted in Chapter 4 that although it's helpful to have the full array of questions as a template, to ask departments to respond to all seven principles for each of the five focal areas is a daunting task. The following questions provide a starting point for the self-study and a convenient place for the auditors to start when they visit.

Starting Questions

Research outcomes: What outcomes are important, and how does the department compare with peer departments?

- *Define quality in terms of outcomes.* How good is your department's research and scholarship? What types of publications, in what types of outlets, do you reward? Are you willing to consider other outcomes?
- *Base decisions on evidence.* What indicators do you use to track the department's overall research performance, and what does the evidence tell you? Who are your peer departments, and what departments can you reasonably expect to catch up with?
- *Strive for coherence.* Are the department's desired research outcomes consistent with the abilities and interests of the faculty? Are they compatible with the campus's goals and other departmental goals? Do research outcomes systematically inform other departmental efforts (e.g., mentoring doctoral students and new faculty)?

Research environment: Does the department have a vibrant research environment? Do faculty members reflect on the research environment and how to improve it? What steps is it taking to effect improvements?

- *Focus on how things get done.* Do faculty members reflect on ways to improve the department's research environment, and does the department act on the results?
- *Work collaboratively.* Do you consult together on the department's research environment? Do you regularly discuss faculty members'

research aspirations, strategies, processes, and frustrations with colleagues? Does the university listen when faculty frustrations are presented?

- *Make improvement a priority.* Do you reconsider your research environment systematically and regularly? Does anyone else in the university encourage you to do so?

Sponsored projects (where applicable): How does the department's sponsored research compare to peer departments? How effectively does it support principal investigators in proposal-writing and project management?

- *Focus on how things get done.* Does the department have a specific plan to expand sponsored research funding? Does the department or college have an infrastructure in place to help faculty secure funding?
- *Base decisions on evidence.* How is the department doing in relation to other departments on campus and in peer departments across the country? What evidence do you collect, and how do you use it?
- *Learn from best practice.* Do you know what other departments on campus do to enhance research funding? Do you regularly discuss such funding options?

Doctoral programs (where applicable): How good is the department's doctoral program relative to peer departments? How do faculty train and mentor students on research and teaching skills, and how do they monitor progress toward the degree?

- *Define quality in terms of outcomes.* What are graduates expected to do, and where are they expected to go? Are your goals consistent with campus goals? How do you track what actually happens?
- *Focus on how things get done.* Does the department have a deep understanding of how doctoral training should work in your field? Do you act on this knowledge? How do your doctoral students contribute to the department's teaching and research programs? How do you ensure that they are not exploited?

- *Make continuous improvement a priority.* Do you reconsider your doctoral program systematically and regularly? Does anyone else in the university encourage you to do so?

Synergy with education: How does the department's research and scholarship contribute to its educational programs? How does it ensure that time spent on research does not undermine teaching effectiveness and education quality improvement?

- *Define quality in terms of outcomes.* Do you have specific outcomes in mind when considering the contributions of research to teaching? Do your desired outcomes reflect the needs of all or most students, or mainly those who share the faculty's research interests?
- *Focus on how things get done.* Do you reflect on the ways research contributes to teaching? Do you act on the results of these reflections?
- *Learn from best practice.* What do truly successful contributions of research to teaching in your field look like? How do you learn from such examples?

Modifying the Audit Process to Include Research

Adding the research component to audits requires some changes in the design of self-studies, the audit visit, and the audit report. Most are obvious, but there is one overarching imperative: that adding research does not overshadow the all-important teaching and learning component. A major problem in less structured reviews (e.g., program reviews) is that the inherent interest and excitement of research drives the conversation in that direction, leaving insufficient time and energy for the less familiar and often difficult discussions about teaching and learning.

Mitigating this difficulty requires that the two audit components maintain their separate identities throughout the audit process. The separation begins with the self-study, where departments are instructed to write separate sections for teaching and for research. Sometimes different people are put in charge of the two sections; if that's the case, it's essential that the two come together to consider the intersections between education-related and research-related quality work. Including an introductory section in the self-study about how teaching and research contribute to an overarching culture of quality will help participants understand the intersections more easily.

Balancing the needs for separation and integration during the audit visit presents the biggest challenge. The approach in Missouri was to field a single audit panel with separate subgroups for teaching and research. We enlarged the typical audit panel from approximately 8 to about 10 people and increased the length of the audit visit to a day and a half to provide the necessary coverage. The overall panel chair was chosen based on audit experience and without regard to discipline, although it could be beneficial to have a member from the same or a related discipline overseeing the research and scholarship subgroup.

The typical audit visit schedule is shown in Table 7.1. Notice that the expanded duration allows more small group sessions than the typical education audit. Further, the enlarged team permits more subgroups—actually sub-subgroups in this context—because the teaching and research subgroups will further subdivide for the breakout sessions. The schedule maintains the audit's unified character through plenary sessions at the beginning and the end, as well as integrated executive

Table 7.1 **Sample Audit Visit Schedule Incorporating Research**

Day 1		Day 2	
12 pm–1 pm (lunch)	Executive session to compare notes and prepare for the afternoon's small group sessions	9 am–11 am	Third set of small group sessions
1 pm–3 pm	First set of small group sessions	11 am–12 am	Fourth small group sessions; usually includes a small group session with campus leadership
3 pm–5 pm	Second set of small group sessions	12 pm–1:30 pm (lunch)	Executive session to compare notes and prepare for the exit session
5 pm–6:30 pm (dinner)	Executive session to discuss the day's findings	1:30 pm–2:30 pm	Exit session with departmental leadership
		2:30 pm–3 pm	Executive session to compare notes and prepare for writing the audit report

sessions. The audit reports have separate sections for teaching and research, plus an executive summary.

Results From Reviewing Research and Scholarship

Two rounds of audits using the combined approach of examining teaching and learning and also research and scholarship have been conducted at the University of Missouri. The process has been judged as successful. It allows auditors to view a department in its full context and observe how research and scholarship are integrated with the teaching and learning mission. By examining both components, it also allows faculty to discuss their full array of activities, something that faculty complained about during the first round when we only focused on teaching and learning.

We emphasize that several of the audited units displayed outstanding research and scholarship; some ranked high nationally, and at least two likely ranked in the top 25 programs in the country in their research area. At times departments' efforts seemed strategic and purposeful, but in other cases they simply represented the summation of talented faculty members working alone. Improving the latter type of department by leveraging the talent of its best faculty members is one of the primary benefits of looking systematically at how things are done. Such improvements have the added advantage of not requiring extensive investments of time or money.

The more mature research units had clearly focused on the national scene, had explicitly identified their peer groups, and had knowledge of how those units conducted their activities. In one case the department chair had carefully studied the other units—including the number of faculty, the average number and location of publications, what grant funding they had obtained, and how the unit compared with its own peer departments. The chair and department faculty had explicitly discussed what would be required for them to move to the next level and had developed a plan to get there. They had articulated their goal and plan to the campus's central administration and obtained agreement in principle. In another case the department had an accurate view of itself but less clarity on what its peers were doing and how it compared with them. Other departments drew on general and nationally defined notions of research outcomes that had not been specifically tailored for their units. These standards worked fairly well for those units with national prominence but did not represent realistic goals for others.

Few departments had formally examined their research mission in the context of their specific strengths and campus culture. Even fewer had identified the outcomes they would take as evidence that they were meeting their specific research goals. In general, senior faculty had much clearer notions of what constitutes successful scholarship than younger faculty. In some cases junior faculty were not explicitly clear on what they needed to get tenure or where they should devote their precious time. One problem common to most departments was a rather traditional notion of scholarship that had not been expanded to encompass nontraditional outcomes such as patents, licenses, invention disclosures, or other more applied outcomes. This was surprising, particularly for units operating in a discipline or field where the application of knowledge would be viewed as valuable by people outside the academy.

Some units had created a healthy climate supporting research and scholarship, one where both components were fully integrated into the department's culture. Students as well as faculty could articulate the goals of their research efforts and how those goals related to education. In most cases that was accomplished informally, as an accepted part of the culture—through a shared model of what a successful department should look like—and reinforced in explicit hallway conversations. In those places faculty fully engaged their students in their research, talked about it in classes, coauthored papers with students, encouraged national presentations by students, and conducted regular symposia that attracted students as well as faculty. In other departments there was general conversation about the value of research but few explicit activities to create an effective research climate.

When the research and scholarship permeated the educational ethos for doctoral students, faculty mentored them like colleagues or junior faculty—working with them on grants, papers, and presentations. In one case the department created formal weekly research sessions and devised clever ways to help students complete portions of their dissertation before or during the comprehensive exams. Usually faculty in these departments viewed the enculturation of students as a key part of their role.

In other departments the auditors found the climate for doctoral students more traditional, more like an apprenticeship model. In these instances the departments did not seem to have regular meetings with groups of students and instead thought it was the students' responsibility to complete their own work. In some cases the departments did require an annual review meeting where students meet with their dissertation committee, but even here the sole responsibility for determining and spurring progress was too often left in the hands of the dissertation advisor. More effective units delegated the primary responsibility to the advisor while providing a meaningful amount of oversight to the department.

Regarding sponsored research, the auditors found several different levels of activity. Some units were quite successful in obtaining grants, and sponsored research was embedded in their culture. Securing research funding was purposeful and based on faculty who had established grant programs with successive funding over many years. Yet even in these units, the primary funding was associated with a few faculty members—professors who had successful track records and explicit strategies to secure funding for their research and for their doctoral students.

In other departments the scholarship was excellent, but only a few members had obtained grant funding. These departments did not seem to have explicit strategies for enhancing sponsored research nor efforts to share the knowledge about how to increase funding with others in the department. In most such cases there was no real climate to support investigators' grant application and grant administration processes. Further, these units often did not have explicit buy-out processes in place, nor did they have explicit strategies for balancing the teaching and research efforts for faculty who obtained grants versus those who did not have the extra load of funded research.

In the domain of integrating research and scholarship with education, most departments focused their efforts on graduate students. Some departments had active programs where graduate students were involved with faculty research, where discussion of research was an integral part of classroom instruction, and where faculty assertively involved students in their papers and grants. The examples were not as systematic for undergraduate students. Certainly there were cases where talented individual undergraduate students were involved in research with faculty. But systematic attempts to integrate undergraduate students with faculty research were less obvious. The auditors found few if any strategies to ensure checks and balances were in place so that faculty research efforts did not undermine teaching effectiveness for undergraduates.

These observations should not be interpreted to mean that undergraduate instruction was slighted, nor that the combination of research and undergraduate education was not present in other campus units. It does suggest, however, that most departments focused their energy on integrating research and instruction at the graduate level. The difficulty with focusing more on undergraduates was balancing such efforts with an already demanding teaching and research load. Perhaps future academic audits will uncover departmental efforts that have been successful without overloading existing faculty commitments.

Combining the review of quality processes for research and scholarship with those focused on teaching and learning proved to be successful. We have been able to demonstrate that review teams can get a comprehensive picture of these two key departmental activities and how they relate to each other. The audits uncovered some issues that might not have been identified without examining research-related AQW. In most of the units that were reviewed, the auditors found competent faculty conducting their scholarship with successful results. Even so, the auditors also saw many examples where scholarship was a collection of individual efforts performed without departmental reinforcement. Even when the department's research environment was good, it may have been the result of happenstance rather than explicit and purposeful actions. The comprehensive audit allowed the review teams to identify areas where the research effort was uneven and where purposeful strategies could enhance the research results without increasing costs or demanding unrealistic amounts of faculty time.

In conclusion, reviewing research as a component of academic audit can be helpful to academic units where research is a critical component of their mission. The early audit experiences suggest that the most mature research units will have integrated research fully into their departmental culture. These units have focused their research efforts in areas that allow them to develop critical mass of talent and foster collaboration between faculty. Modeling this behavior with colleagues and graduate students provides a powerful message for graduate students, postdoctoral students, and new faculty members. These departments focus on new hires who will round out key research areas and thus build a level of expertise that allows the department to distinguish itself.

The exemplary units protect their successful research faculty from unnecessary administrative or committee assignments, with the tacit understanding that these faculty members will mentor new faculty members and graduate students to get them involved in grant-writing and national paper presentations where they can hone their skills. Further, when such departments focus their efforts they proactively build a network of recruiting connections in their critical areas instead of waiting until openings occur. Another exemplary strategy in mature research units is the purposeful integration of research with undergraduate instruction—which spurs undergraduate students' excitement as they learn about research in the discipline, the methods of examining research questions, and mental habits of successful researchers.

In less mature research environments the selection of faculty and their related research expertise can be more haphazard, based on individual interests rather than a departmental strategy. Professors are busy with their own research but in more independent ways, where they do not collaborate regularly with other faculty, share papers or ideas, or build on colleagues' successes. One good way for a department to develop its research prowess is to discuss the processes that can be used to promote research. Such discussions enable a department to become more systematic about creating a climate for research and integrating it into the mission rather than seeing research as an independent activity of individual faculty members.

Appendix: Concept-Defining Questions for Research

Research Outcomes

How does the department's research and scholarship compare to peer departments? What measures are used to gauge performance? What kinds of research outcomes, for what audiences, are judged to best suit the department's purposes? If the department has a doctoral program, what outcomes are sought? Does the department map the field's current and future priorities relative to its mission, and if so, how? Does it seek critical mass in particular areas?

- *Define quality in terms of outcomes.* How good is your department's research and scholarship? What types of publications, in what types of outlets, do you reward? Are you willing to consider other outcomes—for example, like those described in Boyer's *Scholarship Reconsidered*?
- *Focus on how things get done.* How did you select your peer departments and the departments you are trying to emulate? Do you have a departmental plan for improving research outcomes, or is improvement left to individual faculty?
- *Work collaboratively.* Do you encourage faculty to collaborate with each other and with doctoral students, or is research generally a lone-wolf activity? Does the department care about interdisciplinary research, and if so, how are interdisciplinary linkages being fostered? Do you have a good working relationship with the campus research office?
- *Base decisions on evidence.* What indicators do you use to track the department's overall research performance, and what does the evidence tell you? Have you consulted nationally recognized external scholars about outcomes and indicators? Who are your peer departments, and what departments can you reasonably expect to catch up with? How have the data affected your decision-making?
- *Strive for coherence.* Are the department's desired research outcomes consistent with the abilities and interests of the faculty? Are they compatible with campus goals and other departmental goals? Do research outcomes systematically inform other departmental efforts—for example, mentoring doctoral students and new faculty?
- *Learn from best practice.* Have you checked with other successful units on campus or elsewhere in the country to examine their outcomes and performance measures? Do you contact outside experts to identify successful practices?

- *Make continuous improvement a priority.* Do you reconsider your desired research outcomes systematically and regularly? Does anyone else in the university encourage you to do so?

Research Environment

Does the department have a vibrant research environment? What steps does it take to stimulate such an environment? Does the department or university provide researchers with technical, administrative, and seed money support? To what extent does the department help junior faculty develop their research programs and more senior faculty adapt theirs to current conditions?

- *Define quality in terms of outcomes.* What would a suitable research environment in your kind of department look like? Do you plan for achieving or maintaining this kind of environment?
- *Focus on how things get done.* Do faculty reflect on ways to improve the department's research environment, and does the department act on the results? For example, does it offer research seminars and research paper series? Does it assist faculty with proposal development, gaining institutional approvals, managing grants, and so forth? Are service centers and other support organizations well managed? Are there organized processes for counseling faculty on promotion and tenure criteria?
- *Work collaboratively.* Do the faculty consult together on the department's research environment? Do they regularly discuss their research aspirations, strategies, processes, and frustrations with colleagues? Does the university listen when faculty frustrations are described? Do experienced faculty coauthor grant proposals and papers with new faculty?
- *Base decisions on evidence.* What indicators do you use to evaluate the research environment? Are these well aligned with your desired research outcomes? What are the key outcomes indicators for faculty development? Do these apply to mid-career faculty members as well as fresh PhDs? By what measures do you gauge success?
- *Strive for coherence.* Is your research environment consistent with desired outcomes? With hiring decisions? With resources? To

what extent do faculty development activities promote the department's research goals and strategies?

- *Learn from best practice.* How do peer departments maintain and improve their research environments and faculty mentoring? What measures do they use to gauge progress? Have you adopted any such practices?
- *Make continuous improvement a priority.* Do you reconsider your research environment and faculty development systematically and regularly? Does anyone else in the university encourage you to do so?

Sponsored Projects

How does the department's sponsored research, if any, compare to peer departments? How effectively does it support principal investigators in their proposal writing and project management? To what extent does the department or university support principal investigators with space, cost-sharing, reduced teaching loads, technician and shop time, and the like?

- *Define quality in terms of outcomes.* What are the key outcomes indicators for sponsored research? Are they trending upward or downward? Are the faculty members clear on the goals set for research funding? What would constitute successful funding efforts?
- *Focus on how things get done.* Does the department have a specific plan to expand sponsored research funding? Does the department or college have an infrastructure in place to help faculty secure funding?
- *Work collaboratively.* Are funded researchers working with other faculty to help them secure funding? Do faculty work with colleagues across disciplines to secure funding? Do faculty work collaboratively to secure funding?
- *Base decisions on evidence.* How is the department doing in relation to other departments on campus and in peer departments across the country? What evidence do you collect, and how do you use it?

- *Strive for coherence.* Is outside funding a high priority? If it is, do you have explicit strategies for increasing such funding? How do sponsored projects support other departmental efforts?
- *Learn from best practice.* Do you know what other departments on campus do to enhance research funding? Do you regularly discuss such funding options?
- *Make continuous improvement a priority.* Do you reconsider your sponsored research program systematically and regularly? Does anyone else in the university encourage you to do so?

Doctoral Training

How good is the department's doctoral program, if there is one, relative to peer programs? What evidence is used to make this judgment? How good is the program's student intake, graduation percentage, time to degree, graduate placement, and (if applicable) national rankings? How do faculty train and mentor students on research and teaching skills, and how do they track progress toward the degree?

- *Define quality in terms of outcomes.* What are graduates expected to do, and where are they expected to go—for example, academe, industry, government? Are these goals understood by all or most of the faculty? Are your goals consistent with campus goals? How do you track what actually happens?
- *Focus on how things get done.* Does the department have a deep understanding of how doctoral training should work in your field? Do you act on this knowledge? How do your doctoral students contribute to the department's teaching and research programs? How do you ensure that they are not exploited?
- *Work collaboratively.* Do doctoral students work closely with faculty on research and teaching? Do they work with each other? To what extent do doctoral students coauthor papers with faculty members?
- *Base decisions on evidence.* What evidence do you have that the department doctoral program is successful? What is your graduates' employment history? How do you stay in touch with alumni, and what do you learn from them? What do you do with the results?

- *Strive for coherence.* How is the doctoral program integrated with the department's overall research and teaching goals? What fraction of faculty are engaged in doctoral training? To what extent is your program different from other doctoral programs on campus, and are there good reasons for any differences?
- *Learn from best practice.* What does a successful doctoral program in your field look like? How do you learn from such exemplars? What are the most innovative doctoral programs on your campus doing, and how are you learning from them?
- *Make continuous improvement a priority.* Do you reconsider your doctoral program systematically and regularly? Does anyone else in the university encourage you to do so?

Synergy With Education

How does the department's research and scholarship contribute to its educational programs? To what extent are undergraduates involved in research, and how does research benefit those who are not directly involved? How does the department gauge the benefits of faculty research on graduate and professional education (other than doctoral training)? How does it ensure that time spent on research does not undermine teaching effectiveness and education quality improvement?

- *Define quality in terms of outcomes.* Do you have specific outcomes in mind when considering the contributions of research to teaching? (Or do you rely on the general proposition that "good research begets good teaching"?) Do your desired outcomes reflect the needs of all or most students, or mainly those who share the faculty's research interests?
- *Focus on how things get done.* Do you reflect on the ways research contributes to teaching? Do you act on the results of these reflections?
- *Work collaboratively.* Do faculty work together on improving the contributions of research to teaching, or is this left mostly to individual initiative? Do faculty in your department hold each other accountable for such improvements?

- *Base decisions on evidence.* How do you gauge the contribution of research to teaching? What are the most successful efforts to do so, who is doing them, and can they be generalized? Have you systematically searched for evidence about how research might detract from teaching? Have you consciously tried to mitigate such effects?

- *Strive for coherence.* How do the linkages between research and teaching contribute to your department's overall success? How well do they align with campus goals?

- *Learn from best practice.* What do truly successful contributions of research to teaching in your field look like? How do you learn from these examples? What are the most innovative departments on your campus doing, and how are you learning from them?

- *Make continuous improvement a priority.* Do you reconsider the synergy of your research program systematically and regularly? Does anyone else in the university encourage you to do so?

8

Campus Audits and Continuous Improvement

So far we have focused on academic audit at the department level. This was appropriate for several reasons. First, that's where the primary business of quality work takes place. Second, introducing audit at the department level is easier than at the campus or institutional level because departments are smaller and less complex, and also because one need find only a few volunteer departments in a large institution to start a pilot program. Third, and most relevant for the subject of this chapter, campus- and institution-level audits use departmental audit processes as building blocks.

Shifting one's focus to address quality work above the department level, discussed at the end of Chapter 3, represents the essential first move toward campus or institutional audit. Changes to the audit process itself involve the logistics of the audit visit and how the self-studies and audit reports address the different levels of quality work. The steps of the audit process, the focal areas of quality work, the quality principles, and the maturity definitions translate to campus- or institution-level audits essentially unchanged.

Organizing a Campus Audit Program

Academic audit can be initiated by anyone in the chain of academic responsibility or institutional oversight. Earlier chapters described how senior academic officers organized department-level audit programs. Although these programs were initiated well up the organizational hierarchy, the audited units were individual departments. Because higher-level audit programs focus on quality work above the department level, the audited units must be schools, campuses, or university systems. For example:

- The dean of a large school audits the AQW of departments.
- The provost of a large campus audits the schools' AQW.
- The academic vice president of a university system audits the campuses' AQW.
- A government higher education oversight body or quality agency audits the universities' AQW.
- An institutional or discipline-specific accreditation agency includes audit of AQW in its accreditation program.

We propose the axiom that quality work above the department level focuses on improving and assuring quality work at the next lower level. Hence the effectiveness of quality work at the next lower level provides evidence about effectiveness at the higher level. For example, effectiveness at the decanal level offers insight into the provost's quality work. It's possible, of course, that decanal effectiveness stems from local initiative. But even so, the provost should know about it and be visibly supportive—which can easily be checked during, say, a campus-level audit by an academic vice president or external quality agency. This axiom provides the basis for triangulating evidence from multiple levels in a campus or institutional audit.

University trustees and regents have a key role to play in AQW—one that's usually conspicuous by its absence. The role is very simple: Trustees and regents must ask their academic vice president or provost about the institution's AQW and keep asking until meaningful answers are forthcoming. Board members may not have sufficient academic background to understand the answers in detail, but, like departmental academic auditors who cross disciplinary lines, they can distinguish deeply informed answers from superficial ones. Simply asking the questions and not being satisfied with superficial answers may send a sufficient signal. And in the end, boards can hold the president accountable for ensuring that the institution's chief academic officer gives quality work the attention it deserves.

Academic audit is just one way of focusing attention on quality work but, as the material in earlier chapters amply demonstrates, it is a good one. To organize an audit, one implements the six steps set forth in Chapter 4: preparatory workshops, self-studies, selection and training of auditors, audit visits, audit reports, and follow-up. We will review each step briefly to highlight the differences between department- and higher-level audits.

Preparatory Workshops

Because the objectives of academic audit are mostly formative, it is essential to engage academics at all levels from the beginning. Workshops, with their active-learning components, provide a good vehicle for doing this. As for department-level audits, the workshops aim to broaden the participants' perspectives about AQW—particularly the five focal areas and seven quality principles. The prospect of self-studies and audit visits gives salience to the proceedings initially, but it's intrinsic interest in the subject matter that carries the day. The nuts and bolts of audit come up almost as afterthoughts—"here's what you can expect six to nine months hence." The workshop typically lasts one day, with the morning being devoted to presentations by one or more experts on quality work followed by general discussion and the afternoon devoted to processing the ideas in small groups, debriefing, and considering next steps.

Whether a campus should have one or several such workshops depends on local circumstances. The important thing is to involve enough people to create excitement about quality work and the audit program. Participants should include a cross-section of academic officers (e.g., deans and chairs), people on quality committees and in quality improvement units, and rank-and-file faculty. The audit sponsor (e.g., provost or academic vice president) or a senior delegate should participate actively. Preparatory workshops should be conducted before each new audit round. Although they get easier as more people become familiar with academic audit and quality work, the prospect of a new round provides an opportunity to renew interest, refresh understanding, and involve new people—an opportunity that should not be missed.

Chapter 5 described the introductory workshops at the department level in Missouri and the regional level in Tennessee. Other entities might choose a different structure—for example, workshops for individual schools or, for a very large campus, a university-level workshop followed by school-level workshops. The important thing is to involve the participants in active discussions about quality work. Sending a memo simply won't do the job. For Hong Kong's initial implementation of audit, preparation consisted of a two-hour meeting on each of the University Grants Committee's (then) seven campuses. Although some of the aforementioned objectives were met, the lack of active participation imposed a price on the subsequent audit steps. The University Grants Committee learned from experience, however, and the second audit round included provision for more on-campus discussions of quality work.

Self-Studies

Self-studies provide opportunities for reflection on one's quality work and the possibilities for improving it. For audits above the department level, the question is who should do the reflection and be responsible for the self-study document. The answer usually is some kind of quality committee—for example, a standing committee on academic quality that reports to, and often is chaired by, the provost or dean. Ad hoc committees like those appointed to handle institutional accreditation reviews are less effective because they lack ongoing responsibility. (It's hard to reflect on the activities of others without coming across as judgmental.) The quality committee should be viewed as an extension of the administration for purposes of the self-study because its reflections must include the work of the relevant academic officers.

The self-study should address four kinds of commonsense questions—questions that deal with commitment, information, action, and accountability with respect to AQW:

- What is the entity's understanding of and commitment to AQW? What priority is given to quality work, and how is that priority affirmed and communicated?
- How does the entity inform itself about quality work at lower levels in the organization? Are all five focal areas considered explic-

itly? To what extent do the seven quality principles drive the search for information and the evaluation of results? Has the entity made judgments about the maturity of AQW for each unit that reports to it, and if so, how?

- What actions has the entity taken to improve AQW maturity in the units that report to it? What kinds of action is it prepared to take if units fail to give quality work an appropriate priority? Has the commitment to action been communicated?

- To what extent does the person to which the entity reports care about AQW? What information is communicated upward, and what feedback, if any, is forthcoming? To what extent does the entity feel accountable for its quality work?

Potential skeptics should note that there's nothing bureaucratic about these questions. There are no required procedures or forms to fill out. The questions are simply what one would ask if one *really wanted to know* what's being done to improve and assure AQW. Because well-trained auditors will ask just such questions, it's important that they be considered carefully in the self-study.

Selection and Training of Auditors

Little more needs to be said about the selection and training of auditors. We explained in Chapter 6 why the auditors need not come from the same discipline as the unit being audited, and indeed that is crucial for audits that focus on a whole campus or institution. Augmentation of auditors' training with material on quality work above the level of departments and the self-study questions discussed in the previous section are the only change from department-level auditing.

That auditors propagate the ideas and best practices of quality work is especially important in campus and institutional audits. One should select the audit teams with this in mind. Campus audits can draw from other campuses in the system and institutional audits from other universities, regardless of whether the home entities have been audited or, indeed, whether they have officially endorsed the audit program. The Tennessee Board of Regents included all 18 of its campuses in its auditor selection pool, for instance, even though only 12 campuses participated in the first-round project. Likewise, Hong Kong's University

Grants Committee (UGC) used people from all of its campuses. The UGC had an "intact panel," the same for all institutions—people from the campus being visited simply crossed over to the institutional side of the table for the duration of that visit.

Hong Kong used an additional device to propagate the ideas of quality work and audit around the system: the so-called consultative committee. The committee consisted of two senior faculty members or administrators from each institution who bore significant responsibility for teaching and learning quality. (Examples included vice chancellors for academic affairs and chairs of quality committees.) Many, though not all, also served as auditors. The committee's official assignment was to advise the UGC's audit working group on all aspects of the emergent program. However, its members also served as ambassadors and propagators of best practice within their institutions.

Audit Visits

Campus and institutional audit visits can be done in as few as two days, but three produces better coverage. They typically begin with the campus head and chief academic officer, often in concert with the immediate staffs. Interviews with campus-level committees that bear a particular responsibility for academic quality and representative groups of students usually follow. As in the case of departmental audits, these meetings take place in plenary sessions.

The scope of campus and institutional audits requires the rest of the audit visit to be structured differently from department-level audits. First and foremost, it is not sufficient to limit coverage to the campus or institution's upper-level administrators and committees. The auditors must verify the respondents' assertions and trace the influence of their actions and policies through the organization. This requires interviews and document review at all levels, right down to departments. We'll address three overarching design considerations here: 1) attaining coverage by taking a sample of operating units, 2) increasing sample size by splitting the audit panel, and 3) tracking flows of influence through "audit trailing." The visit schedule will be covered later.

Sample of operating units. Because large campuses may have a dozen schools and many dozens of academic departments, visiting all such units is clearly impossible. The answer, of course, is to select a sample of units to visit. The units usually are drawn from the following sampling frame:

- Schools ("faculties" in some institutions)
- Academic departments within each school
- Special units, like teaching improvement and research offices, that bear a particular responsibility for academic quality

Units selected for the sample are asked to prepare a one-page "talking paper" about their quality work. The paper is used as a conversation starter, not as a definitive description of the unit's activities. Except for the special units, which are sure to be included, sample selection should be deferred until a few weeks before the visit. This is enough lead time for producing the talking paper, and no other preparation is required. Deferring sample selection ensures that all units will take the audit seriously until the last moment.

Splitting the audit panel. Opinions differ about whether all interviews need to be conducted by the whole audit panel. The advantage of doing so is that all members share the same body of experience. The disadvantage, of course, is that keeping the panel together reduces the number of interviews and thus coverage of the sampling frame. Australia's institutional audit program, discussed at the end of this chapter, does not subdivide its panels. Hong Kong's academic audit program did subdivide its panels, and this is the approach we favor. We describe a way to mitigate the shortfall in shared experience when discussing the audit schedule.

There are compelling reasons for the whole panel to interview the senior officers and campus-level committees. Two- or three-member subgroups, with one of each being designated as convener, strike us as being reasonable for the other interviews. Again, one must balance coverage with the number of people listening and interacting with the interviewees. Two persons are the minimum if for no other reason than that one person can take the lead on asking questions while the other focuses more on note-taking. Three persons, the number generally used in Hong Kong, provide more interactivity. An added benefit is that the subgroup remains viable if one person can't participate in a particular session. The same considerations apply to department-level audits as discussed in Chapter 6, but there the coverage trade-off is less pressing.

Audit trailing. The term *audit trailing,* a somewhat distasteful term, was coined by the United Kingdom's academic audit unit to describe the tracking of approval and accountability chains from senior administrators or campus-level committees to the department level. The emphasis was on documented audit trails—whether committee decisions were properly minuted or whether adherence to them was formally demonstrated by departmental paper trails. The inevitable result was that many academics came to view audit trailing as a distraction—necessary, perhaps, for bureaucratic reasons but not a value-adding activity. Paraphrasing Professor Higgins in *My Fair Lady,* skeptics were heard to mutter, "The auditors don't care what we do, exactly, as long as we document it correctly."

Our brand of audit trailing eschews formality. It concentrates on the *flows of influence* between organizational units. This is consistent with Chapter 3's definition of *quality work* above the department level: "Each tier seeks to spur improvement in quality work at the level directly beneath it." Audit trailing seeks to ascertain whether this objective is being met. The auditors still follow trails, but they consider all kinds of evidence. Documented accountability represents a kind of evidence, but so does testimony from the lower-level units and data about the decisions they make and how they make them. The emphasis is on what is really happening, not on bureaucratic formalities.

Hong Kong's design selected sample units with an eye to audit trailing. For example, the departments sampled tended to cluster within the sampled faculties so that flows of decanal influence could be ascertained. (Because each faculty reported to the chief academic officer, that link in the chain of influence could be examined as well.) Special units like teaching improvement offices were always interviewed, and questions about their influence were included in the departmental interviews. This approach of hierarchical sampling and reciprocal questioning ensures a threshold level of visibility about flows of influence.

There is another approach, however, one that is more akin to conventional document-based audit trailing. Conventional trailing identifies a few key quality-related decisions during preparation for or during the audit visit and then requests documents related to those decisions. The auditors follow the trail wherever it leads, often requesting additional documents and perhaps interviews as they go. Such flexibility allows in-depth study of a few events—including some that were identified during the course of the audit itself.

But there is no need to focus on documentation. Instead of "following the paper" one can "follow the influence." All that's necessary is to allow time in the visit schedule when the auditors can request additional interviews, and documentation as appropriate, to trail the impact of particularly interesting policies or decisions. We know of no instance where this feature has been used in a purely academic audit, but it is consistent with Australia's approach to auditing institutional management. Combining it with hierarchical sampling and reciprocal questioning will produce a paradigm that is both powerful and flexible.

Audit Reports

The process of preparing audit reports is similar to that for accreditation and program review reports. The panel chair or an embedded staff member from the organizing body writes the first draft. A semifinished draft goes to the whole panel, perhaps with requests for special attention by panel members who followed certain areas during plenary sessions or served on particular subgroups. A penultimate draft goes to the campus for correcting factual errors and commenting on clarity.

Two features do differentiate an audit report, however. One stems from the fact that subpanels interview a sample of operating units. The interviews produce examples of good and bad practice—indeed, that is their purpose, and it would be illogical never to refer to such examples in the audit report. However, there are two reasons why it isn't fair to cite the identified shortfalls in what should be a public document. First, such shortfalls were identified by a small subset of panel members based on one interview with a few faculty and students. Second, the sample wasn't designed to give all units the same chance to be cited for good or bad performance. The result is a set of examples with sufficient collective reliability to inform the audit panel's overall conclusions but not enough individual reliability to put a particular unit in the hot seat. In addition to basic fairness, assuring the sampled units that their warts won't be publicized makes uninhibited conversations easier to attain.

For this reason it's best to disguise the names of units in citing examples, especially those describing bad performance. Exemplars may be identified, but this should be the exception rather than the rule. Generally speaking, key people on the campus will infer enough of the details to make their own inquiries and take action if necessary, but singling out particular units is not the panel's job. Sometimes a unit will recognize itself in the audit report and take action on its own.

A second difference from program review is that, to achieve full effectiveness, the audit reports should be made public. Transparency furthers improvement, and not only because the private reports produce less incentive for change than public ones. To effect improvement, campus leaders need to communicate the audit's findings to those they are attempting to influence—for example, deans, department chairs, quality committee members, and influential faculty members. Disseminating a report widely within the campus almost surely means it will become public, so it's better to preempt any suggestion of a cover-up by making the report public at the outset. In Hong Kong, for example, the UGC insisted that the campuses publish the audit reports along with their comments and the kinds of improvements planned. Publication serves to extend the conversation about quality work, which is a prime goal of the academic audit process.

Follow-Up Activities

The objectives of follow-up activities are no different in principle from those for department-level audits, and they are no less important. They are 1) to debrief the audit process in order to effect improvements the next time around; 2) to help propagate the ideas of AQW and the purposes of academic audit throughout the institution; and 3) to share best practices in teaching, support of research and scholarship, and AQW itself.

Achieving these objectives requires a two-stage approach. The first stage involves one or more sessions attended by "audit insiders" for debriefing and consideration of improvements. (By *insiders* we mean audit chairs, interested rank-and-file auditors, and a cross-section of people from the audited departments.) The second stage involves sessions with broader participation. Possibilities span the range from large conferences to workshop series that are designed to deepen understanding about AQW and share best practices in teaching, learning, and research support.

Campus Visit Schedule

We noted earlier that campus and institutional audit visits can be done in as few as two days, but that three produces better coverage. We'll describe the basic two-day visit because that's where the schedule is most binding.

Suppose the audit panel numbers 10 people, the subgroups have 2 people each (so there are 5 subgroups total), and four time slots in a two-day visit are set aside for subgroup meetings. This allows 20 separate sessions, which will provide an acceptable degree of coverage. Longer visits or larger panels, as might be fielded if the audit covers both teaching and research, open the way for 3-member subgroups. Hong Kong fielded an 18-member panel but limited the visit to one and a half days, which allowed only three time slots for subgroup meetings. This permitted 18 sessions, which turned out to be just sufficient for the larger institutions.

First Day

Table 8.1 shows a typical schedule for the first day of the audit visit. It assumes coverage of both teaching and research. (The "Research and Scholarship" column should be ignored for teaching-only audits.) Plenary sessions are indicated by merging the two columns. The time durations are indicative only, and coffee breaks are not shown. Chairs may want to consider assigning certain lines of questioning in the plenary sessions to particular people, to ensure they are covered in a coherent way. Also not shown are the working dinners usually scheduled for panel members the evening before the visit and after the first day. The dinners provide time for panelists to compare notes and plan the following day's activities. Such planning is very important.

Table 8.1 **First Day of a Two-Day Teaching/Research Audit Visit**

	Teaching and Learning	Research and Scholarship	Duration
1.	Audit panel in executive session to prepare and look at documents		30 min
2.	Campus head and chief academic officer and their senior staff		45 min
3.	Key committee responsible for education quality	Key committee responsible for research quality	60 min
4.	Key senior academic officer responsible for education quality	Key senior academic officer responsible for research quality	30 min
5.	Students from undergraduate and professional programs	Research students	30 min
6.	Lunch in executive session to process the morning's discussions, look at documents, and prepare for the afternoon session		60 min
7.	Small group sessions	Small group sessions	120 min
8.	Small group sessions	Small group sessions	120 min
9.	Executive session to compare notes on the afternoon sessions		30 min

Session 1 allows panel members to acquaint themselves with the institution, look at the documents provided in the panel room, and process any ideas that emerged overnight. Aside from welcoming formalities, the purpose of Session 2 is to gauge senior management's understanding of and commitment to quality work. Session 3 provides more detailed descriptions, but there is no need to reiterate material already read by the auditors. Although Sessions 2 and 3 typically open with short statements, the presenters should be instructed to keep their comments short—say, to 10 minutes maximum. The importance of this cannot be overstated because the tendency is to describe things in too much detail and thus preclude effective dialogue. The panel chair should politely but firmly stop a presentation that is running long. Important factual material should be included in the self-study or, if necessary, in a supplementary memo to the panel provided at least a few days before the visit. Neither the auditors nor the respondents should forget that the purpose of the visit is structured conversation, not the transmission of facts.

Choosing the committees for Session 3 can pose a problem. The job is easy if, like an increasing number of campuses, this one has created committees with specific responsibility for quality improvement and assurance—as opposed to or in addition to academic policy. If no such committees exit, the curriculum and research policy committees that can be found on most campuses will suffice.

Choosing the academic officers responsible for quality (Session 4) usually poses less of a problem. Associate provosts for undergraduate education, for instance, carry an implicit, if not explicit, quality portfolio. The same is true for the principal research officer. Normally these officers will be members of or staff to the committee met with in Session 3, but they should still be present at this session. One of the purposes of Session 4 is to determine the line officer's view of committee performance and what might be done to improve it.

Session 5 gives the panel an overview of quality work from the student perspective. Typically there are 15 to 20 students in attendance, some from the student government structure and some who have signed up in response to a call for volunteers. Although students aren't privy to most of the faculty's quality work, they do have visibility on some crucial aspects of it. For example, are they consulted on important course design questions involving learning behavior? Do professors seek their feedback and then act on the results? Usually these sessions produce more hypotheses for follow-up in the later sessions than they do definitive answers, but they are important nevertheless.

Session 6 provides panel members with lunch and an opportunity to compare notes and process the morning's findings. Because this time turns out to be very important, one should resist the campus organizer's natural tendency to host a formal luncheon with many faculty and staff in attendance. Such sessions do provide opportunities for conversation, but the cost in terms of the panel's ability to lead *structured* conversations is too high. A large luncheon might fit during a three-day visit, however—say, on the second day.

The afternoon is devoted to small group sessions where two- or three-member subpanels meet with groups of 10 to 15 faculty and students from schools, departments, and support units—that is, units sampled as described earlier. Departmental respondents will include the chair, faculty with assigned responsibilities for quality, a cross-section of faculty mainstays in teaching or research, and a representative group of students. School respondents include the dean, key associate deans(s), and student and faculty representatives from relevant committees.

Students generally compose one-quarter to one-third of the group. It's not uncommon for them to remain silent during the panelists' discussions with faculty, though the convener should try to draw them out wherever possible. Such reticence can be mitigated by having the students remain after the main session and asking them something like, "Does the conversation you just heard ring true? What's your take on the department's commitment to sustaining and improving quality?"

The two hours allotted for each small group session allow up to 75 minutes for the main conversation, 10 or 15 minutes for a post-session with the students, and half an hour for comparing notes, looking at documents, and organizing for the next session. These small group sessions compose the core of the audit visit. They're where panelists can really find out what's happening and trace the flows of influence from one level to another. Top-level officers and committees generally have a rosy view of the campus's quality work, but such views may or may not be borne out at the grassroots. Also, knowing that a cross-section of operating units will be interviewed causes people at the higher levels to take the audit more seriously. Some go so far as to stage mock audit conversations with a cross-section of departments. (They can't target the departments to be audited because the selection isn't made until the last minute.) In addition to preparing for the audit, such conversations help propagate the idea of quality work and thus further the audit's formative agenda.

The final session of the day allows panelists to compare notes on the small group sessions while the ideas are still fresh in their minds. This session merges into the working dinner at which the whole day is recapped and plans are made for the following day. Depending on logistics, it may be desirable to extend the session to include the recap and planning at the campus venue, which leaves the dinner free for informal discussion. Australia's audits, known for the intensity of the auditors' working experience, continue the closing sessions for up to several hours—followed by a relaxed dinner.

Second Day

The schedule for the second day is described in Table 8.2. After a short warm-up, the panel continues with small group sessions. The sessions

Table 8.2 **Second Day of a Two-Day Teaching/Research Audit**

	Teaching and Learning	Research and Scholarship	Duration
1.	Audit panel in executive session to prepare and look at documents		15 min
2.	Small group sessions	Small group sessions	120 min
3.	Small group sessions	Small group sessions	120 min
4.	Lunch in executive session to process the morning's discussions, look at documents, and prepare for the afternoon session		45 min
5.	Meeting with the deans as a group		45 min
6.	Follow-up on audit trails	Follow-up on audit trails	60 min
7.	Executive session to prepare for the exit conference		90 min
8.	Exit conference with the campus head and those who attended the opening session		30 min
9.	Executive session to recap the exit conference and finalize writing assignments		30 min

are debriefed over lunch, which affords an opportunity to prepare for an early afternoon meeting with the deans and the audit-trailing interviews that were discussed earlier. The deans' meeting (Session 5) emerged in Hong Kong's second round as a key element of the audit. Although some deans already will have been interviewed in the small group sessions, this session interviews them as a group. Panelists can ask for comparisons across schools and determine whether the deans talk among themselves about quality work. Another test is how the provost treats AQW at one-on-one meetings and the deans' council. Because the deans are critical for embedding a culture of quality work in academic departments, this session often is the most revealing of the audit visit.

The panel then retires to an executive session to structure its conclusions and prepare for the exit conference. The small group conveners are asked to report on their sessions if they have not done so in earlier debriefings. These reports mitigate the difficulties associated with subdividing the panel, and it's not unusual for overall audit conclusions to emerge during the course of reporting. From this point things follow the familiar accreditation and program review pattern. Preliminary conclusions are aired at the exit conference (Session 8), and after a short wrap-up session the panel departs.

Adding a Third Day

An extra day frees up the audit program considerably, though at the cost of an even more intensive experience for the auditors. Several features can be added to the audit program. The first priority is to add at least one more round of small group sessions. Other possibilities include a second slot for meetings with quality-related committees and a second slot for audit trailing. Yet another would be to adopt the Australian practice of "walk-about." Although panelists don't disappear into the bush for a month or two of contemplation, they do fan out to different areas of the campus, knock spontaneously on faculty doors, and engage the respondents in brief conversations about quality work. Sixty to 90 minutes spent this way can reveal much about the degree to which AQW ideas have permeated the faculty and whether the reaction has been positive.

The third day also can allow for additional debriefing time and a longer session to prepare for the exit conference. Depending on what's been added, the panel's workdays can be slightly shortened as well.

Campus Audits Internationally

Hong Kong, Sweden, Denmark, New Zealand, Australia, and the United Kingdom provide examples of how audit's introduction can change the academic environment (Massy, 2003c, Chapter 8). We'll illustrate the motivation and approach using Hong Kong's experience (Massy, 1997; Massy & French, 2001) and add material from Sweden (Massy, 2000), Denmark, New Zealand, and Australia where it provides extra insight. Although none of these early adopters of audit implemented the methodology exactly as recommended in this book, the spirit and general approach are similar.

Hong Kong's UGC began its comprehensive quality evaluation program in the early 1990s. The UGC is a quasigovernmental body that funds and oversees the territory's eight higher education institutions. (Government funds about 80% of the institutions' budgets.) Hong Kong's universities are self-accrediting in the sense that they can determine their own curricula, but the UGC is responsible for quality overall. In U.S. parlance, the UGC functions as a "strong" higher education coordinating board because of its influence on funding. Antony Leong, then chair of the UGC and later the territory's financial secretary, recognized soon after taking office that public stewardship required performance measurement and that this would become ever more important as Hong Kong transitioned to become part of China in 1997.

The UGC's first foray into quality evaluation took the form of a research assessment exercise (RAE), patterned after a similar exercise in the United Kingdom, wherein every department's percentage of research-active faculty was evaluated by peer review panels (French, Ko, Massy, Siu, & Young, 1999; French, Massy, & Young, 2001). Installing qualitative research assessment triggered a massive shift of attention from teaching to research—a perfect example of the academic ratchet in action (Zemsky & Massy, 1990). Better research spurred improvements in faculty and infrastructure that benefited education quality. However, the UGC was concerned that the shift would move past the point of diminishing returns. Something had to be done to arrest the ratchet before it could undermine the quality of education. That something was the Teaching and Learning Quality Process Review (TLQPR), which we identify as a form of academic audit.

The UGC had known for several years that some type of education quality evaluation would be necessary. Fortunately Hong Kong's need coincided with the emergence of education quality work as a coherent concept. To date the UGC has conducted two rounds of academic audit.

Sweden's academic audit program emerged from events in the late 1980s, when the country concluded that centralized regulation could not spur quality improvement and efficiency. As institutions became more autonomous, professors were asked to take full responsibility for their work and its results, and institutional self-regulation came to be viewed as necessary for continual development: "Universities [were] expected continuously to follow up and evaluate their own activities and take action on the basis of the results" (Wahlén, 1998, p. 28). That, of course, left accountability issues up in the air.

The dominant university viewpoint held that an "invisible hand" would produce education quality as long as research quality could be maintained. Starting in 1993, however, Minister of Education Per Unckel and newly appointed University Chancellor (and former Stanford professor and Silicon Valley executive) Stig Hagström challenged this view. Staffan Wahlén (1998), coordinator of the Quality Audit Programme for the university chancellor, described their agenda:

> Each institution was responsible for maintaining and improving the quality of its own activities, and was accountable to the Government and society for this. [One can say] that universities and colleges have always been quality-driven. What has now been added ... is that they must have (and demonstrate that they have) systematic improvement processes regarding undergraduate education, graduate education, research, and administration. They are required to develop routines for reflecting on their activities, and make corrections wherever necessary for the sound improvement of the institution. (p. 35)

The academic audit program, which began in 1996, sought to verify that institutions were carrying out the education portion of this agenda.

In New Zealand comprehensive academic quality audits of all universities were carried out over the period 1995–1998 by the country's academic audit unit, or AAU (Meade & Woodhouse, 2000). The audits sought to enhance education quality work, strengthen institutional quality improvement units, boost benchmarking, encourage thorough program-level reviews, and stimulate more discriminating use of performance indicators. To keep the process fresh and relevant, the second cycle of audits focused on a smaller number of factors: one selected (system-wide) by the AAU, and one in each individual institution, selected by the institution.

Australia began its audit program circa 2000, when David Woodhouse was recruited from New Zealand to the Australian Universities Quality Agency (AUQA) in Melbourne. The audits involve more than AQW—indeed, they might better be called "management" or "comprehensive" audits. The program is highly regarded for its relevance and thoroughness. Massy and Short have served as AUQA auditors and benefited greatly from the experience. Space limitations preclude our describing the details for the Australian audit process, but some of its best-practice elements were introduced earlier.

Denmark's higher education evaluation agency piloted academic audit at two universities during 2004, an experiment that was generally regarded as successful. (Massy chaired the audit panel for the University of Copenhagen.) It's interesting to note that the idea of shifting from external program evaluation to academic audit was initiated by the Danish Parliament.

We would be remiss not to mention academic audits in the United Kingdom, where the term originated circa 1990. The history is complex, however, and we can sketch it only briefly. The audit idea came from the Committee of Vice Chancellors and Principals (CVCP), an organization roughly equivalent to the American Council on Education (ACE) or AAU, as an alternative to the government's scheme for comprehensive program evaluation. Called "subject-level evaluation," the latter scheme aimed to evaluate the delivered quality of education in every academic department in every university. The evaluations were labor intensive and intrusive. For example, panelists would assess curricula and sit in classes to evaluate the quality of teaching. Worst of all, they disempowered the local academics. Why develop one's own quality assessment methods when evaluators from the funding council will come in and override them? Academic audit, in contrast, places all such responsibilities squarely in the laps of the university and its departments. The reviewers' job was to check the locals' quality work, not do it for them.

The CVCP and the funding council ran the two systems in parallel for a number of years to a growing volume of complaints about waste and duplication. Audit's prospects weren't helped by its reputation, which we alluded to earlier, as a paper-intensive and bureaucratic exercise. In the late 1990s the two approaches were combined in a new Quality Assurance Agency (QAA). Subject-level evaluation was given primacy by the new agency, which caused the level of intrusiveness to increase. Things came to a head in the spring of 2001, when the heads of the United Kingdom's most prestigious institutions (the so-called Russell Group) laid down an ultimatum: reform the QAA or group members would refuse to be evaluated and take the matter to Parliament.

The result was a change of management at QAA and the positioning of academic audit as the United Kingdom's primary review method, with subject-level evaluation reserved for institutions that failed to do well on the audit. The emphasis has fluctuated somewhat since, but audit seems to have retained its primacy.

Finally, in a late-breaking development, Australia and Hong Kong are working to revise their audit processes to place more emphasis on standards and metrics. In Australia, for instance, greater emphasis will be placed on institutional standards, benchmarking activities, and their consequent impact. The second-round audits will investigate how academic standards (such as those relating to student assessment, student progress, graduate attributes, and research) are determined, applied, maintained, and monitored. The institution will be asked to supply auditable evidence about the extent to which these standards are met and (as appropriate) the institution's assessment of its comparative national and international performance. We see this as a logical extension of the ideas presented in this book and look forward to making these areas of emphasis more explicit in our own audit work.

The National Consortium for Continuous Improvement

We pointed out in Chapter 1 that continuous improvement is a defining feature of AQW and that getting such processes started is a central objective of academic audit. Much of the material in subsequent chapters addresses continuous improvement in one way or another. However, we'd be remiss to suggest that our work represents the only serious effort to stimulate academic continuous improvement. Such improvement is the hallmark of the research enterprise at many institutions. Moreover, initiatives are under way to broaden its penetration across large areas related to institutional effectiveness.

As a growing number of colleges and universities seek new approaches to addressing challenges related to institutional effectiveness, they are increasingly turning to the National Consortium for Continuous Improvement in Higher Education (NCCI, and to which we are indebted for supplying the following information). Founded in 1999, NCCI represents a wide range of institutions, with many individuals working actively in quality improvement, assessment, planning, institutional improvement, and organizational development. NCCI is committed to advancing administrative and academic excellence in higher education by identifying, promoting, supporting, and sharing effective organizational practices among member institutions. As a result of NCCI's work, higher education is functioning collaboratively across institutions to employ effective methods for advancing academic and administrative excellence.

Consistent with its teachings, NCCI uses planning and improvement approaches to articulate its own purpose and to chart a course of action. Goals and actions include sponsoring systems and events that promote the sharing of best practices and support professional development of individual members, including use of electronic communication and partnerships with other higher education organizations. NCCI's funding comes from dues of member institutions and from event registration fees.

NCCI is composed of more than 200 individual representatives from approximately 70 member institutions, including the University of Missouri. Members come from various backgrounds and occupy a variety of positions in administration, academic affairs, student life, planning, institutional research, assessment, and continuous improvement. The current membership includes nationally recognized quality experts, authors, presidents, provosts, and chief financial officers, as well as representatives from institutions that have received state and national quality awards. The executive council has representatives elected from member institutions who volunteer their time to advance NCCI's goals. Committees develop and implement action plans for meeting membership, programming, and marketing goals. NCCI collaborates closely with ACE and the National Association of College and University Business Officers (NACUBO) and offers professional development opportunities in conjunction with each group on a continuing basis.

NCCI assists member institutions and provides national leadership in quality in higher education through a number of channels. It sponsors national meetings and conferences, including an annual conference linked with NACUBO, and annual meetings and workshops linked with ACE. A national higher education roundtable is offered in the fall, examining topics such as leadership for quality and implementing large-scale change, and best-practice symposiums are offered in the fall and the spring. Conferences and meetings are held at various venues across the United States.

Additional best practices, case studies, and other useful information can be found on NCCI's web site (www.ncci-cu.org). Members network and discuss common issues formally and informally, through email, via phone, and at NCCI-sponsored events. Initially individuals came to NCCI to help advance efforts in their own institutions. Collectively the group has advanced critical issues for higher education at the national level through shared expertise and commitment to organizational excellence.

We hope that recently initiated discussions with NCCI will help in disseminating the ideas and techniques presented in this book.

9

Policy Recommendations

Our final task is to synthesize the ideas presented earlier into a coherent set of policy recommendations. We will summarize the ideas briefly and then link them to the current debate about quality and return on investment in higher education. The importance of this linkage cannot be overemphasized. Unless colleges and universities can link quality and attentiveness to return on investment in all areas of their activity, in teaching and scholarship as well as scientific research, some of that investment is likely to go elsewhere. The report of the Spellings Commission will surely sharpen the debate, and it may bring higher education to a tipping point in terms of public support. This should be a powerful motivator for adopting the ideas we have put forward in this book.

Summary of the Book

Chapter 1 laid out the case for AQW—that most colleges and universities could become better than they are without additional spending. In addition to our own experience, we cited works by Bok (2006); Hersh and Merrow (2005); Massy (2003c); Ruben (2004); Vedder (2004); and Zemsky, Wegner, and Massy (2005)—and noted the many earlier critics of college and university performance. Any serious reader of Bok, in particular, should come away feeling uncomfortable, that something significant needs to be done.

Chapters 2 and 3 introduced the idea of *education quality work* (EQW), the term we use to describe the processes departments use or should use to improve and assure teaching and learning quality. Attacking the problems posed by Bok and others requires this kind of work, whether it's called "EQW" or something else. We believe that giving the processes a name and organizing them in a systematic way will help achieve what has eluded so many institutions over the years—significant and sustained improvement in teaching and learning quality, especially at the undergraduate level. It's only when the processes for sustaining and improving quality are examined carefully and themselves made the subject of improvement that the shortfalls can be observed and corrected. Identifying EQW as a necessary element of departmental activity is a prerequisite for recognizing and rewarding the units that do it well.

Chapter 4 described how faculty can become engaged in EQW—that is, how change agents can alter departmental conversations to include quality work through structured questioning and peer review. We focused on academic audit as the best way to begin and then sustain the momentum over time. Chapters 5 and 6 provided a road map for how an institution can audit EQW at the department level. The methodology follows the familiar pattern of self-study accompanied by a site visit and report. Unlike a conventional program review, however, academic audit structures the conversations around the focal areas and principles of quality work. As a fundamentally formative exercise, it seeks to inform and motivate improvement. Evaluations of departmental EQW maturity emerge inevitably as a byproduct of the exercise, but they do not interfere with its formative objectives.

Chapter 7 extended AQW to include research and scholarship. The extension allows audit to be substituted for conventional program review in most situations, except when an institution wishes to evaluate a department's *capacity* to do good work as opposed to the way it uses the capacity it already has. (In other words, audit seeks to maximize the utilization of existing resources, and program review tends to ask whether new resources or leadership is needed.) Adding research and scholarship to the regimens of quality work and audit is not very difficult. The chapter explained the focal areas, principles, and methods needed to do so. It is the addition of research and scholarship that converts *education* quality work to the broader *academic* quality work.

Chapter 8 described AQW above the level of the department and extended the audit methodology to cover whole campuses or institutions. The AQW task of deans, provosts, academic vice presidents, and higher education oversight or quality agencies is to ensure that departmental AQW is being performed effectively and is continuously improved. Each level in the hierarchy needs to address performance at the next lower level, but to do that the performance at all levels—down to the department—must be made visible. The chapter presented a program for doing so—namely, the campus or institutional academic audit. It ended by describing how campus and institutional audits were introduced and are being used internationally. The increasing numbers of countries that use academic audit view it as a method for increasing the return on their investments in higher education.

Return on Investment in Higher Education

Is higher education a good investment? For decades the answer has been yes, both in regard to the core funds being put into higher education and to incremental money that covers new enrollments, research, and quality improvement. Now, however, people are questioning the United States' investment in its colleges and universities. Some go so far as to say that higher education should be "defunded" through reductions in state appropriations, price controls, and limitation of the tax exemption (cf. Vedder, 2004). Such proposals have been heard before, but they seem to be growing in stridency. Indeed, the United States may be approaching a tipping point in political perceptions about the sector's cost, productivity, and quality.

The irony is that universities have never been more important for sustaining the nation's competitiveness and defending our quality of life. Tom Friedman, Pulitzer Prize–winning columnist for *The New York Times* and author of *The World Is Flat* (2005), points out that the global playing field is being leveled and that America must adapt and innovate to keep up. He describes the attributes of the "new middle-class jobs" that must emerge to offset the transfer of the traditional ones overseas. To protect American jobs, workers will need to be great collaborators, leveragers, synthesizers, and explainers. They must map global ideas to local circumstances, be sensitive to environmental issues, and be great adapters. They must be passionate about what they do. They will do more with their right brains (the right brain is critical in the flat world because so much left-brain work will be done by computers or in India). Friedman's formula for success in the new middle-class jobs is CQ+PQ>IQ: One's "curiosity quotient" and "passion quotient" will trump the intelligence quotient. Above all, workers in a flat world will have to teach themselves if they're to keep ahead of the competition.

Where better to acquire these attributes than at a college or university? The case for return on investment should be stronger now than ever before—but only if higher education can demonstrate that it can truly deliver the goods. Derek Bok (2006) cites example after example where undergraduate education fails to deliver or where it could be dramatically better than it is today. And as we pointed out in Chapter 1, he's not the only critic. A growing sense of malaise undermines the case for investment, even though failure to support America's colleges and universities will turn out to be dysfunctional in a flat world.

People who study change emphasize that a *sense of urgency* is important. We believe a sense of urgency about AQW ought to exist now. One cannot read Bok and the other critics we've cited without concluding that America's colleges and universities can and should be a great deal better than they are—that at least some of the money being poured into them is not used as effectively as it could be. Vedder's solution is to defund the sector. The alternative is to spend the resources more effectively.

This book makes the case that AQW can improve teaching and research quality without additional spending, which means we need to spend today's resources more effectively. Ironically, to summarily defund higher education would be to compound the difficulty of introducing AQW. Universities under siege find it difficult or impossible to call forth the collegial discussions that are essential for quality work. One can make funding increments contingent on progress or perhaps suggest that indifference might lead to defunding, but to defund first is sure to be counterproductive.

The Spellings Commission

In Chapter 1 we cited two of the areas for improvement put forward by the U.S. Secretary of Education's Commission on the Future of Higher Education in its 2006 report (U.S. Department of Education, 2006):

- The quality of teaching and student learning
- The amount and quality of information about teaching and learning that is available to the public

Improving quality work through the use of academic audit aims to achieve both objectives. It's important to note, however, that our approach differs markedly from what we perceive to be the main thrust of the commission's recommendations.

Recommendation 2 under the heading "Postsecondary education institutions should measure and report meaningful student learning outcomes" states:

> The Federal government should provide incentives for states, higher education associations, university systems, and institutions to develop interoperable outcomes-focused accountability systems designed to be accessible and useful for students, policymakers, and the public, as well as for internal management and institutional improvement. (U.S. Department of Education, 2006, p. 23)

We read this as advocating a regimen of standardized ("interoperable") tests that would measure graduates' knowledge, skills and abilities, and perhaps other desiderata. By extension, tests of this kind, if reliable and valid, also could be administered during, say, the freshman year and thus used to measure value added.

We agree in principle with the measurement of learning outcomes—or, better, value added—and with using a combination of market and administrative action to hold institutions and departments accountable for results. The problem is in the implementation. Is it possible to develop outcomes tests that would be reliable and valid when applied to all kinds of graduates from all kinds of colleges and universities? We think not. Furthermore, to apply unreliable or invalid tests would be worse than useless. Such tests would drive higher education in undesirable directions, and for this reason, they would be vociferously opposed by faculty. Trying to hold institutions accountable for misconceived test results would be a national disaster.

We do not challenge the commission's recommendation as a knee-jerk reaction to the idea of accountability. The fact that we believe in accountability is amply demonstrated throughout this book and in our earlier work. Nor do we mount the challenge from a position of ignorance about education quality evaluation. Massy, for example, has studied academic quality and accountability issues for more than a decade, has participated in policy-making, and has contributed heavily to the literature (cf. Massy 2003a, 2003b, 2003c, 2004, 2005). We formed our conclusion on the basis of extensive experience and after careful consideration of systems around the world, including the United Kingdom's subject-level outcome standards and evaluation initiatives and Brazil's national testing initiative (cf. the Public Policy for Academic Quality web site, www.unc.edu/ppaq). Given our experience, we can't help but wonder whether the commission's presumption of feasibility for its recommendation was based on evidence as opposed to, say, ideology or wishful thinking.

Our view of the way forward can be summed up as follows: The federal government, state governments, university systems, and accreditation agencies should provide incentives and other encouragements for campuses to mount effective programs of AQW and to make results of the student assessments inherent in such work public as soon as possible. Accountability should require that 1) academic departments demonstrate maturity in their quality work, and 2) student learning assessments compare favorably to benchmarks and/or show steady improvement. This view is based on two propositions that we believe have been well demonstrated in earlier chapters:

- Every academic department and program in every institution should be able, with reasonable effort, to develop reliable and valid outcome evaluations that can be understood by people outside the unit and, indeed, outside the university. This contrasts with the difficulty or impossibility of developing interoperable measures across the higher education sector.

- The evaluations should be embedded in a feedback loop, like the one described in Figure 1.1 in Chapter 1, that spurs departments to continuously improve their quality. Because the evaluations would first and foremost benefit departments, their development and use would be taken more seriously by faculty than would any externally imposed measure.

Our approach does not let faculty and their institutions off the hook with respect to accountability. Governments, the general public, and especially prospective students will have the information they need to judge performance. The evidence will deal with outcomes rather than the inputs that mainly compose the nation's current rating systems. Nor is our approach limited to common denominator measures as would be inevitable with interoperable testing—measures that although useful for certain kinds of students would be irrelevant or misleading for others. And in addition to improving market performance, the evidence will be maximally relevant for institutional improvement. In other words, what might seem to be lost in direct comparability across institutions would be offset by increased reliability, validity, and relevance to decision makers inside the academy and in the marketplace.

None of the above should be taken as questioning the commission's endorsement of initiatives like the Collegiate Learning Assessment, the National Survey of Student Engagement, and the National Forum on College-Level Learning. In fact we strongly encourage universities to adopt one or more of those initiatives and make the results public. Our point is that such tests don't eliminate the need for developing learning assessments and value-added evaluations at the department and program level. Coupled with data on graduation rates, the two approaches taken in combination can eventually produce the kind of internal and market information so many have sought for so long.

Our final comment on the commission's report concerns its recommendation that "accreditation agencies should make performance outcomes, including completion rates and student learning, the core of their assessment as a priority over inputs and processes" (U.S. Department of Education, 2006, p. 24). Although we understand the desire to focus on outcomes, global best practice in quality evaluation *includes* consideration of process. The United Kingdom, for example, has during the past few years shifted from outcomes to process evaluation as its primary assessment method, with the more intrusive and costly outcomes evaluation reserved for cases where an institution's processes are found to be unacceptable. Australia's institutional audit program provides a fine example of process-oriented evaluation. Combining such an audit with graduation rates and similar measures and, as is the case in Australia, a systematic employers' survey provides a powerful suite of relevant, reliable, and valid information. To recommend that the United States go against this important element of global best practice appears to be the product of uninformed and shallow thinking. Ironically, to downgrade process issues in accreditation would make the improvement of AQW that much harder.

Recommendations

We hope that, by this point in the book, our readers have become convinced of three things:

- Teaching, especially at the undergraduate level, and departmental processes for supporting research and scholarship can be significantly better than at present without material spending increases.
- AQW provides a way, possibly the best way, of effecting improvement, and results can be achieved quickly.
- Colleges and universities ought to feel a sense of urgency for moving forward with improvement and demonstrating to higher education's investors and other stakeholders that they are doing so.

Therefore, to cite a familiar action-oriented phrase, one might ask, "What should I do Monday morning?" We offer suggestions for members of key groups inside and outside the academy.

Campus and System-Wide Academic Officers

Initiate discussions aimed at developing pilot programs for enhancing AQW through academic audit. Relying on local resources and the materials provided in the book can eliminate the need for costly consultants and thus allow one to hold the program's costs to negligible levels. What's needed is a sponsor and a champion: the former to provide impetus and to legitimize the program, and the latter to learn and then to apply AQW and audit expertise. (In Missouri, Vice President for Academic Affairs Steve Lehmkuhle was the sponsor, and Associate Vice President Steve Graham was the champion. Vice Chancellor for Academic Affairs Paula Short played both roles in Tennessee.) Once AQW has gained a foothold within the institution, one continues to roll out and reinforce the ideas with successive rounds of audit.

Deans and Department Chairs

There's nothing to prevent individual academic units from developing their own program of AQW enhancement. Again, the materials in this book can provide an initial resource package. Departments can study their AQW activities, make commitments for improvement, and then ask for a peer review by colleagues in other disciplines. Deans should encourage and support such initiatives. They also can institute mini-audit programs for the departments within their schools. Once again, the cost of such programs is negligible.

Trustees and Regents

Ask the president and chief academic officer about academic quality work and what's being done to improve it. Keep asking, and don't be satisfied with vague answers. Learn the academics' views about what it takes to sustain and improve teaching and research quality, and whether these views take account of the concepts and principles expressed herein. Insist that quality work gets a high priority throughout the institution, by deans and department chairs as well as by high-level officers and committees. Press for some kind of systematic process, within the institution, for evaluating the maturity of quality work and spurring its improvement. Don't be put off by grumbles about micromanagement. Assuring demonstrated performance in key areas is a responsibility of the central board; micromanagement occurs only when the board specifies the details of how acceptable performance levels should be achieved.

Higher Education Oversight Boards

Learn how the institutions under your authority view AQW and what they are doing to assure and improve it. The suggestions for trustees and regents apply to you as well, but you have an added opportunity and hence an added responsibility: to mount your own program of institution-level academic audit as described under the international rubric in Chapter 8. The efficacy of audit doesn't depend on whether you currently evaluate performance in other ways, though it does make sense to take account of audit findings in performance-based funding programs. Boards that have embraced student assessment will find academic audit particularly attractive. The problem with most such programs is that assessment is considered in isolation from the other elements of AQW. Shifting the emphasis from "assessment as required by others" to "assessment as part of the department's own quality work" changes everything. Hence academic audit achieves all the objectives of an assessment program and others besides.

Higher Education Associations

Encourage your member institutions to focus on AQW and the development of value-added measures. Include these subjects in annual meetings, and consider special programs to further the ideas. Where applicable, bring institutional representatives together in working groups to develop standards and measures appropriate for their type of institutions—for example, as the National Association of State Universities and Land-Grant Colleges and the American Association of State Colleges and Universities have done in the development of a Voluntary System of Accountability for Undergraduate Education (McPherson, 2006).

Accreditors

Ask whether it's sensible to accredit an institution that is truly immature in its AQW. After all, to accredit is to certify that the institution can and does produce quality. Traditional accreditation, happily now mostly a thing of the past, concentrated on the "can" part of the equation by ensuring that the institution's financial, human, and physical resources were sufficient to deliver quality. Having an ethic of quality work and the know-how to perform such work is a key indicator for the "do" part of the equation—that is, whether the resources are being used effectively. A number of accrediting agencies have embraced this view and blazed trails of good practice. This runs counter to the practice of allowing institutions to choose the areas that will be evaluated during accreditation. In-depth study and peer review of self-selected areas can be valuable, but they're no substitute for covering *all* the areas of quality work. Individual accreditors and their umbrella associations should ask, and be asked, how visibility on these matters is being obtained, and whether academic audit or a similar process should be instituted as a routine part of accreditation.

The Press

Reporters who cover higher education can do much more to further the cause of quality improvement. In addition to writing about teaching and research quality, per se, you can ask institutions and faculty about the evidence they use to gauge quality for their own purposes—especially the purpose of diagnosing difficulty and effecting improvement. This book offers up many appropriate questions, ones for which the interpretation of answers needs no academic or disciplinary background. Two kinds of stories are possible here: that the sector, or a particular institution, is doing well or doing poorly on particular aspects of AQW. Both are newsworthy. A second role is to help propagate best practice. A third is to add the effectiveness of an institution's quality assurance and improvement processes to the attributes considered by prospective students and their parents. A fourth, the Holy Grail of market information and an objective of the Spellings Commission, is to spur institutions to develop good measures of value added—which in due course can be made available to the public.

What Everyone Can Do

The fundamental message of this book is that America's colleges and universities should become more self-conscious about quality. The three of us believe strongly that once the academy is more conscious of quality matters, improvements will follow. There is no need for coercive regulatory measures, though such may be forthcoming if the current shortfalls aren't corrected. The desire to produce top-quality academic work exists in full measure within the academy. What's missing are systematic grassroots processes for attaining it. Such processes depend, in turn, on collegial efforts, mainly at the department level, to develop clear and meaningful learning objectives and value-added performance metrics—in other words, to develop effective feedback loops that will produce virtuous circles of continuous improvement.

What all thoughtful Americans can do is ask, quietly but persistently, for progress on this agenda. Such progress requires no additional funding. In fact, attention to AQW can be synergistic with efforts to control cost. The barriers are mainly cultural. Our experience shows, however, that simple questions like "What are you trying to do?" and "What evidence do you use to judge your results?"—if delivered in a friendly way—can break down the barriers. Such questions can be addressed to faculty, academic administrators, and nonacademic staff as well as to presidents, provosts, and deans. We believe that improvement will be forthcoming if enough people ask such questions often enough.

The nation's ability to compete in a flat world depends on its educational system, and especially on higher education. Some say the 21st century will belong to Asia, and China in particular. But again to paraphrase Tom Friedman, "We shouldn't cede a century to a country that censors Google. America's ability to innovate, to adapt to the flat world, should not be underestimated. But we won't win by default." Nor can our higher education system play its vital role by leaving quality to an "invisible hand." The time has come to give AQW the attention it deserves. We urge everyone, inside and outside the academy, to strive to make that happen.

Bibliography

Argyris, C. (1991, May–June). Teaching smart people how to learn. *Harvard Business Review, 69*(3), 99–109.

Association of American Colleges and Universities. (1985). *Integrity in the college curriculum: A report to the academic community.* Washington, DC: Author.

Berry, T. H. (1991). *Managing the total quality transformation.* New York, NY: McGraw-Hill.

Bias-Insignares, H. (2005). *Reflections on the TBR academic audit pilot project: An orientation guide.* Nashville, TN: Tennessee Board of Regents.

Bogan, C. E., & English, M. J. (1994). *Benchmarking for best practices: Winning through innovative adaptation.* New York, NY: McGraw-Hill.

Bogue, E. G., & Saunders, R. L. (1992). *The evidence for quality: Strengthening the tests of academic and administrative effectiveness.* San Francisco, CA: Jossey-Bass.

Bok, D. (2006). *Our underachieving colleges: A candid look at how much students learn and why they should be learning more.* Princeton, NJ: Princeton University Press.

Boxwell, R. J., Jr. (1994). *Benchmarking for competitive advantage.* New York, NY: McGraw-Hill.

Boyer, E. L. (1990). *Scholarship reconsidered: Priorities of the professoriate.* Princeton, NJ: Carnegie Foundation for the Advancement of Teaching.

Brown, J. S., & Duguid, P. (2000). *The social life of information.* Boston, MA: Harvard Business School Press.

Camp, R. C. (1989). *Benchmarking: The search for industry best practices that lead to superior performance.* Milwaukee, WI: American Society for Quality Control Press.

Cohen, M. D., March, J. G., & Olsen, J. P. (1972, March). A garbage can model of organizational choice. *Administrative Science Quarterly, 17*(1), 1–25.

Creech, B. (1994). *The five pillars of TQM: How to make total quality management work for you.* New York, NY: Truman Talley Books/Plume.

Cyert, R. M., & March, J. G. (1963). *A behavioral theory of the firm.* Englewood Cliffs, NJ: Prentice-Hall.

Davenport, T. H. (1993). *Process innovation: Reengineering work through information technology.* Boston, MA: Harvard Business School Press.

Deming, W. E. (1986). *Out of the crisis.* Cambridge, MA: Massachusetts Institute of Technology, Center for Advanced Educational Services.

Deming, W. E. (1994). *The new economics: For industry, government, education.* Cambridge, MA: Massachusetts Institute of Technology, Center for Advanced Educational Services.

Dill, D. D. (1992). Quality by design: Toward a framework for academic quality management. In J. Smart (Ed.), *Higher education: Handbook of theory and research* (Vol. VIII, pp. 37–83). New York, NY: Agathon Press.

Ehrmann, S. C., & Milam, J. H., Jr. (1999). *Flashlight cost analysis handbook: Modeling resource use in teaching and learning with technology: Version 1.0.* Washington, DC: The TLT Group.

French, N. J., Ko, P. K., Massy, W. F., Siu, F. H., & Young, K. (1999, Spring). Research assessment in Hong Kong. *Journal of International Education, 10*(1), 46–53.

French, N. J., Massy, W. F., & Young, K. (2001, July). Research assessment in Hong Kong. *Higher Education, 42*(1), 35–46.

Friedman, T. L. (2005). *The world is flat: A brief history of the twenty-first century.* New York, NY: Farrar, Straus, & Giroux.

Hammer, M., & Champy, J. (1993). *Reengineering the corporation: A manifesto for business revolution.* New York, NY: HarperCollins.

Harrington, H. J. (1991). *Business process improvement: The breakthrough strategy for total quality, productivity, and competitiveness.* New York, NY: McGraw-Hill.

Hersh, R. H., & Merrow, J. (Eds.). (2005). *Declining by degrees: Higher education at risk.* New York, NY: Palgrave Macmillan.

Hopkins, D. S. P., & Massy, W. F. (1981). *Planning models for colleges and universities.* Stanford, CA: Stanford University Press.

Joiner, B. L. (1994). *Fourth generation management: The new business consciousness.* New York, NY: McGraw-Hill.

Jones, D. (2004). *TCM handbook: Version 2.0.* Boulder, CO: Western Cooperative for Educational Telecommunications.

Juran, J. M. (1989). *Juran on leadership for quality: An executive handbook.* New York, NY: The Free Press.

Juran, J. M., & Gryna, F. M. (1993). *Quality planning and analysis: From product development through use* (3rd ed.). New York, NY: McGraw-Hill.

Lareau, W. (1991). *American samurai.* New York, NY: Warner.

Lovett, C. M. (2002, March/April). Cracks in the bedrock: Can U.S. higher education remain number one? *Change, 34*(2), 11–15.

Manz, C. C., & Sims, H. P., Jr. (1993). *Business without bosses: How self-managing teams are building high-performing companies.* New York, NY: John Wiley & Sons.

Massy, W. F. (Ed.). (1996). *Resource allocation in higher education.* Ann Arbor, MI: University of Michigan Press.

Massy, W. F. (1997). Teaching and learning quality process review: The Hong Kong programme. *Quality in Higher Education, 3*(3), 249–262.

Massy, W. F. (2000). *Energizing quality work: Higher education quality evaluation in Sweden and Denmark* (Technical report). Stanford, CA: Stanford University, National Center for Postsecondary Improvement.

Massy, W. F. (2003a, April). *Access to what? Putting "quality" into national QA systems.* Keynote address presented at seventh biennial conference of the International Network of Quality Assurance Agencies in Higher Education, Dublin, Ireland.

Massy, W. F. (2003b, June 20). Auditing higher education to improve quality. *The Chronicle of Higher Education,* p. B16.

Massy, W. F. (2003c). *Honoring the trust: Quality and cost containment in higher education.* Bolton, MA: Anker.

Massy, W. F. (2004). *Academic audit for quality assurance and improvement: Report for the public policy for academic quality research program (PPAQ).* Chapel Hill, NC: University of North Carolina–Chapel Hill.

Massy, W. F. (2005). Academic audit for accountability and improvement. In J. C. Burke & Associates, *Achieving accountability in higher education: Balancing public, academic and market demands* (pp. 173–197). San Francisco, CA: Jossey-Bass.

Massy, W. F., & French, N. J. (2001, April). Teaching and learning quality process review: What the programme has achieved in Hong Kong. *Quality in Higher Education, 7*(1), 33–45.

Massy, W. F., Wilger, A., & Colbeck, C. (1994, July/August). Overcoming "hollowed collegiality." *Change, 26*(4), 11–20.

Massy, W. F., & Wilger, A. K. (1995, July/August). Improving productivity. *Change, 27*(4), 10–20.

Massy, W. F., & Zemsky, R. (1994, January–February). Faculty discretionary time: Departments and the "academic ratchet." *Journal of Higher Education, 65*(1), 1–22.

McMurtrie, B. (2000, July 7). Accreditors revamp policies to stress student learning. *The Chronicle of Higher Education,* p. A29.

McPherson, P. (2006). *Toward a public universities and colleges voluntary system of accountability for undergraduate education (VSA).* Retrieved December 13, 2006, from www.nasulgc.org/vsa-8-31-06%20_7_%20_2_.pdf

Meade, P., & Woodhouse, D. (2000, April). Evaluating the effectiveness of the New Zealand academic audit unit: Review and outcomes. *Quality in Higher Education, 6*(1), 19–29.

Melan, E. H. (1993). *Process management: Methods for improving products and service.* New York, NY: McGraw-Hill.

Milam, J. (2000, May). *Cost analysis of online courses.* Paper presented at the 40th annual forum of the Association for Institutional Research, Cincinnati, OH.

Miller, G. L., & Krumm, L. L. (1992). *The whats, whys and hows of quality improvement: A guidebook for continuous improvement.* Milwaukee, WI: American Society for Quality Control Press.

Nettles, M. T., & Cole, J. J. K. (1999). *State higher education assessment policy: Research findings from second and third years.* Stanford, CA: Stanford University, National Center for Postsecondary Improvement.

Orsburn, J. D., Moran, L., Musselwhite, E., & Zenger, J. H. (1990). *Self-directed work teams: The new American challenge.* New York, NY: McGraw-Hill.

Pascale, R. T., & Sternin, J. (2005, May). Your company's secret change agents. *Harvard Business Review, 83*(5), 72–81.

Pitt, H. (1994). *SPC for the rest of us: A personal path to statistical process control.* Reading, MA: Addison-Wesley.

Quality Assurance Agency for Higher Education. (2000). *Code of practice for the assurance of academic quality and standards in higher education.* Gloucester, UK: Author.

Revolution or evolution? Gauging the impact of institutional student-assessment strategies. (1999, September/October). *Change, 31*(5), 53–57.

Rosenbluth, H. F., & Peters, D. M. (1992). *The customer comes second: And other secrets of exceptional service.* New York, NY: William Morrow.

Ruben, B. D. (1995). *Quality in higher education.* New Brunswick, NJ: Transaction.

Ruben, B. D. (2004). *Pursuing excellence in higher education: Eight fundamental challenges.* San Francisco, CA: Jossey-Bass.

Scholtes, P. R. (1988). *The team handbook: How to use teams to improve quality.* Madison, WI: Joiner Associates.

Senge, P. M. (1990). *The fifth discipline: The art and practice of the learning organization.* New York, NY: Doubleday Currency.

Sonnenberg, F. K. (1994). *Managing with a conscience: How to improve performance through integrity, trust, and commitment.* New York, NY: McGraw-Hill.

Spendolini, M. J. (1992). *The benchmarking book.* New York, NY: Amacom.

Stark, J. S., & Lattuca, L. R. (1997). *Shaping the college curriculum: Academic plans in action.* Boston, MA: Allyn & Bacon.

Sykes, C. J. (1988). *Profscam: Professors and the demise of higher education.* Washington, DC: Regency Gateway.

U.S. Department of Education. (2006). *A test of leadership: Charting the future of U.S. higher education.* Washington, DC: Author.

van Vught, F. (1995). The new context for academic quality. In D. D. Dill & B. Sporn (Eds.), *Emerging patterns of social demand and university reform: Through a glass darkly* (pp. 194–211). New York, NY: Elsevier.

Vedder, R. (2004). *Going broke by degree: Why college costs too much.* Washington, DC: AEI Press.

Wahlén, S. (1998, December). Is there a Scandinavian model of evaluation of higher education? *Higher Education Management, 10*(3), 27–42.

Walvoord, B. E., & Pool, K. J. (1998). Enhancing pedagogical productivity. In J. E. Groccia & J. E. Miller (Eds.), *New directions for higher education: No. 103. Enhancing productivity: Administrative, instructional, and technological strategies* (pp. 35–48). San Francisco, CA: Jossey-Bass.

Warren, R. G. (1997). Engaging students in active learning. *About Campus, 2*(1), 16–20.

Watson, G. H. (1993). *Strategic benchmarking: How to rate your company's performance against the world's best.* New York, NY: John Wiley & Sons.

Western Association of Schools and Colleges. (2002). *Evidence guide: A guide for using evidence in the accreditation process: A resource to support institutions and evaluation teams.* Alameda, CA: Accrediting Commission for Senior Colleges and Universities, Western Association of Schools and Colleges.

Whiteley, R. C. (1991). *The customer-driven company: Moving from talk to action.* Reading, MA: Addison-Wesley.

Wilson, J. M. (1997). Reengineering the undergraduate curriculum. In D. G. Oblinger & S. C. Rush (Eds.), *The learning revolution: The challenge of information technology in the academy* (pp. 107–128). Bolton, MA: Anker.

Zeithaml, V. A., Parasuraman, A., & Berry, L. L. (1990). *Delivering quality service: Balancing customer perceptions and expectations.* New York, NY: The Free Press.

Zemke, R., & Schaaf, D. (1989). *The service edge: 101 companies that profit from customer care.* New York, NY: New American Library.

Zemsky, R. (1989). *Structure and coherence: Measuring the undergraduate curriculum.* Washington, DC: Association of American Colleges and Universities.

Zemsky, R., & Massy, W. F. (1990, November/December). Cost containment: Committing to a new economic reality. *Change, 22*(6), 16–22.

Zemsky, R., Massy, W. F., Shapiro, D., Shaman, S., Dubrow, G., & Giancola, J. (1999). *Market, price, and margin: Determining the cost of an undergraduate education.* Philadelphia, PA: University of Pennsylvania, Institute for Research on Higher Education.

Zemsky, R., Wegner, G. R., & Massy, W. F. (2005). *Remaking the American university: Market-smart and mission-centered.* New Brunswick, NJ: Rutgers University Press.

Index